"*The Peril of Remembering Nice Thin[g]s* [is...] father, a self-exiled Southerner's investigation of his homeland's (and maybe his own family's) history of murderous racism, a frank assessment of humanitarian progress in the United States and abroad, a loving collection of stories as likely to horrify and shock as they are to provoke a laugh, and an American emigre's honest-to-God attempt to make sense of his own identity. Beautiful, heart-wrenching, sometimes horrifying, and haunted from cover to cover."

– Hugh Sheehy, author of *Design Flaw and The Invisibles*

"Black Americans have been diving into their family histories for so long, knowing that their lives and their positions in society today are inextricably connected to the past. White people haven't done much digging, scared of what they'll find or persisting in comfortable denial about how history reverberates today. But denial isn't comfortable, looking away isn't comfortable, exactly because of the direct lines between then and now. Jeff Gibbs' journey into his father's life and death and the choices of generations before him, make that painfully clear. This book is not just brave and honest, it is also exceptionally well-written. Gibbs' curiosity, his eye for detail, his skill to ask all the right questions and carefully pull threads to unravel the past, turn The Peril of Remembering Nice Things into an intriguing, disturbing, at times haunting experience."

– Fréderike Geerdink, freelance journalist for the *Independent*, author of *The Boys are Dead: The Roboski Massacre and the Kurdish Question in Turkey*

"Jeffrey Gibbs combines investigative journalism with storytelling to reveal his father's suicide and a region's hidden history, exposing the lasting effects of historic crimes. He courageously delves into hidden histories, from the American South to Japan and Turkey, offering insightful literary documentation."

– Jiyar Gol, BBC World Affairs Correspondent

"While searching for meaning in his father's life and suicide, and tying both to a broader history encompassing the American South, Turkey, and Japan, Gibbs marches unflinchingly up to his subjects, yielding light and a way forward for himself and his readers. Beautifully written despite the horrors Gibbs explores, The Peril of Remembering Nice Things is a powerfully honest and important book about family, community, and race."

– David Joiner, author of *The Lotus Eaters, Kanazawa and The Heron Catchers*

THE PERIL OF
REMEMBERING
NICE THINGS

by JEFFREY WADE GIBBS

edited by LANCE ÜMMENHOFER
designed by THEO HALL

APRIL GLOAMING

Publisher's Cataloguing-in-Publication Data

Gibbs, Jeffrey Wade
The peril of remembering nice things / written by Jeffrey Wade Gibbs / de-
signed by Theo Hall
ISBN: 978-1-953932-29-7

1. Memoir I. Title II. Author

Library of Congress Control Number: 2024944910

For my wife, Delal, who made writing this possible, and for my son, Robin, with whom rest all my hopes for a nobler future.

ONE

The old man's face crinkles into a mask of irritation—furrowed brow, lips upturned in a slight snarl. He settles back into his armchair and asks his question.

"So, why did your daddy kill himself?"

His daughter, my second cousin, Lisa, winces. She warned me this might be coming. Upon our arrival, she explained in her elegant Georgia accent, "Daddy's really excited about meeting y'all, though he might be more direct than we'd like."

But I welcome the candor. Clearly, the question has weighed on his mind all these years, too. I have taken this trip to my father's hometown of Tifton in south Georgia for many reasons, but at the heart of them all is my father, the mystery of his suicide and the life that led to it. This is speed research. I have only three days to collect whatever pieces of the puzzle I can scrabble together, too little time for Southern delicacy and restraint. The old man is Clark, my dad's first cousin, who at one point was also his closest friend. Dad was alone for as long as I can remember, with no friends to speak of, close or casual, though he was charismatic and made admirers wherever he went. Even now, Cousin Clark cannot help but remark how bright my father was.

"Bob sure was smart," he assures me. "Way beyond all of us, and we knew it. I wonder if you got his brain?"

"People say so," I answer politely.

I've never met Clark until now, but I heard a lot about him from my father when he was alive. They'd grown up together in the tiny farming community of Omega (pronounced O-mee-gah), Georgia. As teens, they had pulled lots of pranks which my dad enjoyed recounting in vivid detail. Once, for instance, they had stolen a toilet and set it on the lawn of the Tift County Courthouse in the middle of the night. Beside it, they'd staked a hand-painted sign that read, "The new county seat, full of shit like the old." Later, they'd both lived their early twenties in Jacksonville, Florida and had been rather wild apparently, two small-town boys drunk on the relatively cosmopolitan city. For years, my dad ended every story about their hellraising with a smirk and this request, "If you ever meet him, I want you to say, 'Cousin Clark, how is every little thing?'" This, I got out of him one day when I was older, was a reference to a pesky case of crabs.

But I never got to ask the question. Dad never tried to introduce me, and as far as I know, made no phone calls, wrote no letters, paid no visits to his cousin, though for years this one-time buddy, childhood playmate, and partner-in-crime had resided in Eustis, Florida, just an hour and a half south from where my father lived with my grandmother in the small town of Keystone Heights. Now that I am finally in the presence of the man, of course, I don't think it tasteful to allude to pubic lice in front of his daughter, however funny Dad might have found it.

Of all the people in the world, I think, *Clark will know my father in the ways I did not.* He is the expert on a time before me, before my mother or even my dad's first wife, before the drinking and doom. He will have answers, though right now, he has a question, one that reveals a startling ignorance of the basic facts of my father's life. Anyone who knew Bob Gibbs, however few and limited a group we are, knows the deliberate misery in which Dad lived those final years. I'd been hoping Clark could help me figure out how he'd gotten that way.

"Well," I say to Clark. "I'm not sure what to say. There's no simple answer."

Where to start? The hatred between him, his brother, and mother? The decades of joblessness? The isolation, the drinking, the homelessness? The utter lack of purpose? The general propensity toward doom of generations of men in our family? The big brain that had nothing to do but grind itself to death in the benighted ignorance of backwoods Florida?

"Well, start somewhere," Clark says, the irritated-looking curl still on his lips. It's an expression Lisa refers to as the "Hamner snarl," a family trait Dad and his mother carried as well.

***

This memoir is an answer to Clark's question, though I don't know if "memoir" is the right word. I cannot promise flawlessly accurate memories. The deeper I dig, the more I wonder how accurate any memory can be. Details are always shifting beneath me, changing mid-story like a dream sometimes does. For example, the incident I described with the toilet on the courthouse lawn: I'm not sure anymore if that was with Clark or with a high school buddy or with a friend from his time in the army reserve. Clark himself denies having done it,

2

but adds, "I'm losing all my memories now. It could be true. It sounds like something we'd do." My father's narration of this story feels more like a fact I've learned than a scene I remember. The only actual moving image I can conjure is the profile of Dad's face with his Magnum PI mustache and giant, tinted bifocals as he pronounces his command, "Ask Clark, 'how is every little thing?'" A two-second clip of speech maybe, but Dad is sitting in his chair on the back porch of my grandmother's house in Keystone, alive again. He's in the corner next to the sliding glass door with the inevitable glass of sweet tea and cigarette. His tea was always in the tall glasses with the Zs etched on the side and mine in the scalloped-top tumblers—the Z stood for "Zillman," the surname of his dead stepfather, Carl. I see the frayed rope strung with rusty bells hanging in the screen window, and in addition to the mustache and glasses, I see his curly black hair and skinny legs stretched out in front of him, crossed at the ankles. I hear his sardonic, slow basso voice, and the twangy bounces he uses to deliver the line. Before and after this is all blank.

I spent a large part of my life in Japan. In fact, I was living in Tokyo when I got news of my father's death, and in that country, there's a genre of writing called *zuihitsu*, which translates as "follow the pen." One Japanese dictionary defines it as "taking your subjective feelings, memories, and things you have witnessed and surrendering them to the movement of the pen, making connections to produce a free-form text." This free association is what appeals to me and what moves me closest to the truth when hunting my dad's ghost, for in writing this, I sometimes wander from memory to history, from me to him, from emotional impression to numerical data, from my life then as a boy in conservative rural Florida to my time in Japan to now as a man married into a family of politically active Kurds in Turkey. I bounce between seemingly unrelated topics, except that all of them have Dad at their core. So, this is not a memoir, but a *zuihitsu*. And in following the pen, I will keep coming back to this center: My father killed himself over twenty years ago.

This is the story.

***

One frosty spring morning before sunrise, Bob Gibbs exited his hotel room in Starke, Florida, a small city north of Keystone Heights famous for the state prison. A city where death row executions were still carried out using a seventy-three-year-old electric chair nicknamed "Old Sparky" made of oak and built by the prisoners themselves—black men, mostly; a city either named after a rich slaveholder and unrepentant Secessionist or, according to others, a rich Northern developer's wife; a city, in short, which neatly summed the historical character of the region as much as my father himself did.

Dad was staying in room 24 of the Magnolia Hotel, a beautiful, if haggard relic of the 19th century that offered discount weekly rates, which meant it was more of a home for people with nowhere else to go than a lodging for travelers. Guests included recovering addicts, wives of death row inmates, vagrants and the mentally ill. The date was April 23rd, just three days before his mom's birthday—the rent was due, and he had no way to pay. His mother, a woman we grandkids called Memaw, had been footing the bill, but she'd just informed him she would do so no longer. He left behind his clothes, pictures of me, my letters and postcards from Japan, and walked down to the segment of train track between Jefferson and Jackson Street. There he lit up a cigarette, sat on the rail, and waited for the CSX morning freight to bash him into oblivion.

I'm not sure about the cigarette part, though it's how I picture him. Maybe he didn't have the money to buy any. I do know, thanks to the autopsy report, that though he was an alcoholic, he was completely sober at the time. The only physical thing wrong with him was a few spots on his kidneys. What I remember of the statement from the engineer is that he had sighted a tall man sitting on the tracks and immediately applied the brakes. At the sound of the sudden screeching, the man looked up into the oncoming light and then away. It's this that sometimes gives me the feeling that he had not planned his death, that the train had appeared, and he'd thought, "Well, there it is and here I am. Why not?"

I forget how many feet he was thrown or whether the body landed in the parking lot or in the ditch or behind the furniture store. I want to say behind the furniture store. These sorts of details were important to me at the time, but I've lost all these reports, the box of documents I once had that explained the facts. I do remember the generic drawing of a human body covered in red ink marks showing the locations of the many contusions and lacerations. The human being had become a police outline. Gone were his potbelly, the mustache and long white legs, the deep voice, and the big brain.

When I got the news, I was living just outside of Tokyo. I was in my bedroom, the door closed because I was not getting along with my roommate at the time. That I clearly remember because I heard her calling my name, and annoyed, I put my headphones on. But she kept calling and finally knocked on my door. I knew from the look on her face—the way her features contorted as if trying to find a suitable expression—that it wasn't a dirty dish or a dropped sock that demanded my attention. Something serious was happening. She said my sister, Michele, was on the phone. When I say my sister, I have to make clear Michele was technically a half-sister. We didn't share the same father, and therefore, this news was mine alone.

"Mom doesn't want me to tell you this," she said. "But your Aunt Nancy called. Your daddy's dead."

My Aunt Nancy was the wife of my father's older brother, Gene. She had seen an article in the Starke paper explaining that Robert Lenward Gibbs had been killed a few days earlier, an apparent suicide. She spruced up the story just a tad, as she often did, adding a flourish about him lying down across the tracks and resting his head on the rails as if on a pillow. "Closing his eyes like he was getting ready to take a nap," she said. Horrified, she'd immediately begun phoning around to find out what had happened only to discover my grandmother, with the complicity of my uncle, had already had his body cremated. They'd been about to dump his ashes on their own without telling another soul.

"So, I called your memaw," my sister told me. "To make sure it was true. I told her she'd better not do anything with those ashes until you got here. She said it was her right to do whatever she wanted, and I reminded her that he had a son. Then I told her it was her fault. He did it because of her and everyone knew it. She cussed me up one way and down the other. I've never heard such filth. Said she was coming down to kill me and had her rifles loaded."

I was deeply and profoundly shaken but not surprised. Dad's life had become like a book you could predict the ending to halfway through, a series of events propelling him inexorably toward suicide for a long time.

One such event was my college graduation, three years before his death.

It was a hot June day in Orlando, and my friends and I were burning up in those black robes. I had just gotten the news that I'd been accepted on a teacher's exchange program to Japan and was beyond thrilled. My whole family had assembled in the parking lot of the university, and I was snapping pictures with my best friends and various combinations of relatives. My mother's side from Lakeland was all there, my sister and brother-in-law, nephew and niece, my mother and her own best friend whom I had referred to all my life as "Aunt Sue." The car carrying my father's side down from north Florida pulled in a bit later, but the only representatives to step out were my grandmother and my cousin, Karin, the daughter and youngest child of my Aunt Nancy and Uncle Gene.

Three years my junior, Karin and I had grown up together. We'd gone through all the various family dramas together and so had always been close. Our relationship was the reason I had assumed Uncle Clark would know more about his own cousin.

Dad himself was nowhere to be seen.

"So where is he?" I asked Memaw. I knew this day meant more to him than to me. I was going to be the only college graduate in the family, maybe the first, period. The Gibbs men before me had been drunks and drifters. You had to go back to my great-great-grandfather to find a Primitive Baptist minister, someone with a proper calling.

"I went by to pick him up, darling," Memaw said. "He refused to come."

But I knew my grandmother. This was not the full story.

My father had not owned a car for years, and whenever he wanted to see me, he had to rely on his mother to drive him down to Lakeland. When I visited him in north Florida, we stayed at Memaw's house in Keystone Heights because he never had his own place either. He couldn't. If he was on his own, he drank too much and lost whatever job was sustaining him. In fact, he'd been living with her off and on for twenty years. Just prior to my graduation, she'd kicked him out for drinking again. The police had come, Karin told me. They'd had to drag him out by force, and he'd even spent a night in jail. Apparently, he'd been hiding booze in the mouthwash.

I knew she'd given him the boot again. He'd called me a few days before and told me he'd gone to take a piss one night during a storm and found Memaw outside the bathroom window with an umbrella, watching him. "Imagine taking a leak and looking up to see your mama peering in through the rain," he'd said. "I can't abide living with that lunatic anymore." His version, of course, made it sound like there was absolutely no reason for such odd behavior, no special additives to the Listerine, but I knew he hid whiskey around the house. I'd discovered it many times myself over the years — stuck in the knolls of trees, in empty sugar canisters at the top of the refrigerator, in the back of cabinets or under the bed. It was not the first time Memaw had kicked him out, nor would it be the last. It had been a regular feature of their relationship since he first moved in with her. It's why he was staying at the Magnolia Hotel in the end.

At the time of my graduation, he'd found a free bunk at an Evangelical Christian ranch set off in the swamp on Route 100 between Keystone and Starke. I remember white shell roads winding through the pine woods. He shared a cabin with a couple of other down-and-outs, freeloading off the Bible thumpers, as he put it. In exchange for room and board, residents had to attend prayer every morning, do odd chores around the camp, and accept Jesus as their Lord and Savior. This last item marked a distinct change that I immediately took notice of. He had always been a staunch atheist and argued vociferously against the inanity of all religion, yet this place required of him a public plea for Jesus to come into his heart and full immersion baptism. For proud Bob Gibbs to submit to this ceremony meant an unprecedented surrender of dignity. He glossed over this fact when I ribbed him about it, said it was a necessary evil. People were always laying on hands around the place. What to do but offer a warm surface to lay them on?

"At least they leave you alone when all the religious hoohaw is over," he said. "You get a lot of quiet time then. Unlike with your memaw." He also liked the various animals they kept around the compound. A pair of flying squirrels lived in a cage right outside his cabin. A raccoon couple down the boardwalk. They were looking for bears. He said they'd been capturing local fauna in twos in anticipation of the end of the world, with the hopes of preserving species just as Noah had done.

With all the celebrating, it wasn't until the day after graduation that we finally managed to speak. He phoned me from the compound to explain his absence. My grandmother had indeed come to pick him up, he confirmed. When she arrived, he was getting dressed. She marched through the door, picked up one of the socks he had lain on the bed and said, "I suppose this is your masturbating sock."

"I couldn't go with her after that," he told me. "I just couldn't."

I can imagine the scene of Memaw's arrival at this swampy Apocalypse boot camp. Dad would be sitting outside in a lawn chair in the garden next to the white sand parking lot, smoking a bummed cigarette or a butt scrounged from the ground. He wouldn't bother getting ready until she showed up, whether out of spite or simply because he wasn't sure she would come. When her car pulled in, the tires crunching the shells, he would have continued sitting and smoking until she climbed out with an impatient sigh, put her hands on her hips, and said, "Well? Aren't you ready yet?"

"No," he would have answered in his basso voice, then risen with deliberate slowness.

I can picture her following him along the trails to his cabin and standing in the door, hands still on her hips, chuckling contemptuously in that way she had of expressing her disgust and disappointment, the family snarl on her face as she watched him piece his outfit together. He put a lot of care into his appearance. He would have had a button-up Western shirt laid out neatly on the mattress along with a pair of slacks, both recently ironed. His shoes would have been at the foot of the bed, old but shined and turned to face the door. His roommate might even have been there, watching the whole process when she delivered her line about masturbation.

And as she pulled out of the drive without him, I can imagine what he felt as the opportunity to see his only son's achievement faded into history. One more failure, he would have thought, and it was her fault. She had known just what button to press to get the reaction she wanted. He must have also understood it was his fault, too, but so many different threads had come together to weave the fate he now wore, and he felt she was somehow the source of them all. Yet, a few months later they were living together again. He had nowhere else to go, no other way to be.

***

I tell none of this to Cousin Clark in answer to his question. There is an unspoken agreement among us. I feel it. We will not dishonor the family. In turn, I press Clark for any recollection that sheds light on my father's early years, but he always answers, "I don't know" or "I can't recall." I can't tell if he doesn't remember, or if he simply feels recounting would be improper.

"Daddy sometimes has trouble remembering last week," Lisa explains.

"Don't we all," I say.

"Hell," Clark says. "Sometimes I don't remember my own name. I tell people I'm Paul Jones."

Lisa rolls her eyes. "Oh Daddy, if you keep saying that, you're going to start believing it."

I've been reading memoirs of people who, like me, are connected to the old South. For hundreds of pages, there are detailed anecdotes with flowing dialogue and settings elaborately described. But that's not how memory is truly experienced nor how it exerts its power. It is memory cleansed of chaos and uncertainty, augmented with old photographs and films, with numerous interviews, with some poking around in libraries and the Internet. Memory and history are much more piecemeal than a well-crafted book implies. Writing about memory is like archaeology. You dig a few deeply buried fragments of ancient lives out of the ground and do your best to fill in the gaps for the rest.

Occasionally, you discover something extraordinary, a panel, a scroll, a mural well-preserved, something that gives you a trove of key information all at once. Even then, the meaning is tough to establish without the context of the civilization that once existed around it.

Most people are similar to Cousin Clark and me. I have imperfectly remembered fragments of my father's stories, last heard more than twenty years ago and at the time, unrecognized for the significance they would later possess. Clark, on the other hand, is struggling with senescence.

"I'm sorry my memory is so shoddy," Clark says, sitting up in his chair to turn in my direction. "But by God, I will say, you do look like him."

I can't exaggerate how this makes me feel. It's as if I suddenly crystalize into a sharp picture from a murky smear. It's clear who and what I am. I'm Jeff, the son of Bob Gibbs. I still grieve. And I will become the expert on my father I came here looking for.

All sorts of old internal machinery switch on and lunge into motion. A momentum builds.

I get so caught up in thoughts of my father that I momentarily forget the other reason I've come to Tifton and to Cousin Clark, the one I've told no one about. I plan to research another death Memaw was involved in, a murder; the lynching of a black man named John Henry Williams. And as I dig out facts of that brutal and ghastly history, I find unexpected pieces of my father's as well. Nothing too direct, nothing too obvious, but in the South, a white man's suicide and a black man's murder can have roots that coil together deep, deep beneath the earth.

TWO

My first memory is of a lightbulb exploding.

I am standing in the kitchen doorway, looking in from the hallway. I see a blue flash, and the room goes dark. I have nothing from before or after, but if I don't look directly at the moment itself, at the visual that forms in my mind, I can tease out other details. I'd heard yelling and was walking in from my bedroom. I had a baby bottle in my hand. My mother was glaring furiously up at my giant of a father. She had the haircut I remember almost exclusively from old pictures, her brown waves short on the sides and puffed up on top, an attempt at a kind of Carol Brady beehive. And then the sound of broken glass, that burst of blue light and the blackness followed by a red afterglow on my retinas.

If I try to focus on any of these things, my mother looking up, the bottle, the walk from the hallway, the images seem to slide away off-camera. Maybe my mind is filling in those parts to cover the blanks. I must have been about two years old.

For years now, I've narrated this memory to my eighth graders in the Istanbul school where I teach English. We have a unit on the book *I Am the Cheese*, a young adult novel partly about the tricks memory can play. Before we start reading, we do a little research on memory formation, then share our earliest recollections to see if they have something in common. Most of the kids tell a story much like mine, a blip of a scene—someone is fighting, hurt, or in danger. A few kids relate tales of simple joy, playing with the family dog when it's still a puppy, tossing a ball in the garden with their father. These memories all share two things in common. One is emotion. More often than not, the first memory is one of negative emotions. The second is isolation, none of us remember what comes before or after.

For years now, I have told kids about this memory and not known anything about it. When it happened, why, who did what. I had assumed it was just a brief fight between my parents, but recently, as I researched this book, I was able to put the whole story together. I want to share this process. Not only for what it reveals about my father but for what it demonstrates about how the archaeology of memory works, how you can collect a few more artifacts than you had before and tease out a whole world, how some can mislead you for years while others solve lingering mysteries with a sudden and startling vividness. In fact, this process is integral to the structure of this narrative. It's how I finally piece together the lynching of John Henry Williams, for example, and it's how I now reassemble the story of my family's first collapse, the first event that sent Dad cowering to his mother's side and launched him on the road to suicide.

***

A story that pops up whenever the word "Memaw" is uttered in family gatherings is the one about how, with the aid of my Uncle Gene, she tried to kidnap me. My mother has always said I was a baby when it happened, which is why I have never tried to recall the event. I even forget the story as Mom tells it, so I have to ask her for the details one night during my weekly phone call from Turkey. She recaps the tale grudgingly, launching into the general outline readily enough, but becomes hesitant once I start questioning the specifics—the kinds of things you need to make a story coherent.

"I like to remember nice things," she says.

I get it. The whole ordeal still makes her feel guilty somehow, like she was duped into betraying her own child. But I push anyway.

"Well, we were living in Lakeland," she says. "In that house on Tradewinds Avenue and your memaw shows up out of nowhere with your Uncle Gene at the wheel."

Lakeland is a small city in Polk County, the geographical center of Florida, famous for citrus groves, the primordial Green Swamp, baseball spring training, and bass fishing on the Chain of Lakes. It's also where my parents met and I grew up. I remember fragments of our cinder block house on Tradewinds Avenue, the green shutters, riding my tricycle on the sidewalk outside and getting stuck in the wet cement, the older neighbor kid with the Italian last name and his closet full of cool toys. Mom had lived on Tradewinds with her first husband and all the neighbors were like sisters to her. When she moved back with her new husband, my father, it was like she was bringing him home to a compound occupied by a vast extended family.

"Was Dad around when Memaw and Gene came to get me?" I ask.

"Oh, he was off doing his thing," she says. This meant that he was drinking again and had walked out on the family for a while. Or been kicked out, I don't know. The "family" back then was not only me and my mother but my older brother and sister, too, Mike and Michele, who were his stepchildren from my mother's previous marriage. Except for me and Dad, they had all lived on this street before.

"And don't ask me where he was either," my mom says, "Because I don't remember. Maybe that was when he was in the hospital. Wait. No, the hospital was later. I think."

She was referring to the time he went into the psych ward of Lakeland General to "cure" his alcoholism. In any case, Memaw had journeyed south from her lake home in Earleton, Florida, with my uncle at the wheel. She wouldn't have been sixty yet, completely fine to drive on her own, and yet she dragged her eldest along as if he were security detail, which I suspect he was. Both my father and his brother were huge men, standing over six feet tall with broad shoulders and jaws like a Superman drawing from the forties.

Earleton is a small community on Lake Santa Fe in north Florida, just fifteen minutes from Uncle Gene's place in Keystone. When I was a child, Memaw lived there in a large lake house with her second husband, Carl. From Earleton, it was a three-hour trip to Lakeland and never undertaken without careful planning, so it was highly unusual for no one to have called to let my mother know they were coming. Memaw brought with her a sense of emergency intervention.

"She said she was worried about you being in that kind of situation," my mom explains. "And she thought it would be good for you to get away from it for a while. I agreed for some reason. But then she wouldn't bring you back."

I ask my mom what "that kind of situation" had meant or why Memaw thought that I, specifically, would need to get away from anything, and not, say, my brother and sister?

"I don't know," she says. "Nothing was happening. Your dad was drinking again, that's all. He was never abusive, just drunk. Don't you forget that. It was just some story your memaw had cooked up."

Memaw had that power; she could always make you feel that what she wanted had ample justification.

"I should have known better than to trust that crazy old bat," my mom continues. "I had to go get you myself."

My mom drove up to Earleton with her own mother in the passenger seat for support. Her mom, whom I called a proper "Grandma," was a tough, practical, West Virginia mountain woman and had little stomach for bullshit. She also despised Memaw and used to refer to her as "Old Puckerpuss" for the snarl her face always wore.

When they arrived at Memaw's lake house, Memaw met them outside with Carl, whom I called "Grandpa" before I knew we weren't related at all, and who, in fact, had only been around a few years at that point, marrying my grandmother a year before I was born. With her husband behind her, Memaw ordered them to get off her property and "go right back where they came from."

"I've called the sheriff," she said. "He says you have lost your legal rights to this child."

"You'd better go inside and call him back," my mother answered. "Because I'm taking my son if I have to knock your ass on the ground to do it."

"Now look here," Carl began indignantly. "I was there when she made the call, and he—"

My mother cut him off, "I said call him back."

Carl went inside and phoned the sheriff, or pretended to. When he came out, he grudgingly informed his wife they were legally obligated to turn me over to my mother.

"That made your memaw so mad," my mom says. "She was about to spit fire. She was so used to getting her way."

"So, what happened then?"

"Well, she gave you back! She knew she was full of shit. All I remember was how on the way home you kept saying how hungry you were. And your grandma just cried and cried."

I don't know exactly what to make of this part of the memory. In Turkey, moms and aunts and grandmothers find any excuse to cry and fret over children. My wife's aunt will stand in the doorway as I leave her house if she thinks I haven't eaten enough, repeating over and over, "May I be struck blind!" (if he goes away hungry), though I've just stuffed myself sick, and here I am a forty-seven-year-old man. So, I tend to dismiss my grandmother's tears as an American example of this, evidence that I was hopelessly spoiled and my every discomfort a crisis. However, Lela Nesbitt was no softie. I never saw her cry. Not this woman who had broken horses, played baseball, and hunted with her brothers. What was it, then, that so affected her? What puts that hesitation in my mother's voice?

"Your memaw hid food from you," she reminds me by way of explanation. "Remember how she used to put the sugar in the safe so your dad couldn't make tea?"

"Why did Uncle Gene come with her?"

"Oh, Gene knew who buttered his bread," she says. "He was the oldest and did what Mommy said. Or maybe he had no idea what she was up to. Maybe Carl didn't either. I don't know. I do know that she just couldn't stand that she didn't get what she wanted. And that's why I've always liked your Aunt Nancy. She would tell that woman where to go. Your memaw might have controlled all the others but not Nancy. No, ma'am."

She pauses.

"I still can't get over how upset your grandma was."

I want to draw a distinction between "Grandma" and "Memaw." "Grandma" meant all that the word should mean. She was a white-haired old lady who cared for me while my mom worked. She took me everywhere she went, to her friends' houses, to the Methodist camp meetings or to the old civic center on Lake Mirror where she had covered dinners with other emigre women from West Virginia. My mouth still waters at the memory of all their casseroles. Grandma taught me to read, showered me with presents, and switched me when I was naughty.

But "Memaw" was something else altogether, a quaint old-timey name for a woman who was more like a demonic force, a name, that even today, two decades after I last spoke with her, casts a shadow every time it's uttered.

The kidnapping story still has a lot of holes. Where was my father when it went down? What was "the situation" my mom had mentioned? Where were my brother and sister? How much time passed before Mom realized I wasn't coming back? What was Memaw thinking? So, I decide to ask my sister about it. Michele has a sharper memory for family drama than any of us. When I was writing about my graduation, for example, I had trouble remembering whether it had been my high school or college ceremony that my father missed. I asked my cousin, Karin, and she wasn't sure either. I asked my mom, and she said first one, then the other. But Michele knows and can tick off details of both days that don't set off any sparks for me at all.

"Do you remember the time Memaw and Gene kidnapped me?" I ask. I summarize the story as Mom has told it.

"I don't remember that," she says. "But I do remember the time your father threw us all out of the house."

"When was that?"

"When you were just a baby. One day, he pushed us outside and locked all the doors and windows. He wouldn't let us have you."

"I was inside?" I had assumed I was part of the "us."

"Yes. The police had to be called finally."

"Who called the police?"

"I don't know, Jeff. Mom did, I guess."

"Was he drinking?"

"I don't remember that, either."

This is the first time I've heard this story, and yet it resonates. It's a telling statement my sister makes: 'He' wouldn't let 'us' have you. He had gotten rid of them and kept me. In his mind, Bob and Jeffrey were separate from the others. I can picture him sitting in his armchair, pretending to watch the TV as they all banged on the window. The neighbors would be helping, my mom's gang of friends. He would be wearing that expression that I so often saw on his mother and brother, the scowl, the nose in the air, a kind of righteous but beleaguered aloofness. He would have seen himself as the bastion of tradition and good sense against the mob beyond the walls. My sister says, "one day," and so I picture all this happening during the daytime. Everyone is on the front porch peering in. The sun is Florida bright. The kids are outside playing kickball in the street. Some of them stop to wonder what the hell the adults are doing.

I try to confirm the details with my mom on our next video call.

"Michele says that Dad locked you all out of the house one day and wouldn't let you have me."

"Yeah, I remember."

"And?"

"And what?"

"What happened?"

My mom sighs. "We were fighting, and he tossed us out."

"Fighting about what? Did he physically push you guys out or…?"

"Well, we were trying to wean you off the bottle, but you were crying, and I wanted to just go ahead and give it to you. He told me no. He got pretty mad about it. He grabbed me by the arm and threw me out of the kitchen, and that's when your brother came out of his room with the baseball bat."

"A bat?!"

"He was going to protect his mama." My mom is clearly proud of this.

"Did he hit him?"

"Yeah, he went rat-a-tat-tat."

The sound she makes is so silly, I can't help but laugh.

"Rat-a-tat-tat?"

"That's right."

"You make it sound like an episode of the Three Stooges."

"Well," she says. "That's what it was like. He didn't take a big swing you know, just a few little blows to the head. Rat-a-tat-tat."

"Jesus Christ."

"Your dad was bleeding pretty bad. I remember the scar he bore from it later. Your brother hit him rather hard. And your dad was drunk, of course."

"But you just said he *didn't* hit him hard. Rat-a-tat-tat."

"Well, it was in the head. It doesn't have to be that hard."

"Michele said you had to call the police?"

I hear the doorbell from her side of the phone.

"Do you know what the difference between Wi-Fi and the internet is?" she asks out of the blue. The man from the internet company has arrived and she needs to know what to tell him.

"Just hold on," she says and disappears from the screen. I listen to her open the door and greet the man who's going to install her service. I wait impatiently, staring at a view of the ceiling as she asks him the same question she asked me. She wants to know if Wi-Fi drains her phone battery more than the internet does. In the meantime, I am re-imagining the scene my sister had painted with the new details. My brother would have been fourteen at the time, already a powerful athlete and baseball player. Any honest blow he struck with a bat could have been deadly. The whole scene feels like some kind of final showdown. What had happened before this that the first thing my brother thinks of is a possibly fatal attack? Everyone constantly assures me that my father was not and had never been physically abusive, and I certainly never saw anything that made me doubt that. Ever. So, what sort of emotional storm was finally breaking over all our heads?

"I'm back," my mom announces. Her face fills the screen again.

"So, you called the police?" I repeat.

"That was the internet man!"

"No, I mean when Dad locked y'all out."

"Oh, that! I did. They came out but said that technically they couldn't do anything because I was the one that left the house. So, I went across the street to Trudy's, you remember her?"

"Sort of. I remember calling someone Aunt Trudy." An image of a black-haired woman in 60s flared pants flashes through my mind.

"I stayed at Trudy's living room window all night long watching our place because I was worried your dad would try to take you somewhere. The next day the police came again, and they arrested him this time."

"But why would they arrest him then and not before?"

"I don't remember. I try to block these things out. I like to remember the pleasant things."

"So, you've said. And did he go to prison?"

"Yes, but not for long."

An idea strikes me. "Could this have anything to do with 'that situation' that Memaw said she thought I was stuck in? The reason she came down to get me."

She pauses. "You know, now that you say it, I think it did."

"I remember you telling me that kidnapping story once a long time ago, only in that version Dad was in Memaw's house when you and Grandma went up there."

"Now I'm not sure about that. I don't think so. But I think you're right about the other thing. The two incidents were connected."

"So where did he go then? After he got out of jail?"

"He lived in a trailer on Arizona Avenue for a while. I remember that."

Arizona Avenue was and still is known for being one of the worst areas to live in Lakeland, a road lined with aging, mildewed trailer parks. The police are always going there for drug busts or domestic violence calls. Most recently, one of its female residents became a viral internet sensation under the headline, "Crystal Metheny Fires Missile into Boyfriend's Car." The subhead read, "That's right, folks, the name is real." It's a depressing place, full of what my mom called "white trash." I picture my father exiled there, fresh out of jail, the wound to his pride greater than the one to his head. Had he lost his job? He'd been working as a chemical salesman. My mom can't remember, but if he'd followed the pattern I knew from the rest of his life, then he had. He had also probably called his mother to help make the rent on the trailer.

"You mentioned Mike," I say. "What was Michele doing when all this was going on?"

"She wasn't there," Mom says. "She had already gone to live with her daddy."

"Because of stuff like this?"

"I don't know."

"But she says she remembers it happening."

"I'm sure she remembers hearing about it. She must have it mixed up."

"Is that when Dad moved in with Memaw the first time?"

This is a crucial question, to pinpoint the moment he gave up and surrendered his life to his mother, beginning the pattern that plunged him headlong toward suicide. But neither Mom nor my sister remember anything else. I used to ask my dad sometimes, when I went up to visit him, why he never thought of coming back down to Lakeland, to be closer to me. He always answered that he couldn't bear the bad memories. I never knew what those memories were, but now I have some idea.

The last piece of the puzzle falls into place as I lie down in bed beside my wife that night in Istanbul, forty-five years and five thousand miles away. This whole incident with my father throwing them out of the house, I realize, had not taken place during the day, but at night. I get up, switch on the light, and text my mom. She confirms.

It was the middle of the night.

There's a feeling, then, like when you are blindly turning a Rubik's Cube and suddenly all the sides come out the same color. I said memory is archaeology. A larger picture crystallizes around the exploding lightbulb and the blue flash, and all the disparate incidents fall into a straight line of cause and effect. The memory I had narrated so often to my students was the fight between my parents about the bottle, the fight that triggered everything that followed, my brother with the bat, my father locking the rest of the family out of the house, Mom sheltering at Trudy's, him going off to jail, Memaw abducting me, the final separation and his first move to his mother's.

I keep coming back to that moment of Dad sitting in the armchair—I remember it was brown fabric—as the rest of the family hammered on the windows. For once, the cops had been on his side, and there was a respite. He could breathe, take refuge. He would have me to himself all night, would be finally alone with his flesh and blood while the outsiders were kept at bay—the stepchildren and the gang of his wife's friends, those protective women who had been her neighbors long before he ever came on the scene, when she lived on this street with her first husband. I was the one person there that truly belonged with him, and we were sequestered safely inside this shelter the others had only recently been banished from. We were inviolate.

And yet, I also belonged with the people outside, with my mother and sister and brother and all those adopted aunts—Aunt Gloria and Aunt Trudy and Aunt Marie. I have felt this division ever since, as if I cannot be part of both sides of the family but have to be wholly owned by one or the other. It's a fundamental metaphor of my identity; my mother's side, the noisy, social, crowded outer self, peering through the window at an isolated inner self, the beleaguered soul of my father brooding proudly alone among the dark and empty rooms made to house a whole family. The one is constantly tugging on the other.

***

As a middle-aged man in Istanbul, I have another mode of belonging that joins with my mother's to compete against my father's. My wife Delal's Kurdish family is huge, a crowded clan of relatives both near and distant, all of whom, to my great good fortune, are likable people who adore one another and me. "My family is my refuge," Delal often says. "The only place I can truly be myself." Over the decade we have been married I have slowly come to understand the full import of what she means. Turkish society is extremely racist against Kurds, a large minority who either live in or come from the east of the country. If you are a Kurd, as soon as someone finds out where you're from (that bit of casual information is almost always where the conversation starts), you are in danger. In the worst of times, you could be assaulted, arrested, or disappeared. In the best of times, you are patronized and chided. How often have I heard someone we might have otherwise befriended tell my wife, "But you don't seem Kurdish," meaning it as a compliment, or "But you speak so clearly," or "I had a Kurdish friend before, and she was very nice," or my favorite, "Olsun, onlar da insan." *That's alright. They're people, too.* All of these are, of course, classic lines I have heard well-meaning whites back home inflict upon black people. For Delal, the only place to be completely at home, to be sure of her welcome, to be completely safe to say exactly who she is and what she believes, is among her small nation of a family. It's a foreign concept for me, where the last place I would ever call safe was among my father's nightmare of a nuclear family.

Delal and I threw a barbecue at our apartment in Istanbul after we got back from our summer break in America, the trip to Florida and Georgia, and we spread a blanket over our living room floor that accommodated more than seventeen people, all relatives. Aunts and uncles and sisters and first cousins and second cousins grabbed grilled chicken wings and bulgur salad and Kurdish green beans and wrapped us in concern. How were we? How was my family? How had our trip gone? They told stories and jokes and caught up on all that had happened in the summer. But mostly they laughed—at every point in every conversation, laughed at some silly thing someone did or said or just randomly. At some point, I sat back and listened to the resonance of that laughter and marveled that I was so close to all these people and that there were just as many more who had not been able to come—Delal's mother and brother, at least four other cousins and their families. We could have filled every room in the house. My eye wandered up to my dad's picture floating high above the noise on a bookshelf, a black and white of him taken at his high school graduation just as he was ready to launch himself into life. How would that young man's fate have been different had he been born into such a warm family, crowded and unalone? Could he have been saved? Have I?

There was something uncompromisingly isolated about Dad, an isolation that was genetic. When he locked the house against my mother that night, he was pulling up the drawbridge and defending the fortress walls. And oddly, though they all hated one another, I think the fortress sheltered his mother and brother as well, not his wife or friends, or in the end, even his son, just that hard little core of mother and brother.

I've realized a truth about him in talking about all this that I feel awkward putting into words, as if there is something deeply wrong with the grammar or syntax of the sentence itself. Namely, that no matter how miserable he was with Memaw and Uncle Gene, the three of them were, on the most fundamental and invisible levels, united against the rest of us. They each fought to protect the barrier that kept the outside world at bay, a barrier that had formed before any of us came into existence. And like when Memaw and Uncle Gene took me away, sometimes they tried to pull one of us behind the walls, but it could never last. There was something deeply wrong about their inner sanctum, something that cast you out.

Mine was not Memaw's only kidnapping attempt.

Long after her husband Carl had died and she had moved from her house on Lake Santa Fe to one in Keystone, she paid a visit one day to my uncle and aunt who lived only a few miles away. It was during the early afternoon, and Aunt Nancy was babysitting my cousin Ray's two-year-old son, Ryan, while his parents were at work. Memaw came in the house and asked Nancy if Gene was around and left when my aunt told her he was out. The rest of the story I'll let Aunt Nancy tell with her inimitable style. In addition to her thick Southern twang, she has a verbal tic that I can't imitate in writing, but let me describe it quickly here so you can have it in your imagination whenever she takes the stage—she likes to punctuate statements she deems particularly important with a high-pitched and outraged, "Yeah!" I mean no offense with this comparison, but the tenor of that "yeah" sounds like the yip of a small but valorous dog and conveys a challenge, daring you to contradict her.

"Your Daddy was out for a walk, and he sees your memaw's car cruising toward him. She stops in the middle of the road wearing a big, shit-eating grin, which immediately makes him suspicious. Yeah! You'd have to have peanuts for brains not to be. 'What are you so happy about?' he says, and she just nods her head toward the backseat and says, 'Look what I got.' You know, preening like she'd just done something that deserved a reward. Well, there sits Ryan all strapped up in the seat belt. Yeah! On her way out, she'd found him playing in the yard and figured she would show the world what a horrible babysitter I was and just took him. I nearly lost my mind. I ran around the yard and down to the damn lake shouting his name. I had gone back inside to call the cops, ready to slap his face on a milk carton when your Daddy phoned. 'You missing anything?' he says, 'because I might know where it is.' I hauled buggy over there to pick Ryan up, and as soon as I pulled in the driveway, she came prancing out the door to let me have it. Yeah! I was just a piece of shanty Irish trash who let that baby wander the neighborhood all alone, and she was not about to let her precious great-grandson go back to a den of abuse and negligence. Well, I called his momma, Ray's wife, Donna, and Donna told her to give Ryan to me that instant or she'd call the cops and have her ass arrested. That scared her, all right, 'cause she gave him back.

"Anyway, I guess she didn't have enough because that night she came back to my house for round two. She charged right through the front door and into the kitchen like a little bull. 'I'm going to kill you!' she said. Yeah! I was washing dishes, and she was across the counter from me a'cussing me down one road and up the other. I had just finished dinner, and there was this glass bowl of cream corn still sitting there on the counter. I remember I hadn't had enough cream corn, see, and so I'd mixed regular corn in with it, and she reached into that bowl thinking she'd throw something real deadly at me, you know, she was going to show how dangerous she could be, despite being seventy-something years old, and all she came out with was a fist full of that damn corn. I can still see her slinging it across the room. I burst out laughing and turned back toward the sink to finish the dishes. Well, that made her so mad, she came around the counter and grabbed the nearest thing she could find, a big old dish soap bottle, and she clonked me in the head with it. It hurt, too. I saw stars. Yeah! She was about to have another go, and all I could think to do was put my hand over her face and push her away. She was a short old bitch, and her arms wouldn't reach as far as mine. I yelled for Gene, then, told him to come get his mommy or I'd have to kill her. He grabbed her from behind and I remember her legs just a'kicking like a caught rabbit. She was still cussing, too, still describing all the ways she was going to kill me. Oh, she was going to take that steak knife and cut my throat and break my skull with the crock pot. He dragged her out to her car and told her to get her ass home. Yeah! We sent her packing, right back to your daddy. Bob must have been thrilled to see her coming at him in that state."

"Why in the hell did she do it?" I ask. "Why did she want Ryan?"

"To show what a horrible grandmother I was, of course!" My aunt barks out a laugh as if she can't believe I need this spelled out. "I had stolen her beloved Gene from her when I married him, and she'd hated me for it ever since. She didn't give a flying fig about Ryan. She took him so she could finally reveal the truth about me."

What had caused this madness? I want to know. Such hatred didn't just come out of nowhere. What happened before I was born that explained it all? My aunt throws up her hands.

"Jesus, Jeffrey, she was just mean. She had the devil in her from the day she popped out of her momma and was proud of it. Some people are born that way, see? Evil from the get-go. They don't need no reason."

THREE

*"There she stood in the doorway; I heard the mission bell
And I was thinking to myself, 'This could be heaven, or this could be Hell'."*

"Whose song is this?" my wife asks from the backseat of Cousin Lisa's SUV.

"The Eagles," Lisa answers with slow, elastic Southern vowels. "This song is off one of their most successful albums called *Hotel California*, and it's the first song off that album."

I smile at the pedantic detail. Delal is playing the role of bemused foreigner to whom so much of what everyone else takes for granted must be explained. People have fun with it, I think. It allows them to enjoy all the elements of life that have faded into the ambient noise of the day-to-day and see them anew, stark against an unfamiliar background. Like this tired rock song played ad nauseum by every radio station between Lakeland and Tifton, or like the Georgia cotton fields, churches, trailers and pine forests now rolling past us. For Delal, a Kurd from the dry, rugged mountains of Anatolia, who has spent the last two decades of her life in the megalopolis of Istanbul, the dense green and sleepy torpor must look like the landscape of an alien world. And the history which is so intimately tangled in my genes is an utter mystery.

It's the day after our arrival, and Clark and Lisa have been gracious enough to tour me and Delal around the farmland outside of Tifton and point out the places of my father's childhood.

"Look," Cousin Clark says, interrupting Lisa's explanation of American pop culture. He points to a yellow clapboard farmhouse on the left which sits back from the highway in the middle of an open field. We are driving north of the little unincorporated village of Crosland. "We used to live in that house. Bob would come up from Omega for a visit sometimes."

"Now, when was that, Daddy?" Lisa asks.

"Oh, I don't know. I must have been seven or so. I can still see Bob and me hightailing it across that field to hide beneath the porch when a squadron of planes flew over. We thought they were Germans come to bomb the living daylights out of us."

23

Clark is the son of Dorothy, Memaw's youngest sister. Aunt Dorothy passed just a few years before, having made it well into her nineties. She was famed for her kindness, her wit, and her cooking, especially her pound cake and fried chicken, dishes which, sadly, I never got to taste. Dad used to call her the sole sane one in the family. Though we had only met a few times when Aunt Dorothy came to visit Memaw, Lisa assures me that her "grandmama" remembered me. Lisa and I became friends, because of all things, Facebook. Many times over the years she has invited me up for a visit, but I live and work in Turkey, and what time I have for vacation in the States, I generally spend with my friends and mother in Florida.

This year is different, though.

In April, in Istanbul, while sleepily surfing the internet one morning before classes started, I ran across, quite by accident, a blog entry about a lynching. It was one that Memaw had told me about twenty years before, and I had nearly forgotten all about it. Suddenly, she haunted my thoughts again, accompanied by the disturbing bugbear of race and the old South I was still connected to.

She had told me the story a few weeks before I left for Japan. Memaw was taking me around her house asking what I wanted after she died so she could write it in her will. It was a morbid ritual she engaged in whenever I visited. I told her I didn't want much of anything except a book she kept on the family history of the Gibbses. It was a thin volume, bound in red leather and printed by a long-extinct publishing house in Tifton. It looked like a Baptist hymnal. Together we flipped through the pages and found a passage about my grandfather's great-grandfather, James Gibbs. He'd lived on a farm in Ty Ty, Georgia, apparently, and owned two slaves, a man and a woman. There was the usual qualifier exonerating the white master: "He had bought the woman from a Mr. Mitchell, who had been very cruel to her." As if in the end, the purchase of a human being had been a good deed. I mentioned how odd it was to think I was descended from slave owners, and Memaw got a distant look on her face.

"When I was around, oh I don't know, eight or so," she began, "a colored man by the name of John Henry was accused of raping and killing a white girl named Loreena, one of our neighbors."

This had happened near her family's farm in south Georgia. One night, shortly after the girl's murder, Memaw's father and her older brother, Fred, joined a posse to hunt John Henry, leaving her mother and the younger kids alone at the main house.

"People didn't stop with just finding the colored man," she said with some hesitation. "They were burning houses and just all kinds of awful things. All the black folks living nearby came to us because they knew my mama would help them. Their ol' eyes were just as wide as plates and scared as can be and one of them said," she shifts into a high-pitched whine, "'Oh Miss Linnie, Miss Linnie, they burning everything! You got to let us hide in yo' cane field!' So Mama took them out in the sugarcane rows, and they lay there till morning, not daring to move. I can't blame them for being so frightened, either. The posse found John Henry."

She paused, laughed uncomfortably.

"Now this isn't nice to say, but they chopped off his private parts and sewed them up in his mouth. They tortured that poor man and then burned him alive. People came around later and cut off pieces of his body for a souvenir."

I don't know what possessed her to tell this story, then. I had never known her to say anything remotely sympathetic about a black person, and yet this tale clearly caused her shame, however buried, so much so that seventy years later she felt the need to confess it to me. Aunt Nancy denied that Memaw's past explained anything, but what did such an upbringing do to a human being, in a place where extreme violence and hatred were so much a part of the social fabric that no one even thought of them as unusual? Did this have some influence on the kind of person she was to become and thus, the kind of person she turned my father into?

This brutal mob killing, a killing my own great-grandfather may have had a hand in, has haunted my thoughts for years. I needed to see where it had happened as much as I needed to find out about my father's suicide. The violence of both seemed cousins to one another and revolved around the same woman. And so, I had asked Clark to show me the sight of his grandfather's store and farmhouse where Memaw had grown up and where I assumed those frightened black people had come for help. I didn't say a word to anyone about why I wanted to see it, my real motives. This was why we were on that empty highway running through the empty farmland, barreling headlong toward the county line, toward all sorts of borders.

***

My grandmother is an inescapable piece of this puzzle. She is a Nazca line, a face on Easter Island, a megalith at Stonehenge—a relic of a blank and unknowable past whose surface I run my hands over, looking for fresh clues. So desperate am I for understanding that any tidbit counts as enlightening. My cousin Karin's oldest brother, Wayne, for instance, wrote me recently about the origins of the word we used for her, *Memaw*. It was a bastardization of "*mémère*," he'd discovered, a French term meaning "granny" that was brought by the Acadians from Quebec when they moved to Louisiana and became the Cajuns. From there, it spread over the whole South. This was just academic trivia. Still, I couldn't help writing it down in my own notes. It seemed important, another clue. I needed to know more; however abstract, however irrelevant the information was in the quest to explain this woman. Who had given her the name? As the oldest of us grandchildren, I assumed it was Wayne. I asked. He wasn't sure, but he didn't think so. He confirmed with his mother, Aunt Nancy. She says, yes, of course it was him who first called her memaw. He even came up with Pepaw for my father's father.

Wayne is an exception in the family, not one to worry over old grievances and without a negative word to say about Memaw or anyone else. Fifteen years my senior, he seems an obvious source of information about the lives of people I knew only after they had become so twisted, but he remains tight-lipped, never speaks ill, never even recognizes there were problems. Still, the fact that the word tickled his conscience enough to merit delving into its origins suggests to me that, in his own way, he wrestles with her memory and her presence much the way we all do.

Memaw. The name makes friends of mine laugh, but it has a power in our family. There was an inhuman quality about her. We grandkids considered her a kind of elemental spirit, someone who had always been just as she was, unpredictable, cruel, yet somehow ever in control, her "meanness" brilliantly hidden behind the veneer of a genteel, affectionate old Southern lady. No one outside our immediate family knew anything of her dark side, so effectively did she dissimulate. She greeted us with effusive kisses and hugs, bought us school clothes, sent us money for our birthdays, told us she loved us all the time, peppered all references to us with saccharine terms of endearment like "my sweet darling" and "my beautiful doll baby." Her letters to me, even after I turned thirty, were always addressed to "My Precious Boy."

Here is the story I usually tell people when pressed to explain what Memaw was, the one that distills her character without embarrassing anyone else in the family or giving away any skeletons in the closet.

One summer afternoon, she set my cousin Karin and me at the finely polished dining room table and asked us if we would like some iced tea. I must have been twelve, Karin nine.

"Mama's sweet babies must be so thirsty," she said, looking at us with her hands on her hips and a smile that seemed slightly ironic. We both squirmed at the way she addressed us, but we were used to it. Plus, we had been playing outside in the ninety-degree heat and desperately wanted something to drink. We didn't serve ourselves as we would have in each other's houses. We knew better. So, we said yes, of course, and Memaw disappeared into the kitchen. We heard the freezer open, the ice falling from the trays, and then her voice, the low growl we were so familiar with.

"Goddamn kids eating my food. Can barely keep a goddamn bag of sugar in the house."

We heard the tea pouring.

"Like little thieves."

When she reappeared in the doorway, she was chuckling, a glass in both hands.

"Oh, I hope you don't pay this crazy old lady any mind!" she said, setting them down in front of us. "I talk to myself sometimes."

I remember staring at the sweat oozing down those glasses, the ice shifting in the tea, and thinking there was no way I was taking a drink, and yet I would, we both would, because what recourse did we have? This was just how it was. We were trapped in that sterile room surrounded by her China cabinets, each stocked with antique plates and cups displayed on metal stands, delicate floral patterns painted on the surfaces and the edges lined with gold. She liked to talk about how expensive they were, how careful we had to be around them. She took my arm, kissed me from elbow to wrist. This always made me cringe.

"Mama sure loves her precious dolls."

I finished my tea quickly, and she reached for the empty glass.

"Lord, that was fast," she chuckled. "No wonder all your mother's kids are so fat. Let me go get you some more."

Karin and I flashed each other a look. *Here we go again.*

***

Her real name was Ruby Vernell Hamner. There's a story my Aunt Nancy tells from back before my father met my mother. Whenever Memaw came to their house and wore out her welcome ("Took about a minute," my aunt assures me), my uncle, father, and she would sing Waylon Jennings' "Ruby, don't take your love to town."

You've painted up your lips and rolled and curled your tinted hair...

"We'd just croon at the top of our voices," my aunt told me. "Nell would storm out with her ass in the air, all in a huff like a little bull and calling us every name in the book. She hated that name of hers, couldn't stand it! Yeah! She despised her parents for giving it to her."

This story has always stuck with me because it featured my father and his older brother acting in unity against her. I never saw anything like that myself. My father and uncle had hated each other for as long as I can remember. When I ask Clark if he remembers when Gene and Bob were friends, he says, "I wouldn't say they were ever friends." It's the only negative comment Clark speaks about family the whole visit. More often than not, Memaw would pull in Uncle Gene as an ally against Dad. He had helped her kidnap me after all. And whenever she kicked Dad out of the house, she called Gene to come down before she ever phoned the police.

***

I asked Memaw once what her first memory was. "A whipping," she answered. She had been playing in front of the homes of the children of her parents' sharecroppers. Her mother Linnie caught her running back from the "n—— cabins," as she called them, and beat her across the legs with a razor strop she kept behind the piano.

"Oh," she said, laughing at the memory. "Mama was fit to be tied, and you didn't see her angry very often. I didn't stop running, either, but kept on going just as fast as my feet would carry me. She wore my legs out good. But I sure loved playing with those n—— kids."

The attacker in this story, "Miss Linnie," remains a revered figure in our family, paradoxically renowned for her gentle nature.

"Oh, she was the kindest, meekest creature on earth," Aunt Nancy is fond of saying. "How that other thing came out of her is anyone's guess."

Other members of the family described both Linnie and her husband Claude as the "sweetest people," adored by the whole community. When I post a picture of their old store on the Facebook page of the Worth County Historical society, I get a flood of gracious comments and fond memories from older people.

"Everyone in Bridgeboro knew who your great-grandparents were. Just real good people. We loved them dearly."

"I remember Mrs. Hamner more than anyone in the family. She was so good to all us kids!"

And a cousin writes, "I remember Miss Linnie. She saw the world through rose-colored glasses, always so upbeat and sweet-spoken! And I remember

Linnie's piano. She would play and sing the hymns 'When the Dew is Still on the Roses' and 'This Old House.'"

I immediately write back and tell her the story of Memaw's first memory.

"Oh, I remember that old razor strop. What I remember most is your great-grandfather using it to sharpen his razor, which looked like a long knife, but I just can't imagine someone like sweet Miss Linnie using it on a little girl!" A page from the Census adds some clarity to Memaw's first memory. Her father, Claude Hamner, was overseer on a farm in Colquitt County, hired to supervise several black families listed as "laborers." These are the people who must have been Ms. Linnie's sharecroppers. Seeing their names brings them into focus a little as human beings, fleshing out the wide-eyed caricatures from Memaw's story. There were the elderly Joe and Clora Brown, Bob and Lizzie McCray, Garnie and Josephine Mathis, eighteen-year-old Mary Stubs and her two-year-old daughter Queen, Joe and Tilda Johnson, Frank and Rachel Peterson. The children Memaw had been playing with could have been Ellina, youngest daughter of the McCrays and just three years older, or Dan, the youngest son of the Mathises, who was two years her senior, or Franklin Peterson, who was the same age.

It's hard to imagine Memaw as a little girl, as an actual child played with others and cried and called someone Mama and Daddy. Yet, this little scene did seem to provide an explanation of how she was created. This is how I think of it, too. *Created.* I was always reading comic books as a kid, and I was expecting her to have something along the lines of a supervillain origin story. The complicated, destructive woman she became later in life *was* created just as surely as any Lex Luthor or Joker.

In 2007, in the Istanbul neighborhood of Harbiye, an Armenian journalist and humanitarian named Hrant Dink was assassinated on the sidewalk by Turkish nationalist, Ogun Samast. The reason? Dink was Armenian and had spoken openly about the Genocide committed against his people during World War I. Turks have always denied the Genocide, and to mention it is still taboo. A great deal of history is taboo. When Dink's killer was caught, instead of looking like a hunted criminal finally apprehended, frightened or contrite, he posed proudly with police at the station behind a giant Turkish flag. At her husband's funeral, a grieving Rakel Dink spoke of this racist, unrepentant killer, and indirectly of those officials who posed with him, and of their flag.

"I know at one point Samast was an infant. If we don't question the darkness that turns a baby into a murderer, then nothing can ever be done."

The darkness.

Picture four-year-old Nell, not yet *Memaw* the supervillain, as a child running home across the fields. She's flushed and sweaty, breathless, her reddish brown curls sticking to her forehead. Now, picture any little girl you know and let Nell wear her smile, speak with her voice. I automatically see my niece's daughter, Linleigh. She likes to play rough sometimes, wrestle with the boys, but at the same time, she's very sensitive. Any cross word can make her feel guilty for weeks. She's also indefatigably cheerful. She wakes up every morning by Facetiming my mom, her great-grandmother, and saying "It's a beautiful day!" It's a girl like Linleigh I see rushing home across those Georgia fields in 1921. Maybe she's been wrestling with the boys, with Franklin or Dan. Maybe she and Ellina were fussing over the baby named Queen. Or maybe the whole gang of kids was fresh from a game of hide-and-seek or chasing minnows in the creek. Nell wears a huge grin thinking of something funny one of them said. Then out of nowhere comes the attack, a beating. The world goes upside down. Her normally gentle mama is shouting furiously at her, wielding a razor strop that she brings down on Nell's small legs again and again until she raises great bleeding welts. And for what? What does Nell understand as her crime?

"I told you not to play with those n——s," her mother hisses.

***

Memaw told me about the lynching of John Henry in the early 90s, before the magic of Google and Wikipedia. I went to the public library in Lakeland, checked out all the books on lynching I could, but found no mention of a John Henry. Once I had access to the internet, I did a few tentative searches. All I ever turned up was an article on the lynching of a Virginia man named John Henry James. The story was so similar I assumed my grandmother had read about it somewhere and got it mixed up in her old age with some vaguely remembered news item out of her own childhood. A black man was accused of raping a white girl outside of Charlottesville, Virginia in 1898. A mob seized him from the jail where he was being held, took him to a tree, and hung him. They shot him over seventy-five times for good measure. Locals came by to visit the murder site, taking souvenirs off the body. As the Richmond paper put it at the time, they cut off "some portions of the clothing, etc." It's the "etcetera" that nags.

Then this April, some twenty-five years later, I stumbled on that blog entry. It started with a recommendation that popped up in my daily newsfeed under the heading "articles you might like," utterly random and utterly fateful. It was a piece about the National Memorial for Peace and Justice, a museum recently opened in Montgomery, Alabama, which had a database documenting lynchings in America. It had been years since I'd tried researching John Henry, but I browsed the museum's website thinking I might turn something up.

Nothing.

Maybe I had the name wrong. On a hunch, I wrote *John Henry, lynching* and *Georgia* in Google's general search bar, just to see what might pop up, and the blog was the first entry at the very top of the list. In the title bar, the author had typed an introduction: "This started as an attempt to find a lynching for every day of the year. It's a grim reminder of a part of United States history I fear too many find easy to shrug away." She had named her blog "Strange Fruit and Spanish Moss," a reference to the eponymous Billie Holiday song and, in the case of Spanish moss, the symbol of my home state. It was a digital memorial to nearly a century of butchered and martyred black people. In the entry for June 18th, I found John Henry *Williams*, a man who had been lynched in the small town of Autreyville, just a half-hour's drive from Tifton and Omega.

From the Daily Concorde Tribune of North Carolina, dated June 14th, 1921:

> *Word was received here today from Autreyville where Lorena Wilkes, a twelve-year-old white girl, was murdered yesterday morning, that a negro church was burned and two negro women severely beaten last night while parties of white men searched for the wife of John Henry Williams, the negro accused of the crime. The woman was not found.*

After a quarter of a century, the specter of the John Henry my grandmother had told me about had finally surfaced.

The first destination I ask Clark to show us is the location of the fabled store of his grandparents, where I assume my grandmother's tale of the black people coming to her mother for help had occurred. Memaw and her sisters had often talked about growing up there after all. In the scene I've painted of Memaw's story, a scene inspired, perhaps, by dozens of movies about the South, I see the black families standing nervously out in the yard as my great-grandmother greets them on the porch of the general store with eight-year-old Nell hiding among her skirts.

My only resource on the famous Hamner store is my Aunt Nancy, and I grill her about it one day when I'm home visiting during winter break. As it turns out, her mother and Memaw were cousins. Aunt Nancy's grandfather, Downy Bridges, and Memaw's mother, Linnie, were brother and sister. I grew up among rumors that Aunt Nancy and my Uncle Gene were not only husband and wife, but second cousins, and this confirms it. It's a minor victory in family gossip.

"Guess that's what you call 'kissing cousins,'" Aunt Nancy says and laughs dismissively. "I met your uncle Gene when I was a little girl visiting Aunt Linnie. We'd come up from Savannah. Yeah! Wish we hadn't. Might've saved myself a few decades of hell living with that beast I married. Anyway, Momma would haul us all up there for the weekend. Aunt Linnie lived in the store, see. It was just a little old country grocery. There was a swing out front, and we'd all sit out there of an evening and chat with that red sun setting over the fields. She had a pie-safe out back, a kind of china cabinet with a screen over it to keep the pies cool. There was a pot-bellied stove that always had a pot of coffee boiling. We kids would take turns sweeping the chicken yard or getting wiggle worms out of the well."

"Out of the well?" I ask. "Their drinking water had worms in it?"

"I guess they filtered it or something before they drank it. Keep the worms out of your mouth. Anyway, I remember Gene one time asking his mama when 'them people with all the noisy kids' were gonna leave. Yeah! He was talking about us, of course. Couldn't stand that there was anyone else in the world but him. He wanted to annihilate everyone except himself and his precious mommy. That's what his problem with your daddy was. Bob was born, see? Gene wanted Mommy all to himself."

I've heard this line of thinking from her before. I'm not sure what to make of it. It sounds a bit like the bitter ranting of someone who lived with a man she hated for forty years, and so I try to ease her back toward a subject on more solid ground. "And this store was in Sparks?"

"No. Sparks was where Nell was born. The store was near Bridgeboro. Oh, we had a ball at Aunt Linnie's! I remember they had a gas pump out front and in back was the house where they kept an old pee-ana we liked to bang on. We had ourselves a good time with that pee-ana!"

***

Cousin Clark has us turn left onto a dirt road that plunges west through cattle land sectioned off with barbed wire. Rolls of hay dot the fields. Trailers sit in yards with much older wooden houses behind them falling into ruin. We cross a highway, and Clark points to a blue doublewide with a wooden deck added to the front. A clapboard garage stands next to it, leaning precariously to the right. Out front, a black SUV is parked under a crepe myrtle. The tree drops bundles of pink blossoms onto the hood.

"That's the old site of the store," Clark says. "Though it was torn down long ago. I think one of the cousins lives in the trailer, but I'm not sure which one."

We stop and I roll down the window. I snap a few pictures. Is this the place, I wonder? I try to imagine a crowd of black people standing where we are parked, pleading with my great-grandmother to save them even as my great-grandfather marauded with a lynch mob.

"Did they always live here?" I ask Clark. "I heard they lived in Bridgeboro."

"Bridgeboro is up the road," he answers.

"How close is Autreyville?"

"Oh, about half an hour's drive south."

Half an hour seems too far for Memaw's family to have been so closely involved in John Henry's lynching. Yet, I know men from several counties were rallied for the manhunt.

"Grandmama always said she was born out on Tallokas Road," Lisa adds. "I think I know where that is, but she never mentioned any more about it."

Tallokas. I write the name down.

As we talk, a man comes out of the trailer. He looks quite old, wears baggy overalls and a service station cap. Lisa calls out to him, asks him if this was the site of the old store owned by Claude Hamner.

"He was my granddaddy," the man shouts from his front step.

"That's Kenny," Clark says, "Your daddy's and my first cousin! Why, we used to hang out all the time. His dad was Uncle Carlton, who we called Uncle Sleepy, 'cause he was always drunk and stayed passed out in one place or another."

We climb out of the car and introduce ourselves. Kenny takes my hand, and Clark explains that I am Bob Gibbs' son. The old man peers into my face, his eyes bloodshot and watery.

"My God," he says. "He looks just like Bob!"

My face reddens. With those words, I am sucked instantly out of my musings on an old murder and back with my daddy again, consumed by the man and the mystery of his suicide. *This is why you've really come*, a voice in my head says. I am suddenly far from the subject of race and lynchings and historical crimes. Or am I?

"Such hatred didn't just come out of nowhere," I'd told my aunt.

***

33

It's the Fourth of July, a few days before my Georgia trip. It has become a Gibbs family tradition to gather for barbecue and swimming on Lake Geneva in Keystone, where my cousins grew up and I spent my summers. Cousin Wayne, with his methodical attention, brings every accoutrement imaginable for optimum family enjoyment. There are kayaks, deck chairs, insect repellant, hats to keep the Florida sun from frying our faces, paddle boats, water-ski equipment, a cooler full of local craft beers, inner tubes, and, of course, fireworks. My father used to make fun of Wayne's fussy obsession with gadgets, but my oldest cousin's need to do things the "right" way is a welcome contrast to the generation before us who all seemed focused on just getting through the day no matter how much damage they did. Wayne always makes Delal and me feel cared for. He came the week before to mow the beach grass and clear the lake weed along the shore so that a sandy spot was available next to the dock for swimming.

The family abandoned the house on Lake Geneva after my Uncle Gene died of cancer, and it now sits rotting and crumbling on top of the hill, lost in the shadows of the live-oak trees; the windows from which Aunt Nancy used to watch us swim are now eyeless, like the sockets of a skull. The lake was first settled by a white family named Alderman, who built an antebellum citrus plantation, complete with slaves, on the shores. The road leading past the house is named after them. A few orange trees dot my uncle's yard, buried under blankets of muscadine vines.

We gather under the covered part of the dock and chat. On the lake, neighbors water ski and putz around on their paddle boats. My youngest cousin Karin provides the bulk of the food, pulled pork sandwiches and ribs from Dianne's Old Time Barbecue in nearby Hawthorne. We've brought a peach cobbler.

The kids are jumping off the end of the dock, playing a game of copycat where the next person has to imitate the daring jump of the leader into the water. There are cannonballs, cartwheels, and somersaults. Karin and I used to play the same games. We adults are buzzing a little on beer and sun. Delal is eager to take the kayak out and have a go around the lake. It's a lovely thing to do in the late afternoon when the sky turns pinkish-orange and the worst of the heat lifts. The opposite shore is a quiet marsh, and I love to paddle through the duckweed and hyacinth, teasing Delal that I hear a gator grunt.

Into this idyllic holiday, I drop a bomb. There's an old family story told by my aunt that I'm not sure I remember correctly, and it bears directly on my research into John Henry. I have been waiting all day for an appropriate time, but there's never really an appropriate time to bring up torture and lynching. Aunt Nancy is talking about her father.

"Oh, he was a character! They say when he came to ask Mother to marry him, he rode up to her front porch perched on a donkey, said his piece, then put her on the donkey's rump and hauled her off."

"He did not!" my mom says, and then the two burst out laughing for a few seconds, convulsed in helpless giggles.

"You told me once," I say, "that your daddy had a thumb or something in a jar? Do I have that right?"

"Oh yeah," she says. "Had an old n——'s thumb."

The mood changes immediately. My mother's face wrinkles up in disgust, and she turns angrily away from the rest of us, muttering something under her breath. I feel a bit guilty for what I've done. I try to make eyes with Mom, to offer a silent apology. I know how much this kind of talk pains her. Though not enlightened on the current debate about race in America and, in my opinion, a little too dismissive in her views on the subject, my mother has spent most of her life working in the black community of Lakeland. I've seen the respect that community confers upon her, and when I was a child, she made sure that not one uncivil word about black people escaped my lips. This was in stark contrast to the older generation on my father's side who routinely uttered racial epithets that made my ears burn. I am not going to edit the story my aunt told that day on the lake, neither the vocabulary nor the events, though it shames me to tell it. This is the conflict I have always felt, that my mother felt that day, too, just seconds after laughing hysterically with her sister-in-law—love and revulsion, affection and horror, friendship and shame.

"When I was a girl," Aunt Nancy begins, "an old n—— raped and killed a white girl. This was in Savannah where I was born. Back in them days, people didn't fool with trials and appeals and all that malarkey. Yeah! They took care of things themselves. That's when criminals got what they deserved, not like nowadays where we have to be careful not to hurt anybody's feelings, and they got to go to court and have themselves 'a fair trial.' So anyway, my daddy joined the posse to hunt the son of a bitch. I was just a little old thing, outside playing, and I heard something scuffling under the house. So, I went and peeked under the stairs and tried to peer up in them shadows, but all I could make out were two white eyes gaping at me like little moons. Well, damned if it wasn't that n—— rapist! He ran like a bat out of hell, the dogs chasing after him. They found him lying out in a swamp among the logs, which were black like him. He was trying to camouflage himself! Well, it didn't work. Yeah! They got him, and they hung him. And my daddy took that thumb for a souvenir."

There's a slight falter in her voice at this last part, a subtle quavering that betrays the whole idea that such mutilation was the proper carrying out of justice.

"I guess that's what people did back then," she adds vaguely. "Took souvenirs."

None of this squares with Memaw's story of John Henry. It wasn't the right place, wasn't the right time. Nor does it square with any other historical event. My aunt would have been a girl in the early forties. In all my research, I haven't yet found a record of lynching at that time in that area of the state. My feeling is that Aunt Nancy, in her penchant for embellishment, put together a few scraps of memory, some tales from her father, a few newspaper stories and a dash of imagination, then strung them all together into a coherent narrative. I do not doubt that her father had a thumb in a jar. That story I have heard off and on all my life.

Later, Wayne and I wade out past the dock, each clinging to a pool raft.

"My granddaddy told me a story," he says without commenting on the truthfulness of his mother's. "I'm talking about my mother's father. He said that he was with a bunch of men surrounding the courthouse."

"Where?"

"I don't know. Somewhere in Georgia, I guess. He was from Savannah. Anyway, there was this black guy inside, and they wanted to hang him for raping a white girl. The marshals were on the steps, and someone in the crowd said real innocent-like, 'Hey that looks like the guns we use to go hunting. You mind if I take a look?' Well, the marshal let the guy inspect his gun, and the guy realized it wasn't loaded. He shouts, 'They don't have any bullets!' and then the mob charged the marshals and took the black guy away. They tied him with chains to a tree, but the guy was so strong, he broke free and charged them. They all panicked and started shooting. My granddaddy remembers pieces of the man hitting his face from all the gunfire."

This does square with an element of the John Henry Williams story. Aunt Nancy's daddy would have been just eighteen in 1921. Williams had been taken to the town of Moultrie, to the Colquitt County courthouse for a "speedy" trial. The mob waited outside. The doors were guarded by twenty officers, according to the *Baltimore African American*, a black newspaper. Williams left the courtroom with ten on each side. When he appeared, someone from the crowd shouted, "Let's get him!," and his supposed protectors, led by Colquitt's chief of police, J.O. Stewart, yielded him without a struggle, and may have even accompanied the mob to the killing site.

My father always said that Aunt Nancy's dad was, like his daughter, a teller of tall tales, so his connection to the story is a little in doubt. But my great-grandfather, Claude Hamner, could easily have been part of the mob that day. The men threw their victim into a car and drove him south to Autreyville, to the pond where the body of the girl he had allegedly murdered had been found. They tied him to a tree trunk near the edge of the water and piled wood around him. They then siphoned gasoline from their automobiles and soaked his clothes. Not many people gathered at first, and so they passed the time "spitting on him, poking him in the ribs, and calling him names." When an audience of several hundred had amassed, someone lit a match.

"Flames flared up and found their way to Williams' body," the anonymous reporter of the Baltimore paper writes.

Now and then he cried aloud, and his body went through terrible contortions. For a while, the winds carried the flames and the smoke directly into his face so that he could not speak. Later, the winds shifted and members of the mob, unaffected, recognized the hymn he sang as, 'Nearer My God to Thee.' At the trial today, the jury was out less than one minute when it returned the verdict of guilty.

The Washington Eagle, also a black paper, tells another story. It wasn't twenty officers, but fifty sheriffs who guarded Williams. No one shouted, "Let's get him." Rather, a "cracker" by the name of Ken Murphy gave the Confederate yell and cried, "Get the n——!" The mob tore off his clothes as he was shoved in the car. They "unsexed" him and made him eat a portion of his "anatomy" which had been cut away. Another portion was sent to Georgia governor, Hugh Dorsey, who had enraged whites that year by publishing a report that condemned the state's treatment of black people. Williams was then taken to a grove and surrounded by "five hundred people in Ku Klux Klan Ceremonial." He was tied to a stump, and a pyramid of wood piled around him. "The pyre was lit, and a hundred men and women, old and young, grandmothers among them, joined hands and danced around while the negro burned."

The Thomasville Daily Times, the local white newspaper, wrote this about the manhunt:

Many wild rumors were current last night, but the crowd, while determined to punish the guilty negro, was orderly and no disturbances occurred.

There was no reason, you see, for those frightened people to seek a hiding place in Miss Linnie's fields. It was all 'wild rumor' and my grandmother's imagination. The writer continues, describing the mob's torture and immolation of Williams.

The men from Colquitt County were perfectly sober and restrained themselves at all times. The crowd was as orderly as they could be under such circumstances. Not a drop or smell of whiskey was detected. There was no noise or excitement apparently.

I like the "apparently" and how the lack of alcohol seemed to sanctify the event.

Four different stories about the killing of this man, each contradicting the other, even when they were on the same side. Perhaps none of them were told by people who were actually present. The black papers added that amid the flames, Williams asked for a cigarette and then calmly blew the smoke in the face of his tormentors. Some of the white papers mentioned this detail, too, but put a different spin on it. Rather than showing a man stoically refusing to allow the monsters who tortured him to see his pain, it represented his indifference to the brutality of his crime. The white papers were also careful to describe his unrepentant gaze, the cold way he confessed to the murder of a child as he burned. Black papers emphasized Williams' stubborn insistence on his innocence. A confession was only extracted after extreme torture. One side was trying to scrabble together some dignity, the other to deny their butchery. I wonder where my great-grandfather and his son were. In the crowd? Wearing white sheets or trying to keep their distance from this orgy of violence? Where was my grandmother's mother, the fabled Miss Linnie who had saved her neighbors by hiding them in her cane fields, the "gentle" woman who had switched her daughter for playing with those same "n——s"? Did she approve of this? Had any of her boys gone out to the field and cut a "souvenir" off the body? Did anyone join in that macabre dance of "old and young" around the fire?

Those who were actually there do not speak so freely, I think. They do not give interviews with newspapers or write accounts themselves or seek out a platform to make these atrocities public. The people who suffered the horrors wrestle with fear and threat, with trauma, with shame even, and with the frustration that so few who hear the tale will really be able to understand the gravity of what happened.

***

Throughout these three days in Georgia, Delal was ever at my side. I am judicious in mentioning her, because she loathes any kind of spotlight. But she has witnessed her share of atrocity. Being Kurdish in Turkey is a lot like being black in the States. There's a history of violence and persecution constantly denied or minimalized. For instance, if you tell people, as did a Kurdish friend of ours, how your rally for civil rights was attacked by an ISIS bomber, and the Turkish police, instead of helping you escape, blocked the ambulances from reaching you, well, you'll be called a liar or arrested or worse, even though the shrapnel of those bombs are still lodged in your leg, even though you still limp years after the fact. "The President publicly condemned the attacks," you're told. "The police are investigating to find the perpetrators. How could they be part of it?" Our friend must be twisting things. She's paranoid, a radical. What was she doing at a rally anyway, stirring up trouble?

It's better to stay silent.

My wife has stories like this, too. The worst I find out secondhand or by accident or not at all. That reticence is a truth that fills this narrative. You have to pay attention to how the story is told. The real voices are not the ones speaking the loudest. The past has an edge that still cuts.

Black and white, the people who were present at the lynching of John Henry Williams seem to keep what they know to themselves, until, say, for the perpetrators at least, they near death. Then they might be seized with the need to confess to someone, like their grandson. In the case of the victims, they might wander the streets in a haunted, half-mad daze until someone stumbles on them quite by accident.

The Harlem Renaissance artist, Lois Mailou Jones, painted a portrait of a man about to be lynched called "Mob Victim." An older black man dressed in shades of blue, his hands tied, stands against a background of green foliage. The sky is dark. It's night. There are clouds lit by a luminous moon. He is between two trees, looking off canvas to the right. He wears an odd expression for a man about to be lynched, the look of someone from an old Renaissance painting, eyes on the crucified Christ.

Apparently, the painting was meant to portray the lynching of John Henry Williams. I say "apparently" because I can only find a reference to the interview where Maillou Jones states this on a website selling college essays. The source is well-documented—an interview given to Ken Oda in his art magazine KOAN—but it's accessible only through old-fashioned means. I would have to go to the library at Howard University in Washington, D.C. or the University of Minnesota and physically check it out. I do find an interview in Callaloo where she describes to editor Charles H. Rowell her meeting with the model for "Mob Victim."

"I did another impressionistic painting of a man about to be lynched," she explains. "I was very much disturbed by the many lynchings taking place in the United States, and I felt I had to make a statement on canvas. I needed a model, and I recall walking down U Street and discovering this tall, black gentleman. I remember he had two guitars on his back, and he was rather a clochard-looking type with a slouched hat and a long black overcoat, a curious-looking individual. Under that hat, I caught the expression of his eyes and his bearded face; he was just the type I needed. I asked him if anybody had ever painted his portrait. He didn't quite understand what I was talking about, and I said, 'Come to this address; I want to make a picture of you.' In two days, he came to my apartment here in Washington, and I mentioned that I wanted him to pose as a man about to be lynched. I said, 'You have to open your shirt and take the look.' He said, 'But daughter, you know I worked in the South, and my master took me and the other workers in the wagon to see one of our brothers lynched.' I said, 'Tell me about it. How did he look?' 'Well,' he said, 'he just had his hands tied and he fastened his eyes on the heavens.'

Jones says she was moved to make the painting by the many lynchings taking place throughout the United States. I can't help but wonder if it was her model who told her about Williams, if the lynching his "master" took him to in the back of that wagon was the same one my family participated in. In the book, *A Voting Rights Odyssey: Black Enfranchisement in Georgia* by Laughlin MacDonald, the author finds an eyewitness to John Henry's murder named John Cross living in Moultrie, Georgia. Cross said Williams "was tied to a tree about three feet off the ground. They castrated him and put his genitals in his mouth, then showed the picture of his charred corpse in the black community as a warning."

The pictures of the charred corpse. The wagon trip to see the castration and burning of another human being—lessons for the good black men and women of the region. They would behave and keep their mouths shut or risk the same fate.

This is the atmosphere Nell breathed as a child.

***

When Lisa, Clark, Delal, and I leave the site of the old Hamner store, I still have a lot of questions. And I know they are easy for me to ask because I am white. What do I risk recklessly roaming this countryside exploring the history of a black man's murder?

I feel certain of Memaw's story. Yet, I know she was born in a town called Sparks thirty miles east of Autreyville. If the family moved to the site of this store, they still would have been a good thirty miles north, both places too far for frightened neighbors to seek them out for help when the local whites began their assault. The only other clue I have is the mysterious "Tallokas" road that Lisa has mentioned. Where's that? In Sparks? In Tifton? My phone is connected to a service in Turkey, and I don't have internet service here to look it up. I have yet to discover that Census page. I've reached a dead end.

We hit the road.

FOUR

I need to go back a day from the tour of the Hamner family store, back to our first encounter with my new cousins in Lisa's elegant north Tifton home. It ended after only two hours, which disappointed me. I had fantasized about embarking on a trip with Clark to the site of the old grocery that very afternoon. Everything was going to magically come together by nightfall, all the answers to Dad and John Henry Williams would fall into my lap.

"People have lives," Delal said, dragging me out around five o'clock. "We'd run out of things to say, if you hadn't noticed."

"We only have three days!" I protested.

"We can wait till tomorrow. Besides, we have plans."

The plans she spoke of were a bacchanal of Southern food at the Olde Time Buffet on the edge of downtown Tifton.

***

One of the critical bonds that brings Delal and me together is the mutual appreciation of a good meal. In Turkish, there's a picturesque phrase to describe our condition, *boğazımıza düşkün*, meaning "addicted to our gullets." We aren't picky. I love eating a snack of fresh yogurt and tandoor bread on the balcony of her grandfather's house in his tiny Kurdish village as much as I enjoy the labor-intensive pilafs whipped up by her aunt from Şirnak. Delal loves pulled pork on cheap hamburger buns picked up from a roadside stand as much as she loves the elaborate Creole dishes I learned at my father's side.

Dad, who was also addicted to his gullet, gave me my passion for food, and thus planted the root of this fundamental bond with my wife. I feel him most near when I sit down to a good meal, and to this day, I share the details of such meals with him in a kind of whispered prayer to the dead. It's perhaps a Southern thing, in that he taught me that good food has to have a story. For example, the yogurt and bread I mentioned earlier, *mast û nan* in Kurdish, is not just yogurt and bread, it's Delal's grandfather's history in a bowl, part of the rhythms of his ninety years in Kurdistan. For centuries, the village of Conag orbited two stars

42

from its hiding place tucked into a pocket of the rugged East Anatolian mountains. The first was the stone mill by the stream. There, villagers ground the wheat they grew into flour. The second was the *zozan*, or high pastures. Each family had a herd of animals, goats or sheep or cows, which provided milk for yogurt, butter, and cheeses. Every summer, the animals would be led to the *zozan*, and the people who watched over them would have festivals, sleep in the mountain cottages or out under the stars and find romance. This way of life ended, perhaps forever, when the war began with the Turkish government in the 80s. People fled the region in droves.

We called her grandfather "Dede." Most of Dede's stories of times past start with a journey to the mill or the pastures. These personal memories, this entire collective past and its subsequent loss are just as much essential ingredients to mast û nan as flour and milk. The first time I ate it was around midnight, on a wooden stool at a low table on Dede's balcony in the village. The house, which he had built himself out of local stone and trees, perched on a steep slope that overlooked the valley of the Peri River. The view stretched for a hundred miles. Delal's aunt had baked the bread that afternoon on the iron surface of the wood-burning stove. The yogurt had come from a neighbor who raised cattle.

"This is the best late-night snack," Dede assured me. "Easy on the stomach."

"*Pir̄ xweş e*," I'd said, testing my Kurdish. *It's delicious.*

He loved that I loved it. But what was not to love? The warm crisp flatbread slightly ashy from the stove, the coolness of the yogurt, the scene of the valley below, the stars like a spray of glittering glass, the melancholy call of the little owls from the garden. It was a meal that was only there, only then, and that summer night, as I lay in bed, I described it to Dad. I imagined him by the door in the shadows, smoking and listening and understanding as no one else would.

Dad taught me to appreciate this link between food and place, food and time. He was a brilliant cook, and each of his signature dishes came with a story. Whenever we had seafood, he described with relish a deep-sea fishing trip he had taken with friends out of Jacksonville. He painted a picture of the sun and the blue Atlantic and the leap of the boat on the waves. They'd caught mostly red snapper, and he said the fish just seemed to throw themselves out of the water onto the deck. "We caught so many that at one point we were kicking through layers of their bodies just to get from point A to point B. It took a whole army of us hours to clean them all. We grilled a few right there on the beach that night over a fire we built in the sand. A little salt, a little butter, a nice buzz on a couple of beers and the sound of the surf—I don't think I've ever had a better *sooopper*."

He always said "supper" like this, mimicking some long-ago relative and the way he would bellow for his nightly meal. To eat fish with him was to take part in that long-lost day.

Delal, for her part, developed a taste for Southern food for a few reasons. One is my sister, Michele, who still can recreate all the time-honored dishes her Florida granny used to fix. Another is a trip my brother, Mike, and his daughter invited us on the previous year. We went with them to their hunting camp in south Georgia where we plunged through the pine barrens and helped them set up the corn-feeders they used to attract deer. We'd climbed the tree stands, practiced shooting on the sand roads, and rode in the back of Mike's pick-up, like I'd done as a kid. On the way back to Florida, we'd stopped at a Southern buffet called Hometown Restaurant in Pearson, Georgia, and Delal fell in love with the brisket, with the whole day really, bonding with my taciturn brother and niece, learning about this world alien to her. So, when I mentioned going to Georgia, her first question was "Can we stop at the Hometown? Is it close?"

It wasn't. But as a consolation, I'd found the Olde Times, and it was almost as good.

***

The Olde Time Buffet is a place that knows where it's located. It's a tasty glimpse into Dad's childhood, an all-you-can-eat smorgasbord of Soul Food classics—fried chicken, fried bream, pulled pork, barbecue, chicken and dumplings. For sides, there are collards, cornbread with potlikker for dipping, lima beans with fatback, tomatoes and okra, yellow squash and onions, fried cabbage, and sweet potatoes. And of course, nobody is skimping on dessert. They have the trinity of Southern sweets—banana pudding, peach cobbler, and pecan pie.

When we arrive, there's a mildly long line composed of a pair of crowded black families. Many of the people working there are black, too, and at least half the other customers. I take this as a good sign. One of the first things my foreign wife noticed coming with me to the American South was how segregated life still is. For me, a native white boy of the region, it's so much a part of the background I don't see it until she points it out. We have gone with Karin and Wayne to tube down the Rainbow River in Florida, no black people. We went with friends to Clearwater Beach for a swim in the Gulf and seafood, almost all white. When we drive into Lakeland neighborhoods that have a bit of color, someone in the family will quickly warn us that we are "not in a good area" and lock the car doors. There's a famous fried chicken and biscuits shack on Lakeland's northside we have never tried because no one will drive us there. Why do I always want to go to the black areas, they want to know?

"I feel normal at last," Delal tells me at the Olde Time.

"What do you mean?"

"I'm more comfortable with a minority around," she says. "Probably because I come from one."

I gaze out the window as we eat. The restaurant is near Interstate 75 and surrounded by the usual accouterments of a highway exit, various fast food restaurants, boxy hotels, and gas stations. Under all of that are the streets my father grew up in, as did generations of Gibbs before him and all the various families that married into them. My eyes sweep over customers in the restaurant. One of them is bound to be a distant relative or child of a former neighbor or maybe even a descendant of John Henry Williams. An old white woman with tall blonde hair fusses with her squash, poking it with her fork as her husband shovels in a mouthful of limas. Two black women sit at another table with pie and coffee, bent over an accounts book and adding machine. We sip our sweet teas and gnaw our ribs. I eat too much, have two desserts anyway. Delal rolls her eyes, says, "You Southerners like your sugar!"

***

I have a complicated relationship with the capital S South. In my childhood, it embarrassed me. In my teenage years and early twenties, I thought of nothing but escape, but then later, after years of living abroad, nostalgia started to settle in, and nowadays I hunt for personal connections to the history and culture, however ugly they might be. It grounds me somehow. Yet, I'm suspicious of that nostalgia. I hear the "history and heritage" mantra proffered up by friends and relatives defending the white nationalists who marched on Charlottesville, listen to the "All Lives Matter" sloganeers and the outrage of Southern whites at the removal of Confederate monuments, and I think, *This isn't what I mean. This isn't what I'm seeking at all*. In Lakeland, when a pick-up truck whizzes by with a giant Confederate flag flying from the back and my mother says, "I love it!," I don't understand what she's feeling.

In Istanbul, my identity is diluted. I am American, or sometimes, just a Westerner. It's through food and language that I try to show people something more definitive. On New Year's I'll make a pot of hop'n john or bring deviled eggs to a potluck. At school, I teach my students to imitate a Southern accent and use as many Southernisms as I can when I talk with fellow English teachers, just to let them know what I am.

Honestly, all of this seems contrived at times, like I'm posing, which only strengthens the need to prove my identity. Whenever I catch that scent of self-deception, I'll throw myself even harder into the music or the literature or learn to cook a new Southern dish, but no matter how objectively true any of it is, how authentic, it always fits a bit like an itchy costume. None of it feels like my own skin in the way it does when first Cousin Clark and then Kenny say, "You sure look like Bob." Because ultimately, what binds me to the South is my dead Southern daddy.

Funny. To prove my father Southern, I was about to go into a long list of examples, about how he believed in saying "ma'am" and "sir," about his commitment to manners and adherence to an old code of Southern chivalry. Only none of it would have been true. Not exactly. Yet I almost convinced myself this would suffice to convey what I meant by "Southern Daddy" to someone from wherever you, dear reader, are from. In the end, I would have been ticking a list of stereotypical and meaningless boxes compiled for easy circulation on Facebook, describing no one. "You know you're from the South if…" So now I'm stuck with figuring out what I actually mean. This has been the hardest section to write so far. The answers seep up through layers of grave dirt and forgetfulness, emerging slowly, stingily, one by one.

What about my father was Southern?

He spoke deep-toned, slowly, with a mild drawl modulated by sarcasm. That voice stuck in people's heads, and everyone who knew him remarked on it. It hit the lower registers of human vocal range, a Gospel singer's bass, and he harnessed it to spin tales, mostly true, filled with deeply flawed but funny human beings, people you pitied and loathed at the same time. That same voice loved to tease. He had a pet name for anyone he felt affection for. I was "Bumper" for the number of times I hit my head learning to walk as a toddler. My cousin Karin was "Bird Legs." The son of his friend, Dave, was "Chicken Little" because he "always looked like he thought the sky was falling."

Dad liked to turn his own grotesqueries into fodder for laughs. When he lost all his teeth around the age of forty-seven and his mouth shriveled into an old man's wrinkled gash, he entertained himself by taking out his dentures in front of guests who had no idea his "choppers," as he called them, weren't real. He'd suddenly eject them like a cassette tape and observe the room's reactions.

Dad did believe in basic manners but wasn't much into the Southern tropes of sprinkling "ma'am" and "sir" throughout every sentence he said. It had more to do with the way he moved through the world and the way the world yielded to make room for him. If he popped into town to find an old buddy, he wanted to do it by asking people working in the grocery stores and gas stations or by chatting up passersby in the street. If he wanted to explore the state park that had just closed for the day, he sidled up to the security guard and sweet-talked him into opening the gate. Maybe he'd have to share a cigarette or a joke to get what he was after, but an afternoon had room to stretch your legs in, and closing times and rules didn't matter when faced with a fellow human being and conversation. My father had a deep aversion for situations where rules and systems were valued above people, where no accommodations were made for individual quirk, for the odd surprise or whim.

Dignity was important. He rarely cussed but could eviscerate you with a well-spoken barb. He dressed well even if he were going down to the gas station to pick up a six-pack. His "going out" uniform was a button-down checkered shirt, slacks, and cowboy boots. Sometimes he even wore a bolo tie. He treated everyone with respect and hospitality, whether he knew them or not, whether they deserved it or not. It was a recognition of the inherent value of a human being. When a new family moved into the neighborhood, he paid a formal visit with a covered dish to welcome them. He especially liked to bring people apple cakes, a specialty of his he'd developed from a tweaked recipe out of *Southern Living*. Hosting a guest was a sacred affair. You had to be generous with your time and table, though once he told me the secret to being a great cook was to make just less than you thought everyone wanted. That way, they left wanting more.

He valued quality and liked things done authentically and conscientiously, without the stench of commercialism fouling it up. He hated chain stores and fast food. He despised flashy promotions and marketing tricks. He hated that Mom took me to McDonald's sometimes for a Happy Meal.

"You eat garbage," he said, "in return for a bribe of a cheap plastic toy."

I once spent an hour with him searching the backwoods of Florida for a hole-in-the-wall restaurant where all the food was made fresh with ingredients from the owner's garden.

"The carrots," he told me, "are right out of the soil and cooked in real butter like Miss Hattie used to make." Miss Hattie was his father's mother. "And the ham? My God, son, it's so good you'll wanna slap your mama, figuratively speaking, at least in your case. Of course, there's no gift shop, and no costumed characters, but I think you'll like it anyway."

Of course, we never found it. It had closed or been torn down. That was the pattern with most of what he loved and valued—it didn't exist anymore, replaced by things bigger and brighter.

He seemed almost allergic to the modern America I felt very much a part of. He hid out at Memaw's house, both the one on Lake Santa Fe and the one she lived in later after she moved to Keystone to be closer to Uncle Gene. He never called anyone, wrote anyone, visited anyone. No matter how he complained, he seemed to like where his mother was, miles from anywhere, surrounded by cow pastures and pine woods and emptiness. Even on those few occasions he lived on his own, he was always isolated in a trailer off a highway ten miles from any town or in a house on the edge of a swamp. When he moved into that religious compound in the forest, it wasn't much of a lifestyle change. Still, though he acted the part of the hermit, he would talk to absolutely anyone. He could have a long philosophical conversation with the bagboy at Winn Dixie, the hitchhiker we picked up off a country road or the bum hanging out in front of the Circle K—with anyone who would take the time to chat.

He put on no airs and scorned people who did. They were the endless butt of caustic commentary. "Ms. Bonner splurged on a new leaf blower," he once said of Memaw's dotty neighbor in Keystone. "She spends hours now blowing those leaves back and forth on her tiny sidewalk until she's certain all the neighbors have caught sight of her doing it."

He preferred the down and out. I think sometimes he had a phobia of money and all the corruption and meanness it brought. Maybe that's why he could never hold a job. I don't know. I do know he used to ridicule his brother for being so shabby in his greed.

"He'd kill you just to make an extra quarter," he'd say. "And cheat his own mother, though she would deny it even as she watched him do it."

He had a baseball cap with the Confederate flag on it that he wore sailing sometimes, but he was never "country," never a conscious redneck. He gave the air of someone very urbane and educated. Even so, he kept a distance from any kind of ostentation. He thought it a sign of stupidity and low character.

He valued humility.

He shared cigarettes with barflies, picked up hitchhikers, took in stray cats, and fed street dogs. But it was all quiet, unassuming. He never drew attention to the times he displayed charity to the world's damaged and rejected. The idea wouldn't have made sense to him. He saw too much of himself in them. We'd take long leisurely walks around the neighborhood in Keystone, and all the stray dogs would trail after him as if he were the alpha of their pack, the head stray. The only pets he ever kept had wandered into the yard, lost or dumped. I remember the street cat that appeared out of nowhere one night, limping half-starved up to the screened-in porch and plopping down at the door with a sigh as if she knew someone in this house would take care of her, as if he were a legend among lost and wild things. He took her in, fed her, named her "Poochie," a name which is as good an example of his humor as any—a canine moniker for his favorite tabby.

He doted on Poochie, treated her like a fellow inmate. It was this little gray cat he claimed Memaw killed a few years later. To hurt him, he said.

"She knew Poochie was the only thing here that meant anything to me, so she shot her once I was out of the picture." This was after one of the drinking spells where Memaw kicked him out of her house. That's what "out of the picture" always meant. There was no need to explain it. I knew. Everyone knew.

"How do you know she shot her?" I asked.

"You know your memaw, Jeffrey," he said impatiently. "She claimed Poochie ran away, but she's lying. You can see it in the way she smiles when she talks about it. She'll stand under that gun rack and say, 'Shame about that animal.'"

He said there was a pile of freshly-dug earth in the backyard where Memaw had buried the cat. He led me outside to prove it. There was indeed a bald strip of white sand in the middle of the grass, but what did that mean? I thought he was being paranoid. Still, his believing that of his mother spoke volumes about their relationship.

What else made him Southern? The obsession with lost times and lost causes? This stereotype did apply to him. He treated the past almost like one of his stray dogs. The official stories, the purebreds, were hardly worth knowing. More interesting were the things hidden or forgotten or neglected, the history that wandered up on your doorstep unbidden. It inevitably spoke a franker truth.

"Do you know why all these pines have cuts high up on their trunks?" he asked me once on a walk through the Florida scrub near Lake Santa Fe. I must have been around eight years old.

"No," I said.

"Pick off a piece of that wood and smell it."

I reached into one of the gashes in the tree and pulled out a splinter. "It smells like paint thinner."

"These are longleaf pines, and those cuts were called cat faces 'cause of the shape. See the tin cup under that one there?"

"Yeah."

He pointed to a tree just ahead. "That was to catch the sap. This was the site of an old turpentine farm, what they called 'naval stores.' A hundred years ago, Florida worked its convicts in places like this under conditions worse than a plantation. They were mostly black, of course. See, the government found itself a way to keep slavery going. Arrest them and put them to work in the name of 'rehabilitation.' If you died, well, who cared? You were a prisoner, an expendable nuisance to the high society folks your memaw admires so much. You lived in cheap tents out in the woods, all chained up, and the owner just might give you a spoonful of slop to eat if he was in a good mood that day. The state charged these bosses for the use of its convicts and raked in the dough. That made it a kind of patriotic endeavor, see? You could be a blood-sucking piece-of-shit and feel proud of it. And this whole scam, son, was cooked up by Yankee businessmen colluding with some Southern scalawags. So don't go thinking the Northerners weren't bigots, too. *Capeesh?*"

"What does that mean?"

"That's Italian for 'Hey! Do you get what I'm saying or not?'"

Or in another patch of forest, he pointed to what looked like a shallow ravine and said, "Know what that is there?"

"No."

"That's where the Federal government and some Florida fellows decided it would be a fine idea to slice the state in half with a canal. Gonna make them as rich as the one in Panama made those bastards. They got half-way through, too, until they realized they'd destroy the aquifer if they kept going. Apparently, no one will stay in your highfalutin resorts without water. Don't think the project's been taken off the books, though. No, sir. The digging stopped back before World War II, but the vultures still want to finish it. One thing I've learned about Florida, some greedy son of a bitch is always trying to destroy part of it in the name of improvement."

He always ended these minilectures with the coda, "It's not important, but it's nice to know." This was not a phrase he invented. Like with "soooopper," he was mimicking someone, and though he once told me whom, I can't remember the source. I just remember him saying, "And he always used to say, 'It's not important, but it's nice to know.'" Was it a TV character? A friend from his days in the Army Reserve? An old relative? And I never knew for sure how he meant it. There was always an undertone of bitterness, a submissive snarl, like a kicked dog that held onto a dream of biting back one day. *I told you a story, but you don't care, so I'll pretend I don't either.* I take it now as a sign of the contempt his world held for knowledge and intelligence, and thus for the things intrinsic to who he was. It was a warning, too, for me. As much as he took pride in my brain, it made him worry for me as well. The South did not like people who thought too much, who went poking around in history and hounding folks with facts.

***

I cannot close this without mentioning geography, for the South formed Dad's physical borders as surely as it did any psychological ones. Right before he killed himself, I had offered to buy him a ticket to visit me in Japan for Christmas, and I sometimes wonder, guiltily, irrationally, if the threat to bring him so radically out of the South was what precipitated the final plunge to self-annihilation, as if he were one of those fantastic creatures in my comic books and fantasy novels bound by curse or spell to a certain place and who, once removed from that place, evaporated into the void as punishment for violating its borders.

Dad never set foot outside of Florida or Georgia in his fifty-eight years of existence except for one summer car trip he and I took with Memaw and her oldest sister, Evelyn, to a Hamner family reunion in Virginia. And that was only to educate me on Southern history. He'd agreed to serve as driver for the two old women on the condition that they paid for three side-excursions connected to the Civil War: Washington D.C., which housed General Lee's boyhood home and served as a launching point for a visit to the Manassas battlefield; Fort Sumter where the Civil War had started; and Fort Moultrie in Charleston, which had survived two years of constant bombardment by Union ironclads.

In fact, except for that brief sojourn in Lakeland with my mother, Dad never lived anywhere except the Wiregrass Country, that swath of southern Georgia and northern Florida so named for the wild grass, *aristida stricta*, which once grew in abundance in the region's longleaf pine forests. It's an appropriate plant to form his borders. *Aristida* is a weed that survives in nutrient-poor sandy soil on the kind of land from which no one makes any real money or prestige. 19th-century writers disdained the people of Wiregrass Country as "landless poor whites, squatters living a sequestered backwoods existence." In antebellum days, more aristocratic Southerners referred to the landscape as "barren, oppressive, and starved" and to its residents as "frontier paupers." It was indeed some of the last frontier in the Southeast, sparsely settled even after the Civil War. Historian Ann Patton Malone writes, "Physical isolation reinforced the reclusive attitude of the meager Anglo population and shaped the area's culture. The large minority were white southerners and small farmers who understood the working rules of the society they had left (that of the plantation South) and were in general agreement on how the new one should be fashioned."

Isolated, reclusive, understanding the rules of the culture they had deliberately *left* and held in contempt by that same culture. This describes my father to a T.

What sort of place was I trying to remove him from and how strong was its hold on him? Allow me to hound you with a few facts.

Wiregrass Country only emerged from its isolation and poverty with the coming of the railroad, which enabled those backwoods families to take advantage of the pine forests around them and mine the trees for lumber and turpentine. The Georgia Southern and Florida Railway Company and the Brunswick and Western Company built tracks through the wiregrass marshes and turned their remote little mills into boomtowns. That's how Tifton and Omega were born.

Aristida stricta is a plant with a rugged beauty, bushy wigs of thick green and brown prairie grass undulating like sea waves in the winds that sweep through the empty barrens where it grows. Watching the breezes pass over, from one end of the forest to the other, you feel you are witnessing the movement of an invisible Old Testament god crossing his realm. Wiregrass reproduces itself in the devastation of fires ignited by summer lightning strikes. To make flowers and seeds, it must burn to its roots. It's a hardy tramp on the wild margins of the so-called "black-belt," that land of dark, loamy soil just to the north that made money crops like cotton and rice boom. It's hard to find now in the country that bears its name, the population devastated by development and human expansion.

Not only did Dad never leave the Wiregrass Country, neither had anyone in the family for more than two centuries. He was like the most recent incarnation of a plant that flowered on the surface but sprung from the hidden subsoil base that it depended on, a fixed net of ancient and intricate taproots and rhizomes that branched out from the mainline in organic fractals of genealogy, gathering nutrients from layer after layer, generation after generation, down and down and down. His ancestors were its genesis, launching their sojourn on this geography in blood, on the heels of a ruthless ethnic cleansing. Perhaps the seeds of our violence lie there.

Memaw's Hamners appeared in Wiregrass Country when her grandfather's great-grandfather won a plot of land in the 1805 Georgia Land Lottery. The state was giving away hundreds of acres to pioneering white men after driving indigenous Creeks from territory obtained in the 1802 Treaty of Fort Wilkinson. Memaw's mother, Miss Linnie, was born a Bridges, and both her grandfather and great-grandfather are on the 1805 Lottery roll. Linnie's mother was a Dean, her grandmother a York; Memaw's father's mother was a McCrea, his paternal grandmother a Kirkland; no matter which ancestral surname I follow, down which branching line I turn, they all end up in that 1805 land grab that settled whites on the edges of Wiregrass Country, a land grab made on the back of an agreement in which then-President Thomas Jefferson promised Georgians he would forever "extinguish all Indian title" to the east of the Alabama border.

Extinguish.

When I follow Dad's paternal line, the main trunk belonging to the Gibbs family leads to Thomas Gibbs, who immigrated from North Carolina in 1818 to help found Irwin County right in the heart of Wiregrass Country. The county once encompassed a much larger territory and both Tifton and Omega lie within its original borders. The Gibbs men remained within a thirty-mile radius of Thomas' original homestead for over five generations, digging in their roots, ending their streak only when Dad and Gene moved to north Florida.

And it wasn't just the Gibbses.

When I trace the history of the surnames of every grandmother and great-grandmother radiating off the Gibbs line, I end with yet more pioneering families "opening" lands to white settlement that same year, the Hendersons, the Warrens, the Paulks. Irwin County was war booty, part of millions of acres seized from the Creeks in the 1814 Treaty of Fort Jackson. Their new farms sat on sites of former Hitchiti, Mikasuki, and Muskogee towns. Their new lives meant a Trail of Tears for a people whose ancestors had lived there for millennia.

The families that made up Memaw's line were able to encroach on the edge of the wiregrass through a treaty brokered by Thomas Jefferson. Pepaw's people secured their place in Irwin Country after Andrew Jackson betrayed the native allies who helped him crush Creek rebels. It does not escape my notice that Jackson and Jefferson were also the names of the two streets that set the boundaries in Starke, Florida, on that strip of railroad track where Dad was killed. I don't believe in omens, but sometimes the coincidences nag. Was it just chance that he died between two signs bearing the name of the men who, through blood and treachery, established the borders of the lands that yielded each of his parents, lands that prospered after this theft only because of the very tracks on which he died? Sometimes I feel there are messages written not in ink, but in the way we move through time. I had tried to remove him from that geography and send him across two oceans to Japan. Like us, wiregrass is a species born from generations of violence, fire after fire, conflagration after conflagration. It's particularly adapted to this one ecology and survives nowhere else, defenseless against change. I shudder now at the wounds I might have created in trying to rip Dad out of that two-hundred-year-old root system.

***

I reread the previous pages and wonder if I've really told the truth. I've lost so much, remembered so little. I must have admired him deeply, but there are other feelings crawling up out of the past. Resentment, bitterness, shame. Despite his generous, compassionate, down-to-earth chivalry, something was deeply wrong with my father. Just like with the South itself. Something that starts to coagulate at the mention of history and the Creeks, something that killed him. To speak of either him or his geography means to speak of demons as well as angels. The South I know is a world where violence infiltrates every pang of nostalgia, where women like gentle Miss Linnie have to let black people she calls "n——s" hide in the cane because they fear for their lives.

***

As a boy, visiting Dad also meant visiting my younger cousin, Karin, who was my best and only friend in the family. She lived on Lake Geneva, which was twenty minutes by car from Lake Santa Fe, and after Memaw moved to Keystone when I was eleven or so, just ten minutes on foot. At the start of any vacation, my first trip to her house followed a faithful ritual. My dad or Memaw would drop me off in Uncle Gene's front yard. Neither one ever got out of the car, my father because he hated his older brother, and Memaw because she hated Aunt Nancy. So, I would climb up the brick steps to the little green house alone with my swimming clothes tucked under my arm and bang on the screen door. Karin or my aunt would open, and as soon as I stepped inside, my uncle's voice would summon me into the Florida room.

"Jeffrey! That you?"

I'd hesitate, take a breath. "Yessir."

"Get in here!"

I'd step down onto the brown shag carpet and find him in his recliner with a two-liter thermos full of sweet tea on the end table and the TV blasting on the opposite side of the room. He inevitably had a pipe clamped between his teeth—the smell of his tobacco smoke permeated the house. He'd be dressed as he always dressed, in navy blue coveralls with a white undershirt. Like my father, he was extremely tall. The pants of his suit did not completely cover his legs, so I could see the white socks that he pulled up to his knees. He always gave the impression of having just gotten off work, though this is how I found him no matter what time or which day I arrived. Sunday at 3pm was the same as Monday at 10am was the same as Saturday night. Generally, though the television was on, he held an open newspaper that he would shake and lower.

"Come closer," he'd say, looking down his nose. "Lemme get a look at you."

I knew the steps of this dance. I would dutifully shuffle forward so he could peer up into my face as if performing an inspection. He'd squint and say, "Jeffrey, I see something black around your mouth. Like mud or something."

I would offer some non-committal grunt or shrug.

"You been kissing them n—— gals again?"

"No, sir," I'd say. The n-word burned, like a lit cigarette pressed into my skin.

"You better keep away from n—— gals," he'd say. "You can't wash that black stuff off, you know."

And then he'd raise his paper back up, which signaled the humiliating ritual was over. Karin would usually be waiting for me in the doorway. We'd lock gazes, roll our eyes as if to say, "Who can understand these people anyway?" and then bound through the kitchen, out the sliding glass door and down the steep hill to the lake where we'd swim till dark, the water and sun washing away the memory of the way I'd stood silently as my uncle once again made me complicit in a primitive racism I'd only ever witnessed on TV and in books. I never heard that word or that kind of talk anywhere else, that kind of proud, open bigotry. Why didn't I protest? He started when I was around seven or eight, maybe earlier, and I knew it was wrong from the first, so why did I let it happen? A better question might be why he thought it was so important that he had to do it every time I came. Was it his way of showing affection somehow, acknowledging his brother's child? There was always a playful tone to his voice, a sense he was waiting for me to laugh, punch him good-naturedly in the arm maybe, though I can't imagine he felt much of anything for me. Sometimes I think he did it only to make fun of me. I was fat when I was in elementary school, a reader who didn't like to rough house and was terrible at sports, and he had a malicious sense of humor. It may have tickled his funny bone to picture this chubby "sissy-boy" fighting off amorous advances from lusty black women.

I don't know how Uncle Gene negotiated the world. I rarely saw him leave that chair. He was like a mirror image of my father, withdrawn, reclusive, but crude and brutal at times. He ensconced himself in that house on that lake in the middle of the woods and never left. When the house began to fall apart, he still did not rise from his recliner. When the roof rotted, he threw a blue plastic tarp over it to protect against the rain and kept sitting. When the toilet in the bedroom stopped working, he made do with a white bait bucket set beside the bed. ("Your Uncle Gene let you use the facilities?" my father would ask whenever I got back, referring to that bucket.) He refused to pay for garbage service, and so for years he burned all the trash they produced in a green oil drum under an oak tree. "When that stingy son-of-a-bitch finally croaks," Aunt Nancy would say, "I'm gonna cremate *him* in that burn barrel." For forty years, we watched my uncle decay along with the house. Like my father, he wanted to be isolated from the world. Only occasionally did the outside intrude on him. I remember being in the Florida room once, playing a board game with Karin when a Cosby Show rerun appeared on the TV behind us.

"I'll be goddamned," he said. "They got those n——s all over the TV now. Can't turn the damn thing on without seeing them anymore."

Uncle Gene had a reputation for taking after his mother.

"That temper," my Aunt Nancy would say. "Shouting at the TV. He has the same meanness as his mommy. It's Rosemary and her baby, part two."

Though Nancy herself picked up the habit in later years.

I was in her living room one day after Uncle Gene had passed away. We were reminiscing about Lake Geneva and how it used to be. In the background, a talk show was playing on the TV, and one of the guests was a black woman who, explaining a racist encounter said, "I was shocked at how I was treated. I was not a criminal. I was an entrepreneur and a businesswoman who…"

"No, you're not!" Aunt Nancy shouted, turning so suddenly to the TV it made me jump. "Your nothing but an old n——, and that's all you'll ever be!"

Memaw's views on race were no more enlightened than her eldest son and daughter-in-law's. She rarely said the n-word in front of me but did not approve of black people on TV, and though she had resigned herself to integration, I think, she wouldn't tolerate having a black doctor or dentist or lawyer. She did not focus her ire solely on black people, either, but put a little aside for anyone who did not precisely match her background. Aunt Nancy, for example, came from a family of "shanty Irish." Memaw's hairdresser was "some Jap gal" in Gainesville. My cousin Mark's first wife, a Cherokee adopted by a white family, was "that ol' Indian gal." When one of Memaw's friends dared to bring a British person as a guest for dinner one night, she harangued the poor woman with questions. Wearing her famous derisive smile, she asked, "Just what is this obsession with that old queen of yours?" She hated Catholics and referred to all of my and Karin's friends by their physical flaws. So, Karin's friend Jennifer was that "ol' fat Catholic gal" and my friend Marc was that "big-nosed Catholic boy."

Yet strangely, this woman so generous with her bigotry became Mormon one day, out of the blue. My father pointed to the *Book of Mormon* perched on the end table in the living room.

"This is your memaw's newest hobby," he said. "She met some rich Mormon ladies, and now she's memorizing the exploits of Joseph Smith."

Her Methodist sisters thought she had gone mad. "Grandmama could not stop talking about it," Lisa tells me.

And so, what of Dad? If his older brother and mother were old-school bigots, what was he? How did he look on this particular facet of the South? This answer is complicated. It requires me to tell you two stories my father told me, to set two bookends, and between those bookends, there will be a few consequential volumes about Lake Santa Fe and the Wiregrass Country, a significant 'following of the pen,' for the stories occupy a geography from which they cannot be extracted, a geography that produced the brutal murder of John Henry and the suicide of Robert Gibbs—as well as a few other catastrophes I was about to discover.

FIVE

The summer before second grade, my mother and I moved up to Gainesville from Lakeland to give living with Dad a second try. My brother and sister opted to stay with their own father. I guess they'd had enough. We moved into a trailer on the outskirts of the city in the little community of Fairbanks, named after a Florida officer in the Civil War. I don't remember much about this period of our family history. I was not quite seven years old, after all. I do know it was the first and only time I ever attended a private school. I had just been diagnosed as "gifted," and I guess my parents were feeling cocky, confident that Dad's booze issues were a thing of the past and that we would remain a two-income household till I graduated from Harvard, or wherever they envisioned me going. They enrolled me in the Martha Manson Academy where "my unique talents and vision" would be nurtured. Dad, the former wiregrass poor-white squatter, liked having a son with "unique talents." He was nursing ambitions.

The Manson Academy no longer exists. If you do a Google search on my second-grade alma mater, as I did, you will find, after scrolling through photos of Martha's namesakes, Charles and Marilyn, a quote from a book on desegregation in Gainesville called *We Can Do It* by Michael Gengler. "The school's founder," Gengler writes of Manson Academy, "says there is no policy to exclude blacks, but the school imposed a minimum IQ requirement of one hundred." Gengler leaves that statement without comment. Did the founder or the author believe that the lack of black students was a result of the IQ requirement—itself not a very high bar? Perhaps the answer was in the timing of the founding.

Again, according to Gengler, Martha Manson Academy was one of five private schools that popped up in Gainesville as a direct reaction to integration. Bringing together black and white students forced confrontations in the city. Black students newly bussed to white schools protested for more representation in student government and for more black teachers. They complained white teachers treated them differently, that they would be punished more severely for the same behaviors. White parents complained that classes were focused too much on sensitivity group training and discussion of race rather than academics.

They grumbled about other things, too, long hair and drugs, a lack of attention to "traditional Christian morals" and, in the words of one woman, about being forced to send her child to a black school "just to prove her heart is in the right place." At one point, the school board banned the Confederate flag and black power symbols. Presumably, they were being used as focal points for fights. There were incidents and rumors of riots. Whites wanted an alternative to public schools where they might be shielded from all this confrontation and social change, where they might think only of nice things, so many withdrew into private institutions like Manson Academy which invented indirect ways to bar black children from entering.

I remember very little of the place. Just images, a picture of an old lady with blonde hair ballooning about her head, colorful cards with phonetic symbols hanging around the room and the feeling that I was in someone's living room rather than a proper school. I was fascinated by the funny letters on the cards. My teacher was always on the verge of explaining what they meant.

"What's the upside-down *e*?" I asked.

"A schwa."

"What about the one that looks like a and e got stuck together? And the o with two dots?"

"Be patient. We'll get to it."

"And the backward *3*? How do you say that?"

"Soon, soon, we'll get around to it."

We never did. But those cards were an origin. They launched my fascination with languages. I can still close my eyes and see that curious little o with two dots that I now pronounce every day whenever I speak Turkish.

I have other memory fragments of this time. I remember helping my mom navigate the city, which somehow impressed everyone. "I had to ask you every day how to get to your school," she says. My father had taught me that streets ran north-south and avenues east-west, and I had worked out parts of Gainesville were on a grid. Therefore, I could predict directions if I knew the name of the street we were on and the name of the street where we were going. My mom had me perform this little feat for people—she was always getting lost—and I have an image of myself standing up in the passenger seat and counting the green street signs whizzing by as an observer in the back dutifully marveled at my performance.

I remember being obsessed with a Japanese animation called *Battle of the Planets* about five kids with special powers who flew around in a spaceship called the Phoenix and every week defeated giant alien robots shaped like animals. I used to make dozens of models of the Phoenix every day out of notebook paper and fly them around the yard, sometimes attacking them myself as one of the mechanical monsters the kids battled on the show.

I remember a restaurant opened in Fairbanks. We used to like trying new restaurants—all three of us were "addicted to our gullets"—and we stopped in to give the place a go because the marquee promised "gourmet" food. Dad was working at a car dealership, and I think he had just sold one of the more expensive models and made a hefty commission, so we were having a celebratory night out. We got dressed up in our finest. Dad was eager to show me what "gourmet" meant because, in his view, Mom and Big Macs were ruining my appreciation of food. As soon as we walked in the door, the one waitress' eyes went wide, and she took off running into the kitchen shouting, "Get ready! Get ready! We've finally got a customer!" Dad observed her flight, waited for the kitchen door to swing closed, then shooed us back out to the car. "I don't want to be their guinea pig," he said.

I remember going with Mom, Aunt Nancy, and Karin to the big flea market in the town of Waldo on Sundays.

My mom remembers a panther crossing our white sand driveway one night. I do not.

Nor do I remember Dad getting drunk. I don't remember him losing his job. I don't remember the fights, the disappearances, or the final defeated move back to Lakeland. Though all these things happened.

But I do remember asking him about it a year later.

"Why couldn't you keep your job when we lived in Fairbanks?"

It must have been during one of those long conversations we used to have while fishing or on an extended walk in the woods. I have no idea from what hidden reserve I summoned the guts to voice such a question. We were not a family that invited confrontation. Maybe I was simply desperate for an explanation. I have always hated secrets, especially the kind you have to work extra hard not to know.

"Jeffrey," he answered. "It's just not that easy to explain."

"What do you mean?"

"I think the problem was I was working in Starke."

"What's the big deal about Starke?"

"It's the kind of people you have to deal with on a daily basis. They're either ignorant white trash or greedy swindlers. You remember I was working at the dealership?"

"I remember."

"Well, for example, this couple came in one day in a beat-up old truck saying they wanted a brand new car. I took one look at them and started toward the used lot. I knew they couldn't afford a pot to piss in, much less a new vehicle, but my boss took me aside and told me to show them exactly what they asked for. He wanted me to convince them to buy one of the more expensive ones, a Camaro or something. He said they didn't look smart enough to be following 'a budget' and would probably take the first thing they thought looked 'tough,' whether they could afford it or not. That's how the other salesmen thought, see? They didn't mind seeing people lose their shirts as long as they made that commission."

"Did you do it?"

"I walked them over there, yes, but I told them the deal. I explained the price of a Camaro and what that would work out to a month and then kept nudging them toward a more sensible used model. But you should have seen these two. Lord, the man wasn't even wearing a shirt and the woman had on cut-off shorts and an old tank top and was carrying around this little black mutt that kept barking, some ratty Chihuahua mix. The man wasn't even listening to me. He kept running his hand over the hood of the Camaro saying it was a damn fine ride, a damn fine ride. The woman nodded like her head was on a spring. Then she says, "N—— Puppy has to pee!" That was the classy moniker they'd picked out for the dog, see? That's the kind of people they were. She sets that dog down on the ground and damned if he doesn't trot over to the front of the car I'm trying to talk them out of, lift its leg, and piss on the tire. 'N—— Puppy!' she screams, 'That's a bad boy!' These were the people I was trying to protect from the rapacious salesmen. This was Starke. I just couldn't exist in a place like that, son. It hurts a man's dignity."

At the time he told me this story, he was trying to start up a driftwood business. We would tramp along Hatchet Creek in the woods just east of Gainesville and hunt for the best specimens. Dad preferred the gray twisting knots of cypress. We would take them back to the house, sand them lightly, and remove any rotten bits. He would ponder over what animal the piece most resembled, then glue eyes and other appendages in the appropriate place to accentuate the resemblance. The goal was to open a stand at the Waldo Flea Market and sell them as lawn or patio ornaments, one of his many business schemes.

In any case, I took heart from the tale of the couple from Starke. I figured a man who could be so appalled by a person's use of the n-word that he gave up his job and started gluing eyes on pieces of floating wood had a more enlightened view on race relations than his brother and mother.

This conversation took place at Memaw's house when she lived outside the town of Earleton on Lake Santa Fe. After our lives in Fairbanks fell apart, Dad moved back to his mother's just as he had done when my parents first separated a few years before in Lakeland. I don't remember that catastrophe either—him or us walking out the door of our house on Tradewinds Avenue, our own move into Grandma's house, the sudden change in neighborhoods.

That first move was in 1975 or '76 and Memaw's second husband, Carl, was still alive. The lake house was his. Lake Santa Fe has two segments, the big lake to the south and the little lake to the north. The two bodies of water are connected by a narrow pass where a couple long docks jut through the banana lilies and maidencane grass. On the southeast corner of the big lake is the town of Melrose, where Dad and I would pick up worms and shiners at Chiappini's, a combination bar, bait shop, and gas station. Memaw and Carl's house was on the northwestern side of the little lake.

Santa Fe is a dark-water lake. The decaying plants on shore, the organic matter trickling in from the surrounding swamps, and the roots of the cypresses all release tannins into the water. In the shallows, it's a golden brown, like a glass of tea held up to the sun; farther out, it's a perfect coffee black. The lake is spring fed, connected by a series of limestone caves to Florida's underground aquifer and eventually to the Atlantic. The Santa Fe River runs from the eastern shore of the little lake all the way to the fabled Suwannee, with a small segment flowing underground.

The lake is an essential part of my spiritual geography. I spent every summer and holiday there for the first twelve years of my life drinking in its colors, absorbing the look of white caps during a storm, of cypresses along the shore, of the rock wall where cottonmouths and moccasins made their nests, of minnows darting about in the honey-colored shallows, of moving logs along the edge of the weeds that turned into gators' snouts as they drifted closer.

Memaw's house had a porch facing the water, lined with wide bay windows that gave a magnificent view of the lake. The porch stretched from one end of the house to the other and was full of sunlight. The floor was linoleum tile with a yellow floral pattern. Supper was in the dining room, but we had breakfast on the porch at a small table near the door. Bells hung in the windows tied on frayed twine. They were of all different shapes and sizes, and when the wind rushed in through the screens, the clappers sounded with a cacophony of varied resonances—clangs, tings, cowbell bongs. I'd gaze out those windows of an evening at the opposite shore. There was a tall pine sticking out among the other trees, and in its silhouette, I saw the shape of a Tyrannosaurus Rex, the head with its mouth open, the claws stretching out. I was fascinated and terrified of dinosaurs back then, an obsessive watcher of *Land of the Lost*, and I have nightmares to this day of that tree suddenly turning toward me and charging across the dark lake, all fang and terror.

I nearly drowned in that lake. I was about three, and we were out on the dock. I was at the edge peering down into the brown water, trying to pick out the little bream flitting about in the shadows. I must have leaned too far over. The next thing I remember is gazing up at the surface, the fish above me now moving through light the color of tiger's eye. I wasn't panicked or frightened. I felt suspended in a jewel. Then Dad was swimming down toward me. According to family legend, I was already on my way up, paddling like an otter. I don't remember that, but I do remember the feeling of coolness on the skin, of a liquid quiet far beneath the surface.

***

Dad's first move there must have been shortly after Memaw attempted to abduct me, though I can't be sure. Perhaps it was a direct result. Most of my memories of Dad start in Earleton, and anything leading up to that is a haze. I went up there for school breaks in the summer or spring and sometimes for a weekend or holidays like Thanksgiving or Christmas. I can picture every mile of the drive. Going there from Lakeland was like passing through other dimensions. I went from a suburban kid in a bustling twentieth-century city to something else entirely, something older, more vulnerable and guarded. The physics of the land changed, the spirits, too. To enter that place, it's best to bring you on that same drive now.

***

You hug your mother goodbye and get in the car.

You pass the intersection of Combee Road and US 92 in Lakeland. It's a busy four-lane highway with a McDonald's and strip malls filled with Chinese restaurants, frozen yogurt joints, and a Little Caesars. There's a bar and strip joint, the Peek-A-Boo Lounge, and your sister's cousin's house where you go for crowded pool parties and barbecues, dozens of families at once. You pass more fast food chains and then cross over Interstate 4, which shuttles people by the millions between the Gulf beaches in the west and the Orlando theme parks in the east. There's a constant flow of tourists from all over the world, and the air is electric with the feeling of movement, of people rushing. Rental cars by the hundreds speed past clusters of billboards and neon signs in Spanish and English. They advertise Disney World, Busch Gardens, Sea World, Circus World, Little Cuba in Ybor City.

Your dad hates all this chaos.

After the interstate, it vanishes. You drive fifteen miles north on 98, a weathered two-lane that runs along the southern edge of the Green Swamp. On the left side of the road is pastureland and the occasional trailer set off in the brush. On the right are stretches of dense trees webbed with kudzu and muscadine vines. The trees are broken up here and there by fields filled with standing water, tall grasses and birds, always birds, white ibises and egrets, cowbirds and sandhill cranes. This is the borderland, where the chaotic bustle dies away and a rural quiet starts to seep in. Dad will stop at a pit barbecue shack called Garl's and pick up a lunch of pulled pork sandwiches if Memaw lets him. Sometimes she doesn't want to waste her money on "that garbage." He, of course, has no money of his own, not anymore. If she's hungry, you eat. If she isn't, you move on.

Dad drives. Memaw sits in the back so that you can have time with your father, but she makes sure you know it's a sacrifice. "I don't have to sit here," she'll say chuckling. She asks for your hand. You dutifully drape it over the backseat, and she kisses it from thumb to pinky saying, "My precious boy." She'll spend most of the time reading a book but sometimes will look up if an order needs to be given. Stop for gas, for a basket of fruit from the roadside stand, for a bathroom break, give me that hand again.

From 98 you turn north on 441 and enter the Green Swamp proper. There are no houses anymore, only fields and cattle, and even those thin out until there are no signs of human beings at all, just a wall of forest on either side that goes on unbroken for half an hour. The trees bow over the pavement, vines dripping down in tangled bunches like waves breaking. You fall into a daze staring at the living green. You cross the Little Withlacoochee River (a Creek word meaning "little big water") where your dad used to take the family to spend afternoons watching a pair of otters play. Time stretches and slows. This is the passage to another dimension, the tunnel from one world to another. Things that don't exist elsewhere inhabit this space. On this road, a ghostly semi-truck will appear whenever someone gets in trouble. Your mom says it came to her one night and led her out of an electrical storm. She couldn't see for the rain, and so she followed the red taillights until the main road, at which point the truck vanished. There are unexplored Indian mounds, clear patches of white sand luminous in the dense brush. Your brother tells you there is a bigfoot in the swamp. He says a gang of them attacked his hunting trailer one night, pounding on the metal walls and rocking it back and forth. You eye the brush for movement.

When you emerge from the swamp, there is a rhythmic series of thumps as your tires bounce over the speed bumps. A green sign says "Tarrytown," but the lone building in this "town" is a gas station on the corner. This is the frontier, where human settlement reappears, but subtly changed. In the gas station parking lot, a man lounges in a lawn chair between two cauldrons of boiled peanuts, Cajun and regular. Dad can persuade Memaw to stop for a cup sometimes, other times not. Past the gas station is an abandoned junkyard with a statue of a Tyrannosaurus Rex leaning over the corner of a chain-link fence covered in kudzu. You make Dad slow down. The colors of the dinosaur are faded, one of the arms broken off. At its feet lie the shredded bodies of rusty cars.

The geography is different now. From this point on, you'll pass through little cities that existed before the Civil War. You head north toward Webster and the famous Monday flea market. On either side of the road are pastures as wide as a large lake with scrub cows sheltering from the sun in the blue shade of gargantuan live oaks. You see an occasional white farmhouse, two-story cracker homes with tin roofs and wide, columned porches. It's not just the geography that's changing, but something else, something you can't see—a force, a gravity. There's no more standing water. It's like the elevation is increasing, lifting you farther from the sea. In Lakeland, you are never more than forty-five minutes from the infinite expanse of the Gulf of Mexico. Here, the land seems to close you in with something solid and unyielding. The air thickens.

Now you are passing through tiny towns of no more than five hundred people, some built around forts that served as outposts in the wars against the Seminole. You hit Route 301 at Sumterville and take it north: the highway runs beside the railroad track all the way to Starke. The air here is so humid, the power lines covered in Spanish moss and bromeliads. Dad will switch on the radio. He likes the Carpenters and the old country greats, Willie Nelson, Waylon Jennings, and George Jones. He will sing along to some of the radio tunes, the deep basso of his voice making your chest vibrate as powerfully as any woofer. When Johnny Cash's "Daddy Sang Bass" comes on, he belts out the line written as if just for him, and you sing, "And me and little brother just joined right in there."

"I used to sell farm chemicals to George Jones and Tammy Wynette," he tells you. "Back when the two Nashville bigshots had a house in Lakeland." You've heard this a million times. "George was a bit of a boozer," Dad continues. "One day, they took his driver's license away, and damned if he didn't drive to the liquor store on his riding mower." He pauses thoughtfully for a second and adds, "I liked old George."

"He was nothing but a drunk," Memaw mumbles from the back. You turn around and she chuckles, then reaches out and runs her hand through your hair. "My darling, my precious baby." You wince. You never hear anyone else talk like this.

On those rare occasions when Memaw is not in the car, Dad will make a pit stop at the traffic light in Beville's Corner. Before the Civil War, a businessman named George Beville built a grist mill near here for grinding corn. He was a south Georgian, like your father, and he created a private little fiefdom for himself in this remote area of the state, establishing a plantation to grow Sea Island cotton and raise cattle. You try to imagine the empty fields around you filled with cows and slaves. Only the cows and Beville's name on a shabby road sign remain. There's a liquor store at the stoplight and an empty crossroads where devils walk holding contracts and pens to sign them with. You can't see them in the white Florida sun, but you sense them loitering. The liquor store is the sole inhabited space, itself little more than a mildew-covered white box of concrete in the crabgrass. It has a drive-thru, but Dad prefers to go inside and drink at the cheap bar. There are bits of trash on the red-tiled floor; the cooler has a cage over it sealed by a padlock. Dad will buy you a cherry Chex cola and himself a pickled egg from the gallon jar next to the cash register. He shoves the whole egg in his mouth and winks. You count the number of beers he drinks, compulsively. You memorize the number of ounces written on the can, multiply, add, and add again. You'll tell no one the results. It's never very much anyway because Memaw is keeping track of time and will know of any road breaks that drag on too long. You understand this because it's what you would do, too.

At Ocala, the horse pastures start, rolling green hills and postcard-perfect shade trees with fat branches dripping in Spanish moss. Thoroughbreds graze in the distance. These are racehorses that compete in the Kentucky Derby. Cattle egrets stand vigilant at their sides, snapping up the bugs the animals disturb with their hooves. You see the elegance of wealth in the elaborate signs that name the stables, Hillcrest Farm, Grey Dawn, Padua.

"That farm there," Dad says, pointing to a mansion surrounded by stately oaks, "just sold for seventeen million dollars. Ponder that number for a while, son."

This is also the beginning of Wiregrass Country, strands of it grow throughout the national forest, and you can almost feel doors closing behind you as you plunge inside. It's a land of springs as well. Water in the Florida aquifer dissolves the limestone surface and creates pools and rivers that stay seventy-two degrees year-round. The water is startlingly clear, a glittering refraction of green and turquoise. Silver Springs sports a crumbling theme park with glass bottom boats that cruise over the boils. It's going bankrupt. No one comes anymore; no one cares. There's Disney now, after all, with its neon glitter and cinematic glamour, its roller coasters and electric-light parades and luxury hotels. Silver Springs is a relic, built for Northern tourists right after the Civil War. The TV show *Tarzan* was filmed here in the 1930s, Dad tells you, the Florida jungle a perfect stand-in for the African one. It was also the set for the *Creature from the Black Lagoon, Moon Over Miami, Sea Hunt*. He lists these shows and movies you've never seen but which matter to him somehow. He won't watch modern movies.

Dad tells you that one mile away from Silver Springs was Paradise Park, a twin attraction "for colored only." It boasted "Old Cootchie" the giant alligator, beauty contests, underwater photography. It was listed in the famous Green Book, the travel book for black people in the age of Segregation, and its slogan was "See Silver Springs from Paradise Park." *That's it there, y'all. Right over the fence.*

"That's not fair," you say.

Dad shrugs, "That's how it was." Memaw gives another chuckle from the back. When you turn to look, she's smiling out the window, but her thoughts are on the two of you in the front.

Paradise Park closed just before you were born. Now you're entering the Florida that belongs to the Old South, to a past you've learned is dead but which roams here like a ghost that didn't get the news. This is Marion County, where, just like John Henry, nineteen black people were lynched between 1877 and 1950. According to local legend, many others were "disappeared" into a beautiful spring of sapphire water called the Blue Sink.

You pass a sign for Micanopy, the first town established after Florida became a state in 1821. It was named after the leader of the local Mikasuki tribe to appease their fury over encroaching white settlers gobbling up the territory. "Micanopy" was Hitchiti Creek for "High Chief." In the future, you will go camping near here in the national forest, with some Japanese friends visiting from Tokyo. You will turn down a sandy road and drive straight into a white-nationalist militia camp. There will be nets draped from the trees. Men with long beards dressed in camouflage will scamper up and down like spiders. Another group will stand in front of a trailer with rifles in their hands, wearing sunglasses, and the black lenses will follow you as you pull into their driveway to turn around, panicking but trying not to look like you are panicking, hoping the presence of your Japanese friends won't cause any trouble, too embarrassed to tell them to crouch low. Why? Are you in danger? There will be a huge Confederate flag flying over the trailer. The men in the nets will stop their ascent, dangle by one arm, and watch you drive away.

After the turn for Micanopy, you hit Cross Creek, the site of Marjorie K. Rawlings' cabin where she wrote *The Yearling*. There's a restaurant that serves Cracker favorites like gator tail, conch fritters, and fried green tomatoes. Then comes Payne's Prairie, the vast wetland savannah where the Seminole grazed their cows. You can still find wild Cracker horses descended from the stock the Spanish brought. Cousin Wayne saw a herd of them face down a bull gator on one of the back trails.

At a blip in the highway called Orange Park, you turn east. West would take you to the university town of Gainesville, but your destination lies ever deeper in the countryside, not out of it. Pecan groves break up the grazing land that lines the highway now. On the left, you see a big green building that looks like a barn. This is the feed store owned by Memaw's friend, Faye. You turn here, down a narrow two-lane with a county number instead of a name. Tall live oaks form a tunnel of shade and branch, and you're driving through shadow dappled in sunlight. There's a sign that says "Earleton." The center of the little hamlet contains nothing but an old post office and a small grocery. Memaw stops to pick up her mail. There's a fish camp here, where a boat ramp slants into the big lake. They have catfish fries on Fridays and live country music.

The turn-off to the little lake is on the right. It's hidden by trees and brush, easy to miss. You bounce down broken pavement through the palmetto strands and finally emerge at a row of houses along the lakeshore. The first one with the white weather siding and dark green trim is hers. The yard is full of hibiscus and azaleas. Pink, red, and white blossoms form clusters of color under the pines. When you get out of the car, a subtle dread settles over you like a fine dust. You have dreams about this house, that it's haunted, that it's possessed by demons, that it moves toward you when you're not looking. No matter how much boating and fishing you do on the lake with your father, no matter how much fun you have visiting Karin, nothing will rid you of that feeling.

Ever.

But you love this lake. As soon as you're settled, you burst out the back door, running toward the water. The sun is on your bare shoulders and back, and it's delicious.

Later in college, you will live in a dorm near another dark-water lake just outside of Orlando—Lake Claire. It reminds you of Santa Fe. You'll walk through the woods to reach a little forgotten dock among the weeds. Sometimes you'll see a snake or a gopher turtle, or you'll disturb an armadillo feeding in the brush. You'll go out on the dock—it rocks precariously with each step—and you'll strip down for a dip. You'll swim out until your feet can't touch, out toward the middle, and there you'll play a game with yourself. You'll dive down and grab a handful of mud off the bottom, though it scares you to do it. It's that old dread from Santa Fe, a stupid fear, a pointless fear, and yet as you dive, it builds in your stomach until it takes everything you have not to turn and scramble back toward the light. You keep your hand out ahead of you, fingers splayed because that's the rule. You go down and down and down. You'll do this over and over, every time you go into the water alone. You'll do it because you're afraid and you don't know why, because you despise yourself for that feeling. You'll never lose that fear, but the dive into it will become automatic, something you do just to show you can.

SIX

As Dad would say, here's something not important, but nice to know.

Earleton was named for its founder, General Elias Earle. He was an emigre to Florida and scion of a wealthy Virginia family that later set up shop in South Carolina. Forgive me for putting on language airs, but I do believe "scion" is the right highfalutin word to use, as Earle's grandfather was a five-time congressman and a wealthy South Carolina planter, his great-grandfather an officer of the Revolutionary War, and his cousin a Senator. The Earles mattered. They carried weight in the world, and General Elias brought this ancestral gravity to the wiregrass wastes of the Florida woods, and believe me, this brush with nobility would have impressed Memaw however far back in the past it may have been.

"My house was built on Earle land," she could have said.

Earle earned his rank in the Mexican War as a volunteer and received a land grant in Florida as a reward for his service. He built a two-thousand-acre cotton plantation on the shore of Lake Santa Fe with fifty human beings as property to work it, quickly becoming the largest slave-owner in the region. His fields were located on the west side of Lake Santa Fe, right where Memaw's house was.

She used to tell me and Cousin Karin a ghost story, that when she first moved into this house, she would see two people sitting on the front porch every time she pulled into the driveway, their faces unclear, like dark smudges against the outside wall. They would rush inside as she parked the car, and she would chase after them, thinking them vagrants or thieves, only to find the house completely empty.

"They were ghosts!" she proclaimed. "I got so tired of it all one day I went into the living room and hollered just as loud as I could, 'Listen, you might have died here, but this is my house, now. You'll get out this instant and never come back!' Sure enough, that was the last of them. They'd learned their lesson."

I half wonder if she was being serious, if maybe those fleeing figures were spirits from the old plantation. A life of cotton slavery in the Florida heat would make any soul restless and vengeful.

***

Dad, the great amateur historian, first told me of Lake Santa Fe's esteemed slaveholder three decades ago as we strolled through a stretch of longleaf pine forest among the trails that wound around the lake, accumulating chigger bites and gossiping about neighbors. (The Deans upset the prissy Wallaces because they swam naked even during the day. The Andersons had pot at their parties. The Vicks' new son-in-law was Korean.) Those long walks in the forest were one of the key ways he and I bonded. We'd wander together for hours through the scrub and oak hammocks around the western shore of the little lake, exploring the brush and losing ourselves in conversation. We found the ruins of an old Cracker cabin once, with a tin roof and mildewed walls, each room littered with lumps of rotting clothes and broken furniture. Along the door, someone had attached severed turkey legs to serve as coat hangers. We were always stumbling on construction sites for new houses, too. Dad loved these best. He'd circle the foundations, then go from half-built room to half-built room, running his hands across the empty window frames as if he were a building inspector. He'd complain about the shoddy layout or the crooked doorways.

"Look at where they stuck the bathroom," he'd say. "You can't go two seconds without some idiot who doesn't know squat about design trying to put up a house out here."

I remember one sad-looking site at the farthest end of the last trail. It was blocked off by a cattle gate and a crooked "No Trespassing" sign. A bulldozer sat on the other side, listing into the black muck.

"Some ol' boy over in Gainesville thinks he's going to build a yacht club here," Dad told me. "City boys and their money, forever sticking stuff in the swamp. I give it a month before he's bankrupt and that dozer is sunk up to the driver's seat with a possum at the wheel."

He lit up a Winston as I dug at a chigger welt behind my knee.

"You know who the first one was?"

"The first what?"

"The first jackass to come down to the lake and try to turn this swamp into money?"

"Nope," I answered, still scratching.

"Why Jeffrey," he answered, firing up the accent. "I'm surprised at you! It was General Earle, of course!"

"Who's he?"

"Only the founder of the great metropolis of Earleton, son. Don't you know the esteemed gentleman your memaw's land used to belong to? For shame! Ol' General Earle had himself a plantation 'round these parts with a bunch of slaves and cotton fields, the whole shebang. Once Mr. Lincoln made that illegal, why, God sent the General a vision—to build the French Riviera of the Americas." Dad let out a stream of smoke and dropped the exaggerated accent. "Basically, his plan was to help a bunch of rich folks get richer, so they'd name stuff after him. He rented himself out some convicts to work around the old place—I bet some of them were his former slaves—thus reforming the riffraff while they, in turn, helped him realize his dream for the godforsaken swamp muck. Before it all crashed and burned, sometimes literally, he had laid some railroad and dug a canal for the farmers to haul off their citrus. He'd also put up a fancy hotel for the rich Yankee tourists, the great Balmora, complete with an old-timey paddle boat to ferry them around the lake. Best of all, he had a turpentine farm where the hardest of hardened criminals could work out their penance in the tropical heat, getting themselves nice and rehabilitated."

He regarded me, still scratching violently at my bug bites.

"If you think you got chigger issues after an hour of walking these woods, think about those convicts who lived here for *months*. Probably for doing little more than being caught in public with empty pockets. Capeesh?"

***

Sometimes we looked for arrowheads in the dirt along the trail, or else in the mud by the lakeshore after a storm. We didn't think much about it, though we were, in effect, stealing archaeological artifacts. I never found a whole one of my own but was thrilled to come upon a piece of a hand ax sticking out of the wet sand near the dock. Dad showed me how to figure out the stone had been worked, pointing out the sheer planes where large pieces had been chipped off the sides. He always seemed to find arrowheads when I wasn't around, and one Christmas presented me with a framed pegboard with all his discoveries glued to the surface. He took me to the natural history museum in Gainesville where we learned that these tools likely dated back over ten thousand years and may have been used to hunt mammoth and mastodon, giants that roamed Florida at the end of the last Ice Age.

"Were the hunters Seminoles?" I asked the guide.

"This was long before the Seminoles," she answered. "The Seminoles were actually Creeks who fled Georgia when the whites came. The native tribe in this area were the Timucua. Juan Alonso Cabale, the last Timucuan, died in exile in Cuba in 1767, half a century before Florida became a state."

Cabale had grown up on a mission north of Lake Santa Fe. It was strange to think that Florida's true natives had been exterminated before the US even existed, almost a hundred years before a new tribe replaced them, themselves running from an ethnic cleansing my direct ancestors profited from.

***

Dad loved to sail, and I don't use the word "love" casually. I seldom saw my father express his emotions freely. Every declaration of love to me was utterly sincere but made with a kind of pulling away, as if he weren't sure what I would say back. But when it came to sailing, the passion lit up his eyes and spilled out unguarded. That abandon struck everyone who ever knew him, because we never caught a glimpse of it otherwise. Sailing was something that made him love life not for his son or his wife or anyone else, but for its own sake.

I owe my existence to keel and wind in a way. My mother and father's courtship had consisted mostly of sailing trips. The two of them would, independently, tell tales of that time, each remembering different details from the other. The stories described an outgoing, fun couple I had never seen, and I always wondered if it couldn't happen again, if sailing might be that magic spell that put us back together.

Before I was born, Dad had a roommate in Lakeland named Dave whom he used to run races with on Lake Parker. Parker is the city's largest body of water, bordered on one side by houses, a coal power plant, and a Taco Bell, and on the other side by wetland. My parents-to-be used to sail to Taco Bell to pick up lunch and then cruise back munching on their burritos.

One day, my mom persuaded Dad and Dave to let her take out their little sloop by herself—she figured she had learned plenty from their various sail dates. She loved speed and used to let the boat keel so steeply, catching the violent gusts that rushed over the water before a thunderstorm, that the two men would clutch the sides and beg her to turn into calmer wind.

"You're going to capsize us!" Dave would shout.

Now alone and unhindered, she whizzed past the weeds on the lake's north side and slammed right into a gator head as the animal started to surface.

"At this point," Dad would say dryly, "your mother decided the only logical solution was to jump off the boat."

"All I knew," Mom would say, "was I wanted the hell out of there!"

She leapt into the water and started swimming toward shore, screaming for help. Dad and Dave shouted, "Get back in the boat, Lee! Get back in the boat!" But she was already climbing up the boat ramp as the sloop sped merrily into the lake grass unpiloted, like a ghost ship on the Sargasso Sea.

"Your dad had to swim out and get it," she explained proudly as if this meant some kind of triumph for her. "Right through the gators."

Dad desperately wanted me to learn the craft, and though, as a young kid, I never felt the passion he did, a lot of our time at Santa Fe was spent on the water as he tried to teach me the ins and outs of jibbing and rigging, reading the wind, and recovering a capsized boat. He owned a Scorpion, a small dinghy with a black and orange mainsail that had the image of the eponymous crustacean at the top vertice. That boat was his joy, and he would occasionally enter it in competitions on the big lake, running it against the larger catamarans that the wealthier residents owned.

"It's just for the fun of it," he'd say. "I don't stand a chance against those cats."

I never saw him race that I remember. I have a scrap of memory, a bright but fleeting image of being onshore and trying to pick out his colors among all the distant sails. I don't remember why he was on the water without me. I just see the waves and the white caps and the triangle of orange and black that meant he was coming home. The races themselves he'd describe on the phone—what he'd placed, who the competition had been—and my heart would lurch. His participation was a sign he was in one of his good periods, that he felt strong, and I could realistically entertain the hope that he might leave his mother's house and strike out on his own again, bringing our family back together.

***

One day, I was learning to jibe. For you landlubbers, a jibe is a turn that puts you in the opposite direction of the wind and makes the boom swing swift and hard over the prow of the boat. Before this swing, you must warn anyone that might get whacked to duck. Dad taught me to call out "Ready about!" and wait for the passenger to respond, "Ready." I understood the importance of this because I had accidentally thunked him hard once, sending him spinning over the side. Anyway, we were bearing fast toward the east end of the lake. Gusts were making the sail snap like a horsewhip. A storm was coming.

"Ready about."

"Ready."

Swing, turn, over and over so that we zigzagged northwest until we found ourselves heading for what looked like an opening in the lake grass onshore. It looked like a river.

"What's that?" I asked.

"That's General Earle's canal," he answered. "When Emancipation shut his plantation down, he got together with some other carpetbaggers and decided to cut himself a canal between Santa Fe and Lake Alto."

"Where's that?"

"Over in Waldo where the big flea market is."

"What's a carpetbagger?"

"Northerners who came down after the Civil War to get rich off the ruins. Don't they teach you anything in that old schoolhouse?" He said this often and usually half in irony, but I always took him completely seriously.

"I learn a lot in school," I said defensively. "About slavery and the 3/5th Compromise."

"I bet all those textbooks you use are written by Yankees."

"No, they're not." I had no idea.

"Do they call it the Civil War or the War Between the States?"

"The Civil War."

"That's all I need to know."

"But that's what you just called it!"

"Anyway, the General's canal was one of his harebrained schemes to put north Florida on the map and show the folks back home he was someone to be reckoned with. I guess they'd been having their doubts. He bought a little old steam-powered tug and charged his Northern friends a quarter apiece to chug up and down the canal through the exotic jungle, a pleasure tour on the Florida Nile. They'd slap mosquitoes, ooh and aah at the wildlife, then have themselves a fancy Champagne *sooopper* back at the Balmora. Well, that little operation went on for a few years or so before the swamp shut it down. The shores of the canal kept collapsing, so ol' Master Earle had to give up the tour boat business. The swamp always comes back, son. It's the only thing you can depend on around here. Capeesh?"

After that first sighting of the canal, I could not get it out of my head. I kept asking Dad questions. How long was it? Was it still passable? Could you still go all the way to the railroad in Waldo? How long would it take?

"I really don't know," he said. "But why don't we find out?"

We set out one morning on Grandpa Carl's orange fishing skiff. The little boat was equipped with a trolling motor perfect for shallow water. We puttered along, hugging the western shore, then plunged through the maidencane grass and into the shadows we'd seen from the Scorpion days before. We had an Irish Setter named Ginger with us, one of Dad's strays who had bumbled up to the house one night, half-starved and with rope burns around the neck from where someone had tied her too tightly. Dad said she was one of the dumbest dogs he'd ever seen, something he blamed on her being purebred.

"It screws up the genes," he said. "Like incest."

As an indication of her intelligence or lack thereof, he'd cite Ginger's misshapen nose, a hunk of it missing from where she'd poked it into the shell of a snapping turtle.

The canal was littered with fallen trees overhung with arrowhead vine and briar but still passable. Lush clusters of branches formed a storied canopy overhead that afforded some shade—oak tree and hickory, bay and tupelo. The banks were high, collapsed ledges of beige sand and black mud with roots jutting out like tentacles. The cypress knees looked like curtains of stalactites. On logs, turtles sunned themselves in rows ordered from largest to smallest, sometimes on each other's backs. We bumped an alligator with the bow, and it sank slowly beneath a green carpet of duckweed. Minnows flicked across the surface. We kept expecting to be blocked by silt or shallows, but the canal got deeper and wider instead. At one point we climbed out for a rest, and I poked around in the water. I found some freshwater mussels, species with names like the Florida shiny spike and the paper pondshell.

"Can you eat these?" I asked Dad.

"Dunno," he answered.

We climbed back in the boat. High on the banks we saw a barbed wire fence wrapped in muscadine vines. A faded "No Trespassing" peeked out from the leaves. The occasional scrub cow stared back at us, chewing its cud. The world held no human noise except for the chug of our little motor—the rest was the buzz of cicadas, the croaks of herons hidden in the brush, the plop of water when a fish plucked a water bug off the surface, or silence.

In the end, the canal stretched for six miles before spilling into Lake Alto. When we emerged, we took a tour around the new lake. I felt like we had arrived on another planet and were exploring its boundaries. We found a canal spur on the opposite shore that went a short way to a boat ramp in the town of Waldo and a state park where the railroad used to be. Dad parked the boat. I took Ginger's life jacket off and let her out for a quick pee in the grass. Dad lit a cigarette and stood looking around with one hand on his hip as smoke streamed from his lips.

"I'll be damned," he said to himself. "We're in Waldo. You know what Waldo is famous for besides the flea market?"

"No."

"It's a big one for us Southern boys, so brace yourself."

"I'm braced."

"This is where Yankees seized Jefferson Davis' luggage, captured themselves a whole suitcase full of presidential skivvies."

The sun was reddening and sinking west when we made our way back. We spent the six-mile return in the canal fighting early-evening mosquitoes and late-afternoon yellow flies. By the time we arrived at little Lake Santa Fe, we were covered in bug bites. Dad chuckled as he scratched a welt on his shin.

"What?" I asked.

"Oh, I'm just imagining Mr. Earle's fancy guests gussied up in their suits and petticoats, expecting a pretty paddle-boat tour downriver and getting that bug-infested shit-hole instead."

My God, I miss him sometimes. I miss exploring with him. I miss Florida and that lake. I miss the gold-brown of that water and the sound of it gulping against the sand, the quiet of being submerged and looking up toward the surface. I miss the light and the sight of my dad swimming down to rescue me.

***

Memaw's house had a peculiar design. The porch facing the lake was a later addition, and all the windows of the bedrooms, living room, and kitchen opened out onto the porch instead of directly to the outside. Essentially, you pulled the curtains over the jalousies to close off another part of the house. I usually slept in the middle bedroom. Noise carried in strange ways. I often heard what I thought were footsteps pacing the length of the porch, and the way the dock lights fell first through the porch windows and then through the bedroom ones caused double shadows on the opposite wall. When the wind rustled the bushes outside, it looked like two creatures were converging, one climbing onto the shoulders of the other, I was convinced, to slip into the window and do whatever lake beasts did to children in their beds. Memaw's ghost story didn't help.

My mother came up with me for one visit to Earleton, a most unusual occurrence. I don't remember why, only that Memaw was not around and so my parents slept together in her bedroom which was at the end of the house next to the one I occupied. I heard them arguing one night and padded in to see what it was all about.

"Mom?" I called tentatively. I don't know what the topic of battle was before my arrival, but when I appeared in the doorway, it became about me. My dad gestured toward me with a look of anguish.

"Why doesn't he call for me?" Dad asked. "Why won't he even say the word 'Dad'?"

"He does," she insisted.

"No, he doesn't. He never says it."

"He's just not used to you."

"How is he not used to me? I'm his goddamn father."

"But he only sees you on holidays and the occasional weekend."

"And that's my fault?"

She said nothing. We all knew the answer. He turned to me.

"I want you to call me 'Dad,' Jeffrey."

"Okay," I said.

"Say it now."

I looked at my mom.

"Say it."

I tried to make the word come out, but it caught in my throat. I felt like I did whenever I tried to go to a neighbor's house and knock on the door to call a friend out to play. I would stand with my fist raised, completely frozen, and stare at the surface of the door, frustrated by my fear but too shy to move. I would either linger till someone inside noticed there was a little kid on their front porch, or else I would slink back home and wait for the friend to come knock on our door instead. The word "Dad" cowered deep in my stomach. I knew it hurt my father's feelings. I could see how upset he was—not angry, not mean—but genuinely hurt, and I knew that it was my fault, that I should be able to do this simple thing every other normal kid could do.

"I told you," he pronounced finally. "He won't say it."

So, I forced myself to say it the next day, and every time I talked to him after that. Though it got easier with time, it was always something I had to make myself do. Close my eyes, clear my mind, breathe, then say "Dad," It never came naturally, and it wasn't because I didn't think of him as my father, because I did, and I do. It was something else, some timidity that was an intrinsic part of my personality, a timidity that met the distance he put around himself and crested into a high wave I had to jump over every time I delivered the word he wanted.

I don't know what it was.

***

My mom's stay at the lake set the scene for one of the most popular stories in my family, one far less angsty. The three of us were out on the dock fishing when I saw my bobber lunge hard to the left and then down into the water. I grabbed the pole, gave it a yank, and flying up onto the dock came what looked like a snake with legs. It whipped its slimy black-green body frantically toward me with what I saw as nefarious intent. I can still hear the thump thump thump of it thrashing on the wood.

I fled. I bolted right past my equally-frightened mother, into the yard and up the back steps of the house as my father, calm as always, grabbed the pole from where I'd flung it, lifted the creature, and began working out the hook.

"I'd never seen you move that fast," my mother says whenever she tells this story.

After the initial shock, Dad and I journeyed to the Keystone library to explore the secret of whatever the hell we had caught. We found a tome on marine biology that settled the matter. Our snake-fish was an American eel, a "catadromous" species, meaning it spent part of its life in freshwater and part in salt. "Little is known about these creatures," the article began, deepening the mystery we already felt. We learned the adults somehow made their way from the lakes of north Florida to the Atlantic Ocean where they swam to the Sargasso Sea—a part of the magical and mysterious Bermuda Triangle, I noted, and an infamous producer of ghost ships. The Sargasso was not bound by land like the Black or Mediterranean Seas, but rather by a vortex of ocean currents called the North Atlantic Gyre. Nothing that drifted in drifted out. There, among the ship-swallowing tangles of sargassum weed, the eel spawned and died. At least it was assumed they died, for no eel had ever been observed swimming back. How those eel fry returned over hundreds of miles of open ocean to inland lakes like Santa Fe was unknown, but marine biologists guessed they swam into the subterranean maze of limestone caves in the Florida aquifer through undiscovered openings on the ocean floor.

"Not important, but nice to know," Dad pronounced as we closed the book. But by then, I knew what he meant from the way he always encouraged me to find out. It wasn't just nice to know these things, it was essential, even if we were the only two in the family who thought so.

This incident added a layer of magic to Santa Fe. What else from the Bermuda Triangle might slither through the chthonic dark of those caverns to bite our lines?

Fishing was a mainstay of our life on Lake Santa Fe and a pastime that formed a crucial building block of our relationship.

I paused a moment before writing the word, "pastime." It seems so old-fashioned, but neither Dad nor I ever accepted fishing as a sport. Florida abounds with bass masters in their high performance boats, prowling the weeds in the wee hours of the morning, meticulously selecting lures according to the feel of the weather and the look of the water. They use hi-tech, state-of-the-art reels "machine-designed for the dizzying variety of conditions faced by the hardcore bass man." There is the baitcast, the spinning, the spincast. Then, there are the rods—the Bionic Blade, the Carbon Lite. People enter tournaments all over the state with prizes as high as a hundred-thousand dollars. Anyone in Lakeland who said they "fished" meant this high-octane festival of gadgetry.

Dad and I cut our own cane poles. We walked to a strand of bamboo in the woods around Santa Fe, and when that was bulldozed to put up a house, journeyed to visit Cousin Wayne who lived on an island off Lake Geneva where another batch grew against the wall of his cabin. We took the time to select a stalk sturdy enough for the giant fish we envisioned catching, checked for cracks along the body, and then made the cut just below the thickest joint. Back at the house, we'd let it dry, stain it for waterproofing, then fit it with line and tackle. Dad did the more delicate work, but I got to select the bobber. He let me string the hook and sinker and taught me to choose the sizes according to our prey. I loved it when a pole broke, because it meant we got to go through this whole process again.

There was a white clapboard shed in the backyard, divided into two parts. One section was where Grandpa Zillman kept his yard equipment, the mower, the weeder, the edger, and various sizes of shovels, hoes, machetes, and saws. The other was for his fishing and boating equipment. It had a door with a crescent moon-shaped window, and inside were orange lifejackets, nets, paddles, and boat cushions all hanging on nails. I can still smell that combination of rubber, lake water, and wood. There were rods and reels, too, and tackle boxes full of various lures—purple rubber worms and flies of all shapes and sizes. Every time a fish broke the line, and I had to get a new hook, sinker, or bobber, I would fetch one of these tackle boxes and dig through the colorful array of baits, asking Dad about each one. How does this one work? What kind of fish is that one for?

He'd frown and grumble in a fake cornpone accent, "Jeffrey, we just ain't that fancy. Neither is your Grandpa Zillman, for that matter. He bought all that rigamarole and has not the first clue what to do with it."

We were that image of Opie and Andy at the end of the *Andy Griffith Show*, one of Dad's favorites—a tall, dark-haired man and his son walking through the woods with their cane poles over their shoulders, chatting on their way to their fishing hole. The man was the sole sane person in the whole town, intelligent but homespun, the boy the hapless innocent.

But sometimes, we were something much less conventional.

It was at the Santa Fe house that Dad started teaching me to cook. We prepared dinner together, making big batches of his famous navy bean soup with ham hock, cornbread, and pepper sauce. On some nights when we came in from fishing, we baked a pie. Our favorites were Southern classics, pecan and chess, but when bored, we found variations on the basic recipes, spinoffs like lemon chess and coconut chess or chocolate pecan. He taught me when to cream butter with sugar and when to melt, how to prepare a crust, what order to mix ingredients in, and how to tell when the pie was done. Memaw would sometimes stand at the kitchen door with her hands on her hips and smirk at these baking lessons.

"Is this how a grown man spends time with his son?" she said once.

When she went to bed and left us alone, Dad taught me to play craps and poker. We sat out on the back porch with the darkness of the lake out the window as I learned to bet and shuffle cards. He'd quiz me on the strength of the different hands and what their names were, the flush, the straight, the full house, and the coveted royal straight flush.

"Where did you learn poker?" I asked one night. "From your dad?"

"No," he answered with a dismissive exhalation of air. "Definitely not him."

He was adept at dodging questions about his father.

We also played a game called Wahoo, which, when it became apparent that the driftwood animal business would never fly, Dad made the focus of his entrepreneurial endeavors. Wahoo was played with dice and colored marbles that you moved from your base on one side of the board to your home on the other. We played it constantly with various permutations of relatives—Karin and Mom, Aunt Nancy and Michele, even with Memaw and Carl. One of the only things I have left from my father is a Wahoo board he made forty years ago for my eighth birthday.

"If I can patent this thing," he told me once, "we could make a bundle. I've never seen Wahoo anywhere else in the country. No one sells anything like it."

"What about Aggravation?" I said.

"Yeah, but the rules are different enough," he insisted. "I've done the research and legally, a patent is completely doable. Plus, we could invent variations. Imagine, not one game in a box but seven different ones. It would sell like hotcakes."

81

And so, he began creating different versions named after us. There was Lee's Game for my mother, which was played with only half the marbles due to her infamous impatience; Bumper, taken from my childhood nickname and featuring one marble of a different color that went backward and bumped opponents' marbles off the board; and finally, Run Rabbit, inspired by the way Karin played, ignoring all attempts to harass opponents and just racing for home.

For years, I kept the faith. I believed in this scheme of his, that Wahoo was the thing that would break the spell and finally enable him to move out of his mother's house and embark upon a career. I would brag about it to friends and strangers, tell them about the ancient game passed down through generations of Gibbses that my father was finally going to unleash on the world. He caught me doing this one day. It must have been the year before I left for Japan. I'd driven up with my college roommate, whose family was also from Georgia, and I was regaling him with tales of family tradition when Dad stepped in to correct me.

"Wahoo is not a Gibbs family game," he said.

"But you told me that when I was little," I insisted. "You said your dad or grandfather or someone taught you."

"No, I didn't."

"I'm sure of it."

"I told you I learned it from a group of old World War II vets in Lakeland," he said. "And that they'd brought it back from Germany. I have no heirlooms passed down from your memaw's first husband."

And with that, he took a sip of iced tea from the tall tumbler marked with the Z of Grandpa Zillman, dead for many years.

***

Carl Zillman was my first death, the first corpse I ever saw. I have a memory of the funeral that can't be quite accurate, a few surrealistic seconds that float in my head like a gif flickering in outer space. I'm standing next to Memaw, who is holding my hand. She wears a yellow dress and towers over me; I cannot make out her face. Of all the family members that have come with us, it's me she's plucked out of the crowd to take up to the body. "Face forward," she says. The room is dark, murky. I see blurry silhouettes of other people sitting in rows of fold-out metal chairs; it's like I'm viewing the whole scene through heavy cataracts. The coffin is under a pale yellow light that diffuses around us. Grandpa Zillman's head lies propped up on a pillow inside the casket, his face waxy and fixed in a hard-jawed grimace. Memaw's voice is calm, lecturing. She's telling me to bow my head and close my eyes. "Pray, Jeffrey, pray hard for his soul. It's okay to cry. Your grandpa's dead, but you will see him again in Heaven."

But I'm not crying. No one is. No one seems genuinely upset about anything. In fact, I don't think my dad has even come because I get the sense I'm all alone with her in this dark murk; all I can think about is when I'll be able to get back home.

Carl Zillman was the only grandfather I ever knew. My mother's father disappeared when she was very small, and her stepfather died before I was born. My father's father, Pepaw, passed away when I wasn't quite three, and he and Memaw apparently had been divorced for more than a decade. I never uttered the word "grandpa" in reference to anyone but Carl, yet he never felt like the real thing. I was in none of the hundreds of old pictures he kept. No one I knew nor anyone I was even related to posed in the frames that hung throughout his house. He couldn't tell any stories of my father or uncle as boys. I couldn't inherit anything from him. No one could honestly say, "You get that from your grandfather."

None of this would have mattered, probably, if we had been close in some way. After all, I grew up in Lakeland surrounded by a vast clan of my "half" brothers' and sisters' families, and at some point, both siblings married people who already had kids of their own of no blood relation whatsoever, and we had an extensive coterie of friends we referred to as "aunt" and "uncle." Still, although I'm told Carl was "a nice man" by nearly every older person in the family, I only have two dour memories of him. One is of a stern-faced old man sitting in his recliner in front of the television and the other is of him on the back porch of the lake house. It was after he'd had a stroke, and he was trying to tell me something, moaning and drooling and scribbling with a shaky hand on a pad of yellow paper. I'd been sent to find out if he was thirsty.

His death happened around the time I started to feel my difference from the world. In Lakeland, all the older men in my life were Steeles, the last name of my mother's first husband and a clan of males I was connected to through my brother Mike. It included his cousins and father and their friends around the city, which were legion—the Steeles had helped found Lakeland. "Your Mike's little brother? A little Steele?" random guys would say. All of them were ballplayers and hunters; they got together and chewed tobacco, bullshitted while hunched over car engines or showing off the latest additions to their pick-ups. I remember, for instance, when all the rage was gigantic tires. A chubby kid at eight, I could fit inside the hubcap of my brother's brown Ford and have room to work at my Rubix Cube. Most of them rode in the local rodeos. When my sister married my first brother-in-law, another Mike, he was of the same breed, a professional bull rider raised by an evangelist mother. And there I was, set loose among them—this bookworm with the different last name, clumsy at sports and oversensitive, never at home in a conversation unless it was about space or dinosaurs or whatever fantasy book I was currently engulfed in. I was so clearly not one of them. They called me a variety of good-natured nicknames, "Einstein" and "Little IBM," but however playfully these epithets were meant, I cringed every time I heard them, and not being able to roll with the joke only made me more of an outcast.

The only man I resembled was Dad, but he seemed an isolated phenomenon in the world, too, out there alone on the lake in his boat. Where had we come from? Were there other men like us in older generations?

I used to feel under siege by Carl's last name. He had that set of iced-tea glasses engraved with Zs, a sign in front of the house with the word "Zillman," and a widow that bore his name until her own death twenty-five years later. But there were no Gibbses beyond my father and Gene's generation. Everyone else's line was certainly present and accounted for. I knew Memaw's two Hamner sisters, Dorothy and Evelyn. Aunt Evelyn sent me cheesy Christmas and birthday cards every year from Hallmark, each with a short message and a check for two dollars.

"Save those up," Dad would say, "and you can buy yourself something nice in a few thousand years."

I had also met most of my mother's eleven aunts and uncles and her more than thirty cousins. I knew everyone in my sister's and brother's father's family, his parents and all his aunts and uncles. I even knew Aunt Nancy's family, her mother Ruth, her sister Betty, her brother Jimmie, the illustrious state attorney in Jacksonville and her father, George Patrick, whom Dad called Sparky because, according to Dad at least, he made a living by torching rental trailers and collecting the insurance money. No matter which direction I went on the women's sides, I could find a crowd of relatives and at least one oft-told tale about each of them. Even the ones who had passed on were a constant presence in family lore.

But I never knew the first soul from my male line, no Gibbses. No one told stories about them, either. I never heard my father or even Uncle Gene say the word "father" in reference to anyone. If I had trouble saying the word "Dad," then so did they. There were no pictures of my real grandfather, no documents bearing his name, no invocations of memories. For a long time, I didn't even know his name. I knew Pepaw had sisters but couldn't name one of them and would never meet one either, though it turned out one of my father's paternal aunts lived a mile away from us in Lakeland, something I only found out a few years ago in an online genealogy search. I asked Dad once after Grandpa Zillman died—I must have been about seven—if his father had abandoned them at an early age like Mom's father had abandoned her, figuring, maybe that's why he was such a mystery. After all, it explained rather neatly why Mom didn't know anyone on her dad's side.

"No," he answered. "Lenward was around off and on until the very end." I made a note of that. Pepaw's real name was Lenward, and Dad didn't call him "Dad."

"Then why doesn't anyone talk about him?" I wanted to know.

"That's complicated," he answered, and then fell silent on the subject for several years.

***

Memaw met Carl because she used to stop at the filling station in front of his feed store, the C&L. Aunt Nancy says they got "frisky at the gas pump," though I can't imagine what Memaw being "frisky" might look like. What sort of signals did she give? Did she coyly lower her eyes, absently finger her hair, or, God forbid, giggle? And what did she find attractive about him? His legs? Online genealogy websites reveal an uncharacteristic candidate for Memaw's new suitor. He owned a pig farm on several acres behind the store and was well-known among Florida ranchers because of his purebred Hampshire sows. His name figured prominently in nearly every issue of the *Florida Cattlemen and Livestock Journal*, and so passionate was he about everything porcine that he'd founded the Florida Swine Producers' Association and served as president for over a decade. Memaw fancied herself a bit of an aristocrat—a true Southern "lady." I imagine it nicked her pride a bit that she was dating the local pig king.

"But he had property," Aunt Nancy says. "That was the sex appeal."

"That couldn't have been the only thing," I protest.

"Jeffrey, you better believe that woman had her eye on his house and store. He was ten years older than her with no kids to speak of. She figured she wouldn't have to wait long before it would all be hers. Yeah!"

To make matters worse, Carl Zillman was a Yankee. He'd been born in Indiana but had grown up and lived most of his life in Berrien County, Michigan, and didn't move to the South till he was well into middle age. The curious thing for me is, Memaw had been born in Berrien County, Georgia. Both Berriens in Georgia were named for Andrew Jackson's Attorney General, John Berrien, because they were thankful his boss had driven off the Creeks; in Michigan, because the state was trying to curry favor with the Indian Killer in order to get the new president's help in prying land away from neighboring Ohio.

As Dad would say, this is not all that important but nice to know. Except I keep running into these parallels and coincidences as I research this book. Nell Hamner and Carl Zillman were born a decade and a thousand miles apart in counties with the same name, a name that served as tribute to a man whose conquests opened Wiregrass Country to both the Gibbses and Hamners. The town of Memaw's birth was Sparks, named for a mogul who helped establish the railway on which her son would commit suicide a century later. In Carl's birth state of Michigan, a man with the same name as Jackson's Attorney General, John Berrien, inaugurated the Michigan Central Railway.

Does it mean anything? Probably not. I'm forcing patterns on the chaos to make the impact of my father's death have more significance. It's a Rorschach test, revealing the obsessions I use to interpret the world. But sometimes, it's like I'm sifting the obscure data of distant objects to reveal messages written in the medium of coincidence. Sometimes I think time is a physical thing, a phantom planet that floats parallel to the rock and stone earth, and when an event strikes its surface, the seismic waves radiate outward into the past and future, echoing and echoing. There is a kind of crater on the moon, and throughout the solar system, with concentric ridges called megaterraces that radiate out from the main impact site. They grow fainter with distance, seem less connected, their shape less defined, but you can still discern the reflection of that central catastrophe. To scale one of these megaterraces, to measure its breadth and view the horizon from its summit may not convey the violence of that first, blinding explosion, but it memorializes the impact, it lets you know the whole world shuddered when the meteor hit. That Carl Zillman and Nell Hamner were born in counties with the same name. In towns with names commemorating railroad moguls is not anything so overt as a message, but it is a distant echo in time, a megaterrace in the hinterland pointing inward toward the original site of that extinction-level event, the death of my father on the tracks.

SEVEN

Whenever the subject of Memaw comes up with strangers, one story my aunt rolls out by way of explanation is about how, a few months before he died, Carl had a stroke that paralyzed his left side and left him bedridden. He couldn't walk or talk and had violent tremors in his hands that made it difficult to write.

"Your memaw got stuck playing nursemaid, and she didn't like it one bit. Yeah! She was trying to feed him one time, and he knocked the spoon out of her hand so that the food went all over her quilt. Well, she slammed that bowl down and said, 'Why can't you go ahead and die?' Then she flicked those eyes up at me and just grinned, because she knew I'd heard her, see? She was trying to make out like she was joking. I remember visiting once, and he grabbed my arm like he wanted to yank it out of the socket. His mouth was just a'moving, making all these groaning and moaning sounds. It took me a bit, but I finally figured out he was saying, 'Don't go. Don't go.' He was afraid of being left alone with her."

As I've said, Aunt Nancy often embellishes her stories, so I've never known what to make of this, but my mother, when asked, serves up one of her own.

"I was visiting once, and he was trying to tell me something, scribbling on that pad of his and moaning, but I couldn't understand him. He'd point at the window and at the bed, and then I realized he couldn't see the lake. He'd asked to be put out on the porch so he could watch the water, and your memaw had stuck him back just far enough so that it was out of sight. I pushed him forward, and I never saw the man so thankful, but boy, did it piss her off!"

"How do you know she did it on purpose?" I ask. "I mean why would anyone be so petty as to drag a man out on the porch like he asked and then just barely make it where he can't get the view he wanted? Why not just close him up in the bedroom if you want to be cruel?"

Mom rolls her eyes. "Oh, good God, Jeff, this is Nell we're talking about."

"I'm just saying, we all talk about her like she was some kind of supreme evil, but maybe we're exaggerating. It's hard to care for a person bedridden like he was. You have to feed them and bathe them and change their diapers. Maybe she was just frustrated at times."

"That old bitch wasn't frustrated. She used to fix him food he didn't like on purpose. Nancy told me that once, and I thought she was making it up. You know how she does, so she said, 'All right. Let's go visit this weekend if you don't believe me. We'll turn up around lunchtime.' And sure enough, I saw her take a tray of crap we all knew he hated, smiling like she was serving caviar to the queen, and he spit it out all over the blanket. Anyone with an ounce of love would behave better than that, even if they got 'frustrated.'"

Love is the emotion missing in that memory of his funeral. I knew it was supposed to be there, as young as I was, and I could feel its absence. In its place was this terrible blank ritual, this hollow prayer.

***

Memaw lived in the Santa Fe house for about four years after Carl died, and whenever I was up visiting Dad, she would drag out a Ouija board and make me her seance partner. We would sit on the living room floor near his chair, and she would instruct me to place my fingers on the stylus, then concentrate as hard as I could on Grandpa. Sometimes Karin was there, and though she was only five or six and remembers none of this, Memaw would have her join in, and the three of us would watch as the plastic triangle slid from letter to letter, Memaw reading aloud the words it spelled.

"Are these ghosts?" we'd ask nervously.

"These are good spirits," she would say. "Angels on their way to Heaven."

We contacted lots of transiting angels over the years, but I don't remember how often Mr. Zillman manifested himself. A part of me says never and remembers Memaw's constant disappointment, but another part of me remembers seeing his name appear every time and always with the same message, pronounced by Memaw herself as if she were a medium channeling his spirit. "I'm with the Lord and finally at peace. I love you all."

She never wanted to contact anyone else, not her mother or father, not her mysterious first husband, my real grandfather. Just Carl, as if she were perhaps trying to appease a guilty conscience. Or maybe she did grieve, only none of us knew how to read her.

***

I didn't find a real grandfather until I met Delal's. Dede's full name was Memli Seven, and though he was of an ethnicity and creed utterly different from my own, he was closer to me than any man from the Gibbs or Hamner clans.

To know him, you must picture him. He was lanky and tall—as a child, Delal thought he was a giant. He had wispy hair the texture of those white filaments of spun glass people used to drape over Christmas trees, though it was usually hidden by a brown newsboy cap he wore tilted forward. His large glasses were tinted dark brown, and they were set between cap-rim and nose like a barrier to hide his left eye that sagged slightly at the bottom from an infection he picked up in his youth after using a piece of raw steak to treat a shiner.

Whenever I think of him, I see him at his door preparing for one of his many walks. He throws his satchel over one shoulder so that the strap cuts diagonally across his chest and the scuffed leather bag rests on his hip bone, then he grabs the long shoehorn that hangs from a radiator pipe just above the door. With a grace earned from decades of practice, he deftly slips on his loafers and flicks the horn back in place. It was a dance move, a bit of old-world dash. He was baffled by my klutzy habit of reaching down to work my heel into my shoes by hand.

I have puzzled over why I want to include Dede here almost as much as I agonized over defining my father's Southerness. Something connects; my mind keeps pushing him forward, and so I'm going to follow the pen.

First, we were companions. When Delal wasn't home, he'd call me over for dinner sometimes, having prepared for the two of us *gêrmiya şîr*. The Kurdish translates literally as "milk soup," but it's more of a hot rice porridge. It was the only dish he knew how to *fix*, as a Southerner would say, and he liked to show it off for me, especially in the cold of winter when it tasted best. Sometimes, he came to our house to play cards or chat politics or to tell me stories of the past, which neither I could get enough of hearing nor he of telling.

We had a few essential things in common. First, we both grew up without fathers, him because his dad vanished on a boat to America when he was a baby. Second, we both feared death more than the people around us, or more precisely, we feared losing life. Dede never stopped wanting to *experience*. In his nineties, he came to all our parties while his own children skipped because they felt "too old" to attend. He accompanied us on our travels, on a weeklong road trip through Turkey's Kurdistan, for example, and he was always up for learning a new game. We taught him to play charades, Uno, even to bowl.

He had a library of comic tales from his youth. At the age of six, he trekked seven miles from the village to register himself in the only school in the region, though he spoke not one word of Turkish, the only legal language of education.

"Me and the other Kurdish boys would just sit in the class and nod at whatever the teacher said," he explained. "There was one older kid who understood, and whenever he'd raise his hand, we'd all raise ours because that made the teacher happy. Then, the teacher would get so mad when he called on us and we couldn't do anything but smile that sometimes he'd line us up outside and swat the back of our hands with a ruler."

By the time he reached the end of these stories, the pitch of his voice would have risen to a helpless soprano, and it would break out in a loud laugh as he slapped his knee but always leaning toward you, raucously yanking you into the joke as well.

Even in his nineties, he had not lost his capacity to flirt. He was often over for a visit whenever I Skyped my mother. Once, he asked to say hello, so I plopped him down in front of my laptop and let him talk to her for a few minutes, translating between them. *How are you? How is your family? Is it hot there?* Conversation topics dried up quickly, and I resumed my place in front of the computer with Mom's video on the main screen and mine in a little box in the bottom right. After a few minutes, I noticed movement from that direction, like a fly flicking in and out of my line of vision. I glanced down and saw myself at the center of the image and Dede behind me in his newsboy's cap leaning first past my left side and then my right, again and again like a whack-a-mole, each time giving an enthusiastic wave of his hand.

"I think you may have a suitor," I told Mom.

He was on the opposite side of the race issue from my family, being a minority of a minority, and it was this, more than anything else perhaps, that led me to rethink the issue of heritage and the South.

First, he was Kurdish in a country that, as of 1924, had decided Kurds did not exist. They were deemed "mountain Turks," and their language was officially declared a broken form of Turkish that would be stamped out with a proper education. In his schoolboy years, for example, children were encouraged by their teacher to rat out parents to authorities when they heard them speak Kurdish at home. In the 80s and 90s when Delal was growing up, hundreds of Kurdish community leaders were disappeared or murdered by *faili meçhul*, literally "parties unknown," a phrase that should send shivers of recognition down the spine of any black person with a history in the South. Even today, though restrictions have been relaxed, you risk a great deal asserting your Kurdish identity in public. In September 2019, a man was attacked and beaten in the Sariyer district of Istanbul for telling a mob of football hooligans that he was Kurdish. The opposition papers called it an "attempted lynching," a word Kurds have borrowed from the American South's dark history, having found it useful to describe their own.

Dede also belonged to a religious minority called the Alevis, who were and often still are despised by Sunni Turks and even other Kurds, both of whom regard them as lawless pagans turned from the true faith. Dede's village stands on the border of the old Alevi state of Dersim, where the Turkish government began a campaign on March 21st, 1937 to exterminate the rebellious Alevi clans that lived there, a genocide that continued until an amnesty was declared in September 1938. Dede was ten years old during the massacres, and because my father was born on March 18th, 1937, I cannot help but imagine what was happening at his house six thousand miles away in Omega as the Dersim slaughters began. Pepaw, my real grandfather, must have been welcoming home his newborn son from the hospital while three-year-old Uncle Gene watched (jealously, according to Aunt Nancy). Memaw would have been exhausted and sore, still mostly bedridden perhaps. As she nursed my future father on the other side of the world, Turkish forces began exterminating hundreds of their own citizens and dumping the bodies in rivers.

By 1938, Dede said he and his fellow villagers could hear the planes bombing the mountains just over the border, less than ten miles to the west. Many people were hiding in caves among the crags and canyons there, and the air force was smoking them out. For Dede and his mother, the sounds of fighting being so close meant only one thing—their turn was coming.

"I remember my mother locked up the house," he said, "and we sat awake all night, listening for the soldiers' footsteps on the road. Then, just like that, the whole thing was called off. The government announced an amnesty the next morning, right before they got to us."

This bit of dialogue feels slightly false. It's hard for me to imitate Dede's speech patterns on the page. I have to translate from both a faulty memory and from his own peculiar brand of Kurdish-accented Turkish, since much of his storytelling style derived from that idiom. Plus, there was the performance, or the absence of one in this case. He often dove into a scene and acted out bits of dialogue. He'd sit up straight and exclaim "Allah allah!" if there was a surprise in the plot or lean forward with a triumphant clap and a "Ha!" when there was an "I told you so" moment. Everything was illustrated with wide sweeps of his hands. When he told me about waiting for the soldiers in that locked house, however, his manner was subdued, his hands motionless, his voice hushed, as if he still thought someone might overhear that shouldn't. What Dede and his mother felt that night, waiting for death to march down the road, must have been like what Miss Linnie's neighbors felt when they sought shelter from the lynch mobs, and though they shared neither ethnicity nor creed, I bet they would have known what stilled Dede's hands.

***

Dede's first memory takes place when he was four. His older sister is going to a friend's wedding, and Dede—then just called Memli—wants to go with her, but the adults forbid it. He's too young. He'll just get in her way. So he throws a fit, crying and wailing as his sister walks out. He is completely inconsolable until his grandfather takes him into his lap and shows him his rosary, a pretty string of amber beads that little Memli has had his eye on for a while. "I'll teach you a tongue twister," his grandfather begins in Kurdish.

"*Va û va daweteke xwe kir, çûn bani va u va kirin.* One day this one and this one decided to hold a wedding. They invited this one and this one, too."

At each repetition of the word *va*, "this one," his grandfather pulls a bead.

"*Va û va go ku...* This one and this one said…"

The wails fade to whimpers, and he lets Memli have a go. The rosary is old and beautiful; the beads make a pleasant clicking noise, *tak tak tak*. By the time he reaches the end, Dede has forgotten about the wedding and his sister.

He recounts this memory one night when we're having a barbecue at one of Delal's cousins' house. Out of nowhere, he recites the whole tongue twister, lets out a laugh and slaps his knee. "My grandfather taught me that," he says.

The sister from this story married a man from Dersim. One day in 1938, long after news of the massacres started leaking out, Dede's mother said to him, "We're going to get your sister." So, they walked over the mountains to her new home, straight into the heat of the genocide, and demanded the husband's family release her to them. His sister was five months pregnant at the time.

I don't remember the rest, neither does Delal. Does the sister go with them in the end or stay? How long did it take to walk, and where did they sleep? How did they get home, and what in God's name did they see on the way? I know pieces. I know she survived. I remember a story about a soldier hitting her with a rifle butt after she told him she was pregnant. Or am I mixing it up with someone else? When Dede died last year, the details died with him. And these are not stories that make the history books here but are a past deliberately forgotten. Like Mom, modern Turks just want to remember the nice things, the heroes of Çanakkale, their war of independence, the greatness of their lost empire.

***

If Grandpa Zillman was my first death, Dede was my most recent.

He suddenly took ill one day in the fall, his feet swelling so badly that he couldn't walk. He lived in the apartment building right across from us, and we used to always see him on his balcony, drinking tea and watching the street. We'd wave from our kitchen window. He'd wave back and holler at us to come over. One day, he stopped coming outside. His daughters began to visit every day, spending the night sometimes. They cooked him dinner and brought us the leftovers. They took him to the doctor, cleaned his house, and kept him company. In that last year of his life, he'd often exaggerated illnesses out of loneliness—or so we believed—hoping pity would draw in a few visitors, and so at first, Delal and I did not take any of this too seriously. He'd gotten what he wanted, we figured. Exaggerate a little leg pain and the whole female side of the family was at your command. Then one day, Delal's aunt rang our doorbell and found me alone in the living room, writing. Delal had gone off to a meeting somewhere.

"You need to come quickly. Dede is *not* well at all."

I showed up at the house and discovered him on the couch surrounded by at least a dozen friends and relatives. His youngest daughter, Suzan, was there with her husband, having flown in from Şırnak on the opposite side of the country. I hadn't even heard they were coming, and this finally brought home the seriousness of what was happening.

"We were wrong," I remember thinking. It was almost as if a disembodied voice were speaking in my ear. "This was never a ploy for attention."

Chairs had been pulled from every room in the house to accommodate all the visitors. Whenever you enter a Kurdish Alevi home, you must greet each person there and ask how they and their families are doing, so I started along the far wall, reaching out a hand to Delal's brother first. We kissed lightly on both cheeks, as is the custom.

"How's it going?" I ask. "How's everything at home?"

Then came Cousin Murat, Delal's parents, Aunt Fatma and her son Diyar, Dede's best friend and card game rival, Uncle Duzgun.

"You look younger every day, uncle. How is your daughter? Thank you, my mother is fine."

Family friends, Işıl and Eda. Dede's oldest daughter, Aunt Cemile.

"No, I've already eaten. Thanks."

Then Aunt Suzan and her husband Mehmet. "How's everyone at home? My family is fine. No, I've already eaten, really."

When I finally get to Dede, I kiss his hand. This is a formal custom with older people, a sign of reverence. Normally, I wouldn't do it with him; he's way too familiar to me, but something comes over me tonight. I can see his legs are still swollen, encased in a special kind of sock prescribed by the doctor. Bottles of pills litter the coffee table.

"He's got an embolism," Aunt Cemile explains. "The socks help, but we have to take them off now and then to massage his legs and move his blood."

She reaches toward his feet to begin work, and Dede says, "I want Jeff to do it," and for some reason, this makes my eyes well up. It's only at this moment that I realize how much I've neglected him, how often he called me over for tea when I was walking home from work or passing by on my way to a run, and I had said no.

Dede stretches out his legs. I get on my knees and start rolling the socks down his shins. The skin looks pale and taut, veins sticking out around the ankles. Aunt Cemile explains how I need to do it, and I place my hands gently just below his knee. There's a solemnity to it that I'm not accustomed to in my dealings with Dede. It's almost like I'm about to pray. Normally, there would be chatter and banter, but I am quiet, focused, and he watches intently as my fingers move slowly down his calves to his feet. I have this feeling I rarely have in my life—an absolute absence of doubt. This is exactly what I am supposed to be doing, and I am exactly the person who should be doing it. I'd never done anything like it for my father, nothing to honor him. It's so different from that moment with Grandpa Zillman, too, years before, the old man flailing all alone and abandoned on the back porch.

Dede died two months later, diagnosed with cancer of the gall bladder.

In Turkey, the city provides transportation of the body and any mourners to the funeral, no matter how far it is from Istanbul. Thus, an entire busload of people accompanied Dede's remains to the village of Conag in the province of Bingöl, a fifteen-hour drive in the best of weather. It was January, however, and a blizzard had just slammed the region hard. Roads were caked in ice, and the electricity was out for hundreds of miles. Delal, her aunt, and I took a plane so that we could arrive ahead of everyone else and ready the house for the funeral, as it had been closed up since October. We caught a minibus from the airport, and as we entered the mountains, we saw power lines coated with ice, some of them having snapped and fallen from the weight and lying dead in the frozen brush. It snowed the night of our arrival and kept snowing. Icicles formed long columns from the eaves of the houses to the ground. The power was out, and so in the evening, we lived by candlelight and stoked the wood-burning stoves in every room to stay warm.

The village cemetery is at the top of a small mountain along a ridge. We buried him in the family plot at the edge of a steep slope that plunged down to the valley below. And when I say, "we buried him," I mean it literally. There are no gravediggers in Kurdistan. From the burial site, we could see the twin mountains of Taru and Silbüs that tower on the border with Dersim. After the blizzard, they looked like peaks in Antarctica, white crags jutting from a world of polar snow. Silbüs is an Armenian word, Taru is Kurdish; one mountain for a people already erased from this landscape, another for their vanishing successors. The snow had lifted that morning, and the sky behind both mountains was so pristine, so blue that I felt as I once did learning to dive in the Philippines when I swam over a trench and peered down into a darker blue that seemed absolute, planetary, stretching down into a liquid depth so alien that I shrank back against its vastness.

A snowplow carried the coffin to the gravesite, and we followed on foot, trudging up and up between the high snowbanks. We tried to stay on the tracks cut by the plow, avoiding the smooth patches of ice. Aunt Cemile hung onto my arm. She'd had a hip operation several months before, and each step pained her, but she had refused to ride in the plow. The walk, the physical journey was important somehow. "Bouncing along in that truck would have hurt worse anyway," she'd insisted, but as we kept slipping on frozen mud, I found this hard to believe. The grave had been "opened" days before. It lay in a fenced rectangle of rocky ground along with the graves of Dede's mother, father, and wife. We stood at the edge of the fence as the imam said the final prayers. I looked at the layers of people surrounding us, one row after the other with their heads bowed, weeping. It made me think of Grandpa Zillman's funeral, and I remembered Memaw's hand and her yellow dress, the total absence of tears.

When the prayers were finished, we each took a turn with the shovel. At first, the clumps of wet soil sounded like drumbeats on the coffin lid, but then they softened to the swish of mud on mud. When the grave was filled, we reached into the ground, grabbed a handful of red earth and threw it in by hand. We had to take off our gloves to do it. The touch of that cold dirt, of the land that had birthed and raised Memli Seven and that now took him away, still lingers on my skin. I had buried my father like this, but alone. Here I was surrounded by family. Dede's roots were here. He told us that when he was very small, he'd looked at the mountains ringing the village and assumed that was the whole world. I'm not sure that feeling ever went away.

***

Though fishing on Santa Fe was central to Dad's and my relationship, we rarely caught anything, which suited me just fine. I was notoriously squeamish in those days. When I was very small, we'd hook large bream to fry up for supper, but I loathed cleaning them. Some of my earliest memories are patches of green grass full of bloody fish heads and innards. The sight of them made me retch. I also hated touching the worms and dropped them whenever I jammed the hook into their sides and saw the pinkish guts bubble out of the wound. I recoiled from the slimy bodies of the little shiners we caught for bait, too, and couldn't take them off the hook. Still, Dad was dogged in his efforts to show me how, running his hand over the back of the fish so that the dorsal fin did not cut his palm.

"See, Jeffrey? Like this."

My queasiness around all things fishing baffled and embarrassed me. Why was I physically so opposed to something that felt like a fundamental passion? Like with saying "Dad," body reflexes stood in the way of what I needed to do. I was failing somehow as a boy and a Floridian. I didn't even like to eat fish. All I could picture while sitting over a plate of fried bream was the goopy guts I'd seen scooped out of the stomach earlier in the day.

But fishing provided Dad and me an excuse to hang out on the dock till midnight and talk. I'd spend the whole afternoon, sometimes, composing a list of conversation topics I wanted to run through that night. Dad was the only person to whom I could discuss at length all the interests that made me such an oddball back in Lakeland. The average program might include the Nazca lines, the fugitive slave laws, the square root of negative one, trans light speed, and Communism. He would consider each of my theories, add his own. He, in turn, explained the principles of fission and fusion, gave me math puzzles to solve or else told me bits of history from World War II or the Civil War. Sometimes, he spun stories of his childhood or jokes from long-dead comedians.

"What happened when Poles threw dynamite at Germans?" he asked once.

"I don't know."

"The Germans lit it and threw it back."

"That's prejudiced!" I protested.

He laughed. "That's your mother talking."

But it was me, too. I had started growing sensitive to his family's overt bigotry.

"Anyway, Jeffrey," he continued. "It's a fact. The Poles are a lot like us Southerners, a lot of gallantry but not much sense. They used to have this law called a *liberum veto*, for example. Any bill the parliament tried to pass could be vetoed by one person. The Germans or the Russians would bribe a Pole to use the veto and sabotage the whole country for decades."

He'd read about this in a seven-hundred-page tome by James Michener called *Poland*, which we went to the Keystone library to check out the next day. I must have been eight or nine. I remember the librarian gently suggesting I head to the children's section when I appeared with that brick of a book. Dad stepped right in, "He can handle it."

We would argue often about the Civil War in those chats on the lake. He insisted it wasn't about slavery. I insisted it was. We had this conversation repeatedly, and his stubbornness on the subject nagged, making me suspect that he secretly harbored a lot of the sentiments I heard from his mother and brother. To test him, I'd bring up episodes of shows I'd watched—I was a TV addict— *The Jeffersons, Different Strokes, Good Times*, just to see how he'd react. He never gave much away.

I remember every inch of that dock, the cypress knees and lake grass on the right where I could sometimes see a nesting bass, and on the left, where we swam, the gradual darkening of the water's color and the way sunfish would appear out of the black and float into the gold whenever I approached with bread. The end of the dock widened out and formed a deck with benches on all sides. The railing had orange metal holders for your fishing poles. You set your pole in the braces, tightened the screws, and waited, letting your eyes roam the vastness of the lake. The cypress and pine trees that formed its borders felt like the whole world.

Dad and I had a fishing ritual. In the late afternoon, before dinner, we'd go out to the end of the dock with a white bucket and catch "bait fish" on balls of rolled-up white bread. We caught mostly sunfish or shiners, though baby turtles would sometimes pursue the hook so aggressively that you'd be forgiven for thinking they'd been starved for weeks. The fish small enough to use as bait we threw in the bucket, the larger fish and turtles we tossed back in the lake. My job was to make sure the water in the bucket stayed oxygenated. Nothing but a trash fish would bite dead bait, Dad warned, and so every half hour, I climbed down the ladder and scooped up fresh water from the left side of the dock.

After dinner, we returned to the dock just as the sun was going down, the sky smoldering with the hot oranges of a Florida sunset and the thunderheads like nuclear mushrooms towering over the tree line. My father had led me to believe that the best fishing was done at night. "That was when the monsters came out," he said. I didn't care what we caught as long as it was dramatically big and edible, and in Lake Santa Fe, there were two fish that fit that description, bass and catfish. Each came in a dazzling variety of colors and temperaments, which I loved to hear about as we set up for the evening, replacing the tiny hooks and sinkers of the afternoon with larger ones more appropriate for the heavy fighters we would encounter. There was the great largemouth bass which all the sports fishermen were after. It could grow as long as two feet. This was the fish people shellacked and mounted on their wall as trophies, like Aunt Nancy's twelve-pounder hanging in their wood-paneled living room. More importantly, it was delicious, though Dad warned me that we were unlikely to catch any using the primitive equipment we preferred. Those rod and reel folks knew what they were doing. But we might snag a smallmouth bass, which, though not as big, was more aggressive and just as tasty, and if not the smallmouth, then the white or striped or sunshine or Suwannee bass. And if not a bass, then maybe a catfish, whether channel cat or bullhead, yellow or blue or brown.

"And remember our eel," he would add dramatically, "Santa Fe has caves at the bottom leading to the Atlantic. Who knows what lurks down there in the depths?"

I'd lie down on my stomach at the end of the dock, peer into the dark water, and let my imagination roam the fathoms. I had a thick tome at home called *The Book of Facts* filled with articles about the mysteries of the world like the Bermuda Triangle, Stonehenge, or even right there near Lakeland, Spook Hill, where cars rolled up the slope instead of down when you released the brakes. One article was about the coelacanth, a dinosaur fish biologists thought had vanished eighty million years before, but which had recently been caught in the Indian Ocean. Could one of those fish find its way here? Or maybe another species from an even older time?

"Well, I *have* seen things on this lake," Dad would tease when I mentioned these possibilities. "Things I can't explain."

These fantasies were encouraged by one obliging creature in the weeds. Almost every night, toward the late hours, something would suddenly pull our bobber under so dramatically, it made us both jump. Dad would take the pole out of its holder, and the bamboo would arc perilously down toward the water. I'd eye the straining cane with my heart in my throat. Would it snap? I'd grab the net we kept for just such an emergency and crouch down at the edge of the dock, ready to scoop up whatever came out. Dad would pull and yield, pull and yield, walking wherever the thing on the other end of the line dragged him. Sometimes it would break the surface, we'd hear the loud splash of a beast unimaginably big, and then it would descend again, back toward the caves, I'd think, toward the bottom of the ocean. This fight would go on for hours, it seemed. I'd beg Dad to let me try, and he'd say with gritted teeth that I was too little, it would jerk me right in, an idea which both thrilled and terrified. Inevitably the line broke, or the pole, or the thing escaped with the bait and sometimes the hook.

Night after night, year after year, we *almost* caught this leviathan. As I got older, I realized it probably wasn't a coelacanth, but just an impossibly large bass or bullhead cat, something that would make a fantastic trophy or meal if only we could drag it in. We tried bigger hooks, stronger lines, different bait. I quizzed Dad on what it might be.

"They are rare," he said, "But I know there are sturgeon in these waters. One of your memaw's neighbors caught one nearly four feet long."

Then one night, we did something right. It had gotten late; nothing was biting. Dad suggested we leave our lines in the water overnight. Maybe we'd come out in the morning and find something on the other end, something that emerged only in the hours no human stayed awake for. I thought of the shadows on the wall of the bedroom, the creatures boosting themselves into the window.

"Let's do it," I said.

The next morning before breakfast, before a shower, before anything, I jumped out of bed and ran out to the dock with Dad loping sleepily behind. The pole had been pulled right toward the weeds, the metal holder half-yanked from its post. At the end of the line was the giant that had eluded us all those years, a longnose gar over four feet in length. It floated heavy on the surface, exhausted from fighting against the hook all night. It didn't look like a thing used to being exposed to daylight. It was silver against the brown water with a thick armor of scales and a long snout full of saw-blade teeth. It had two solid black stones for eyes and was enveloped in a cloud of pink where blood ran from the wound in its mouth. It looked dead, but when Dad tried to pull it out of the water, it fought so hard that he had to go get the .22 and shoot it before we could drag it on shore. Dark blood bubbled from the bullet wound.

"Can you eat it?" I asked.

"Gar are trash fish. They feed on dead things. Plus, they're impossible to clean."

"It's huge."

"It should be. They are left over from the dinosaur days. If there's ever a nuclear war, every living thing will be wiped off the face of the planet except them and the roaches."

He wanted a picture of me with my prize, and so he went to the tool shed and returned with an angry-looking hook on the end of a long wooden pole. With the hook, he snagged the dead gar by the gills and had me hold it up while he snapped a Polaroid with an instant camera borrowed from Memaw. She stood on the porch steps, hands on her hips.

"Is that what all the fuss was about?" she asked. "Why, it's just an old gar." It sounded playful enough, but I could hear the note of derision in it, some subtle dig at my father.

"It's the biggest fish Jeffrey's ever caught," he snapped, which made her chuckle and shake her head.

***

I still have that picture. It's a perfect frame of a Florida childhood. I'm barefoot and brown-legged, wearing a blue T-shirt with an R2D2 print on the front. My hair is bleached copperish from the sun. The lake is behind me, blue water surrounded by a wall of green cypresses. I'm struggling to hold my fish up—it's longer than I am—but I'm grinning ecstatically. The gar looks like a mutant cross between a gator and a shark, its gray body dripping with blood.

And here at last is the second story, the bookend to the one about the car lot in Starke.

There was an empty lot next to Memaw's house where we had a horseshoe court. On the far edge was a patch of woods bordered by a barbed wire fence. We buried the gar there in a hole of white Florida sand.

"You're absolutely sure you can't eat it?" I asked as Dad dug. It didn't make sense. We'd finally caught the white whale, and there was nothing useful to do with it.

"The only people that eat gar," he said. "Are blacks."

"Maybe they taste good," I said in defense. "If other people eat them, then so can we."

"Back in Omega we'd catch gar sometimes," he said. "We'd take them into N——town and sell them. A quarter a piece or two for a dollar." He laughed. "They always bought two. The n—— boys would say, 'Ooowee, that there's a bargain!'"

The n-word was like a slap. The whole world leapt into the background—the lake, the birdsong, the swish of the shovel—and my father and I stood alone in an emptiness with the dead fish floating between us.

"That's a bad word," I said stupidly.

"What is?"

It was just as hard to get out as "Dad." "N——," I answered.

"It's just how people talked back then," he said.

"Mom says you shouldn't talk about people that way."

"Well," he said, "your momma's from West Virginia and doesn't know what it was like in Georgia."

He never said it again, whether out of deference to my views or because he had no real commitment to that old Georgia bigotry, but it's something that nags me every time I go shaking his bones. The n-word was part of everyday speech for my aunt, uncle, and grandmother. Could he possibly be unaffected by the racism that drove them to say it?

***

A week after starting this chapter, we have a big family breakfast at our house, and I casually ask Delal's oldest cousin Murat if he remembers Dede's story of going to retrieve his sister from Dersim. He's been sitting quietly at the end of the table, watching all the other conversations going on around him, and I assume he'll either say no or relate a few of the vague details I have already written here. Instead, his face lights up, and I find his eyes focused intensely on me.

"Of course I remember," he says. "Dede's sister had married a man from the village of Taru on the other side of the mountain. You know, the one next to Mt. Silbüs?"

"I've been there," I tell him. "We went once a couple years ago. The whole place is in ruins, but some relatives of yours are rebuilding."

"Those are probably Dede's sister's people. You know, right, that Dersim Alevis were organized into clans made up of dozens of large families, each

101

headed by an elder and centered on a specific territory? Well, Dede's sister had married into the Kureyşan clan, and at the time, the army had organized the executions by geography. They were moving east, working their way forward clan by clan."

His fingers moved across the tabletop to illustrate the motion.

"They were killing the clan on the land next to the Kureyşan when my great-grandmother, Dede's mom, realized her daughter's in-laws were next on the list, so she decided to rescue her. She took Dede, he was like nine at the time, and they hiked over the mountains to the elder's house. 'I want my daughter,' she said. 'Let her come home so that she can survive.' And the elder said, 'I am responsible for whole families, dozens of men, women, and children. Is your daughter worth more than all of them? She joined her life with ours. We'll suffer our fate together.' Have you heard of Kutu Creek? They have restaurants there now."

"We stopped there once for breakfast on a road trip through Dersim."

"That's where they did it. The soldiers lined people up and raked them with gunfire. Row after row, the bodies fell in the river. Once they finished there, they were heading into the area around Taru. They'd even started rounding people up. Anyway, a little girl managed to break away from the crowd and escape into the woods. The soldiers had orders not to leave any witnesses, so they stopped everything to hunt down that kid, but she eluded them all night. The next day, the government declared an amnesty, and the killings stopped. Dede's sister and her people were saved by one lousy day, just because that girl was so good at hiding! Imagine what would have happened if she hadn't run! Those people you met in Taru wouldn't exist."

We stare at each other for a minute, silent in the gravity of the thing we're discussing.

"I've heard this story at least five times," I say, "yet I keep losing the details. It's not like it's the kind of thing that's easy to forget. I swear, I must have the worst memory in the world."

"It's not your memory," he says. "It's different when you grow up in the place where it happened, when you're surrounded by those stories, when everyone around you tells them and lives them a hundred times over. It becomes part of what you are."

I think about what this means for me and my exploration of my father's story, of my grandmother's connection to John Henry's death, and of our family's connection to the history of the black men and women they lived among for centuries. What happens when your collective stories are from the point of view of the killer and not the victim, when it's not memory you must suffer, but forgetting you must defend? Turkey long denied the Dersim massacres just as it still denies the Armenian Genocide. How different is that from our family's restructuring of history? The whole idea that there was never a Civil War but a War Between the States, that it was never about slavery, that the lynching and repression that followed for a hundred years was either exaggerated or deserved, that no trace of that bloody history remains today to haunt us? I see it on social media all the time. I hear it from members of my family, from friends back home. "Why can't black people just get over it already?" It's the same line people use for Kurds in Turkey. "What do they want? Those days are long over, and everyone involved is dead." But if I have to write a book because of one personal trauma in my life, my father's suicide and his fucked up family, if that has so affected my psychology that I struggle daily with its impact, then how do four centuries of constant torture, trauma, and atrocity affect a whole race of millions? Is it ever over?

EIGHT

One day Delal's dad and I are chatting about historiography and civil disobedience around the breakfast table. These sorts of topics count as small talk with my political father-in-law, infamous for starting even sentences about something as mundane as toothpaste with phrases like, "Four millennia ago, when civilization first arose in Mesopotamia..." His name is Kemal, but I, and everyone else, call him *Mamoste*, which means "teacher" in Kurdish, though the word is used more like the Japanese *sensei*, a term to honor an older, revered leader in the community. I've never quite gotten used to the formality of it.

Mamoste knows his family's history, such as his father's tales of the massacres in Dersim, and he knows the broader stories behind it, both official and not. Whole walls of his house are filled with books on sociology, linguistics, and psychology, some specifically Kurdish, some focused on the Middle East and the wider world. He has always been actively involved in politics. People from the village and in Istanbul regularly go to him for advice, and he's served in the various Kurdish political parties all his life. As a result, he's been harassed by the Turkish government since he began working as a schoolteacher in the 70s, hounded ceaselessly for his political activity. In fact, a few months after Delal's and my wedding, he was arrested, swept away in a massive round-up of Kurdish politicians throughout the country.

For three years, he languished in prison, went on hunger strikes, was excoriated daily in the official press. Delal and I went to many of the sham trials and watched as he, his fellow prisoners, and his lawyers attempted to argue rationally against the bizarre case cooked up against them. Our wedding guest-list was presented one day as evidence, of what it was never said. They didn't have to. The presence of foreign names meant only one thing to the paranoid kangaroo court, collusion with secret agents.

They tried all the defendants in one large hearing, nearly a hundred fighters in a solemn non-violent struggle. Men and women, young and old, stood shoulder to shoulder to form an unyielding wall of solidarity against the fury of the Turkish state. Mamoste insisted on giving his testimony "in his mother language." That was the phrase repeated throughout the trials; no one said "Kurdish." This was a group decision, a calculated move. The court objected on the grounds that everyone spoke Turkish perfectly well, and so each "suspect" would take the stand one by one and tell the scowling judge, in Kurdish, that they waived their right to defend themselves until their constitutional right to do it in their mother tongue was honored. I didn't understand at first, thinking very practically, very selfishly, that all I wanted was for our family to be free of this nightmare and my wife reunited with her father. *Just defend yourself!* I thought. But it was about the grander cause, the future generations, a fight for rights I never knew I took for granted.

So, we're at breakfast shortly after he is released, the air celebratory with political victory, and he's asking me about America and the South. He's talking about the history of the Kurds, of the persecutions and of Dede's memories of the Dersim massacres and of the many purges that followed, decade after decade. He speaks of the imperative on every human being to struggle for the greater good. Being part of the fight is as natural as breathing.

"I'm interested in your Civil Rights Movement," he says. "In the end, they were very successful. The whole fight seems so similar to ours."

"For sure," I say. "The main parts were all over before I was born, but of course, I think it's still continuing in many ways."

"Do your parents ever talk about it?"

"Not really," I answer, and then am struck by the oddity of that. They both lived at the high point of the movement. Surely, it affected them.

"What about your dad?" Mamoste persisted. "What was he doing during all the protests?"

"I don't know," I say and shrug. There's nothing to tell my freedom fighter father-in-law, for nothing comes to mind, and this time it's not because I don't remember. Dad, the history enthusiast, never spoke about the two most dramatic decades in the history of the South, not even in passing. I have no idea what it meant to him, though perhaps his silence speaks volumes. And so, Mamoste's question nags. What was the man who taught me to care about history doing during the historical event that transformed his world beyond recognition?

***

When *Brown V. the Board of Education* went to the Supreme Court in 1954, my father had just turned seventeen. Rummaging around in the Tifton

Public Library's historical records room turns up a picture of him in an old high school yearbook from that year. He's a startlingly handsome boy—young, lean, with black hair and the kind of sun-bronzed complexion that Aunt Nancy refers to as "that beautiful olive skin" whenever she dreamily recounts the way the Gibbs boys appeared to her as a girl.

In the photo, his head is tilted to the right while his eyes are cocked up to the left of the frame and slightly narrowed as if to say, "You can't be serious." His lips are bowed in a mocking grin, like some tedious adult has yanked him away from his friends and demanded he account for his behavior. Or is it the grin of an introvert goaded into a smile by the cheesy jokes of the photographer? Or is it something else altogether? Everything I write now is as much preoccupied with Clark's question as it is with Mamoste's. *Why did your daddy kill himself?*

I stare at his adolescent face, a possibly trivial millisecond snipped from one day long ago and embalmed in an image whose permanence gives it the illusion of significance, and I look for a revelation, a clue, an augury perhaps, of his future doom. My interpretations shift. *What are you feeling? What is life like for you at home in Omega?* This is probably the year Uncle Gene left the house, and Dad was alone with his mother for the first time. Or was his father around, too? My mysterious grandfather, Lenward. In older yearbooks, I find a picture of Dad from the year before. It shows a sullen boy, scowling into the camera, the eyes a bit more defiant. What does it mean?

I have few fragments of this time in Dad's life. Lisa has introduced me, online, to another cousin, Lana, who is the daughter of Memaw's war hero brother, Russell. Lana recalls meeting my father and his family one day when they were both on the cusp of adolescence. She sends me a message through Facebook in response to a barrage of questions I've asked her.

"I met your dad for the first time on the front porch of Linnie and Claude Hamner's store," she writes. "We lived down the street and walked over at the news Aunt Nell was visiting. The Hamners had a bunch of rocking chairs, and that's where everyone sat whenever they had visitors. I remember marveling at how beautiful your memaw was! So well put together and elegantly dressed. Bob was a bit on the shy side but not Gene. He was very talkative. I could tell your memaw loved her boys very much because she was always hugging them and kissing them. Bob was closer to my age, around ten or so, and I remember thinking he was so cute! He was quiet and not rambunctious like other boys. Some of the girls would come to the store and Grandma Hamner, ever the matchmaker, would introduce them to Bob, and they would immediately develop a huge crush on him, though he never did pay any attention to them. Silly little girls! He and the family came again and again after that for several years. Later, I even remember going to Omega to visit with your memaw a couple of times. That's when I saw your Granddad Gibbs. I think he had a little problem with alcohol. He was not very sociable. I also remember your memaw had some ruby red tea glasses that just mesmerized me. They were so pretty, I bought some just like them when I grew up."

Those few sentences toward the end stick out with their abrupt shift in tone, from reverence to something akin to distaste or dread. *I think he had a little problem with alcohol.* This is the only mention of Pepaw in a dozen mails full of vivid details about every other member of the family. I get the feeling there's more she could say but is refraining from doing so out of politeness, framing his appearance, as she does, between ruby-red tea glasses and silly girls with crushes. What's not said takes on a gravity that tugs at the image in the yearbook.

She winds up her account. "And I remember the grown-ups, Aunt Evelyn and Dorothy, going on and on about how smart Bob was. They just couldn't get over it."

But on his report cards at the time, all meticulously preserved by Memaw, Dad's grades are mediocre. His teachers write comments like "appears not to try," "inattentive," "capable of doing much better." I know these boys from my own classes. I picture Bob sitting in the back row day in and day out and me talking to the other teachers about what's wrong with him, meeting with counselors and calling in the parents. *What's going on at home?* On the back of one report, Memaw writes an apology, "I work at night and can't teach Bob as I should."

I refocus, come back to Mamoste's question. In the end, I don't know what this intelligent seventeen-year-old in the yearbook, the handsome boy with the troubled father, this doomed boy so popular with the girls thinks of the iconic Supreme Court case and the end of Segregation. He probably doesn't have to think of it at all as every other face in that yearbook is white. The first black student would not set foot in those halls for another eleven years, in 1965, when three other seventeen-year-olds approached the entrance of my father's beloved alma mater to find a wall of white students blocking their path.

I find their story in the February 24th, 2019 *Tifton Gazette*.

In August 1965, Nita Ruth Ingram, Sammy Lee Russell, and Janet Roberts registered themselves at the all-white Tifton High School in an act of bravery and ambition. Tifton High was accredited, the traditionally "colored" school, Wilson, was not, and the three friends had their eyes on college. They had been inspired by the Civil Rights Movement transforming the South and wanted to be part of the revolution. The initial wall of angry white students that greeted them was dispersed by the vice principal, but inside, they continued to face abuse and harassment. Between classes all three would be spat on, called "n——," tripped, or punched by unknown faces in the crowd. On the way home one day, boys driving by in a car whipped Sammy Lee Russell in the back with a belt buckle. The three also remember the occasional flashes of decency. Janet Roberts recalls the girl who greeted and smiled at her every day, and though they never did stop and talk, her simple hello was sustaining. Opposition died down as their presence became normalized, but the three black students remained a fluke, an exception. Full integration didn't come to Tifton High until the 70s, well after I was born.

I put aside the yearbook on a table in the middle of the room, Dad's picture face up, and keep digging. The library's genealogy room is a treasure trove. I discover a 1973 article in the *New York Times* by a black historian from Tifton named J.K. Obatala, who grew up around the same period as my father. Many of his memories crisscross Dad's. Dad used to tell me of Saturdays spent at the Tifton movie theater. He'd go there with Clark sometimes to watch Westerns and eat popcorn in the cinematic dark and in fact, had plucked my middle name "Wade" from one of his favorite cowboy characters. Obatala remembers the same Saturdays, "where we used to watch Johnny Mack Brown and the Ringo Kidd from the balcony because blacks weren't allowed to sit downstairs."

Dad told me about the drug store and soda fountain on the corner of Main Street and 3rd, where he'd go for an ice cream float and check out the girls. Obatala remembers the same place. "It was air-conditioned," he writes, "with stools and booths where whites sat in what appeared to be the greatest comfort while blacks had to stand at the end of the counter, buy what they wanted, and then leave."

Tifton's bus station was segregated, too. As were the hotels. Even the Tifton directory. While researching at the library, I thumb through a 1950s edition of the Tift County phone book. I'm looking for the names of family in an effort to figure out where everyone lived. I need to triangulate locations, confirm addresses. It takes me a few minutes to understand why there are two sets of Gibbses, one in the front and one in the back but both under the header "Tifton." And then I notice the word "Colored" over the second set.

What did my father think of all this? Perhaps he thought what other whites did, that old cliche. It was just the way things were. But what about when it started to change?

***

Dad graduated high school in 1956, the year the Montgomery bus boycott ended with the successful integration of public transportation. It was the same year the first black woman, Autherine Lucy, attended the University of Alabama, and Dad decided to give higher education a shot as well. He took courses in things such as animal husbandry and fertilizers at the segregated Abraham Baldwin Agricultural College in Tifton but harbored absolutely zero aspirations toward farming.

"Then why did you go there?" I asked.

"Wasn't much else to do," was his understated response.

Autherine Lucy was forced out of college by death threats and school riots. Dad dropped out from boredom and to follow his parents in their move to the big city of Jacksonville, Florida. There, sometime in 1957, as a young man of twenty-one, he joined the Army Reserves with Clark and started classes at the Chemical Corp School, the branch that would soon develop Agent Orange for use in Vietnam. He graduated his first year with honors, and Memaw clipped an article from the *Jacksonville Times Union* commemorating the event.

"Private Robert Gibbs, son of Mr. and Mrs. Robert Gibbs, 3526 Silver Street, Jacksonville, recently graduated with second highest honors from the First Chemical Entry Class. He was commended by his instructors and advisers upon completion of the course."

I turn this clipping over and over in my fingers. It's a few short paragraphs but professionally laminated, carefully preserved. It's hard to imagine Memaw taking such pride in my father that she would enshrine this modest little blurb.

Dad dropped out of the chemical corps as well, no more a military man than he was a farmer. Memaw persuaded Uncle Gene to secure him a job at an insurance company downtown called Independent Life, where Gene also worked. It was conveniently only three blocks from the Sears Department store where she manned the cosmetics counter, thus enabling her to keep an eye on both her boys. In a single stroke, at his mother's insistence, the man who would later take such care spinning lectures about the intricacies of nuclear fission and subatomic structure, algebraic equations and Antebellum economics to me on Lake Santa Fe embarked on a career as a collection agent tracking down past-due payments from backwoods Floridians.

He had a favorite story from this part of his life.

"My beat was the sticks," he told me. "I'd spend the whole day cruising down one dirt road after another, pulling up to various trailers and shacks to ask for money. I was the bad guy and met with welcomes that were less than warm. I felt like a jackass. Most of those people didn't have a pot to piss in, and there I was in my white shirt and tie driving in from the big city to demand money for a company that had conned them into buying life insurance they didn't need.

"One day, I turned off the highway onto a long sandy road. This must have been somewhere around Orange Park. The road seemed to wind around and around the woods forever before I finally got where I was going, a little mildewed trailer set off in a weedy clearing. I knocked on the door, and when it opened, I found myself staring down the barrel of a rifle. 'I got ya,' the proprietor of the humble estate said. 'You bastard. I'll teach you to screw around with my wife.' I never did get a good look at the guy. He kept jabbing the barrel into the small of my back, cattle-prodding me all the way out to their shed where he locked me up with the tools and the lawnmower. I spent the whole damn afternoon stewing in there, sweating like a pig and trying to figure a way out, only I didn't know if escape would be the wisest move because for all I knew, he might be parked outside with the gun trained on the door.

"So, I waited, expecting to meet my maker at any minute. About six o'clock, I hear a car pull in the yard. A car door shuts, and my captor starts shrieking at a woman who proceeds to shriek right back to him. 'I got your boyfriend,' he's shouting, and she's calling him every name in the book. 'If you've hurt Ray,' she threatens, 'I'll cut your damn pecker off.' Their voices are getting closer, and suddenly the door flies open. He's still got his gun up, only there's this frizzy-haired woman in front of him now, standing between me and the muzzle. She's gotta be about twice my age with a couple of teeth missing, and I wonder how the hell anyone thought I'd carry on an affair with her. She gives me the onceover and says, 'Not half bad, but it ain't him!' The man lowers the rifle as she marches up to the trailer. 'Come on out,' he says sheepishly and then offers me a cigarette. 'Thanks, but I think I'll just be moseying on home,' I tell him, but he's set on commiserating. 'She keeps bragging she's got a rich younger fella she's going to run off with,' he explains. 'I was just sure as all hell it was you in your tie and all. Why you out here anyways?' I start to mention the insurance bill, but about that time, his missus opens the door and bellows, 'If you want supper, get in here already!' He mumbles a hang-dog apology in my direction, then trudges up to his front door. I feel bad for him, but then, that's a typical day working for your Uncle Gene at old Independent Life. I never did manage to collect much from anybody."

He soon quit his brother's firm and moved to another just like it, Gulf Life, a few blocks away in downtown Jacksonville. And I wonder, was this one of the turns in life that set him down the path to the tracks that morning? He never spoke of his various sales jobs without a bitter disdain creeping into his voice. He was a man with a hungry and curious mind built for academics. He had the kind of intelligence everyone noticed and seemed on track to great things. "We were sure," Cousin Clark told me, "Bob would become something important." But instead of finding a way to harness his intellect, of making a break and moving, say, to Athens for the University of Georgia just a few hours away, he chose to stay bound to his troubled nuclear family and maintain his existence with a career in sales, a field and way of life, which, like farming and the military, had absolutely zero appeal to his sensibilities and for which he would be forever ill-suited.

***

In 1960, Gulf Life was housed in an Art Deco building in downtown Jacksonville on Hogan Street. For lunch and coffee breaks, the salesmen and secretaries popped into one of the lunch counters at the nearby department stores or five-and-dimes. There was Sears, where Memaw worked, four blocks west on Broad Street; Kress two blocks south and west on the corner of Main and Adams; and Woolworth's three blocks due south on Hogan, right next to Hemming Park. My guess is that Dad preferred either Sears, where his mother might pick up the check, or the Kress, if only because this was his favorite restaurant in Lakeland. When I was very young, he'd take me there for barbecued chicken and Spanish rice and say it brought back memories.

The Kress lunch counter served some of the best donuts and coffee in the city. It was also whites only. In 1960, the year Dad started working at Gulf Life, the local NAACP led by Rutledge Pearson targeted Kress and the other department stores for an anti-segregation protest. Inspired by the success of their counterparts in Greensboro, North Carolina, black students made small purchases at each store then sat at the whites-only counters and attempted to order food. Predictably, all hell broke loose.

Demonstrations went on for weeks. Many of the lunch counters closed. Reactions in the white community were mixed. A few were sympathetic and boycotted the stores while Navy wives from the base even saved seats for black demonstrators. A white student from Florida State University named Richard Parker, a Yankee from Indiana, joined the sit-in, and when local boys tried to drag him away, a cordon of protesters formed a human shield around him, then escorted him to safety in the "colored" section. The local newspaper, for its part, portrayed this protective wall as a black mob threatening a white youth, and the city police arrested Parker for vagrancy, giving him a stiff jail sentence, communal revenge for his race betrayal.

I mention these things not to focus on the "good white folk," but to list the options people like my father might have had when confronted with these events. Most whites were pro-segregation. Memaw's employers, Sears and Roebuck, in a rather ominous turn, found themselves swarmed with customers buying baseball bats and pretty much anything else that could be used as a weapon. One clerk recalled selling fifty ax handles in just fifteen minutes. I've seen enough demonstrations in Turkey to know that that kind of thing is not a spontaneous shopping spree but part of a carefully laid out plan. Did Memaw watch these armed white men that day as they filed past her cosmetics counter? Did she know what they were going to do?

Sure enough, on Saturday, August 27th, a group of Klansmen and White Citizens Council members from south Georgia and north Florida—Wiregrass country—marched through the downtown streets brandishing those same Sears' ax handles, baseball bats, and golf clubs. Several in Confederate uniforms handed out these weapons to passersby near Hemming Park. They ranted about defending their heritage and protecting their freedoms while warning store owners not to give into black students' demands. Reports say police did nothing to deter the heavily-armed marchers. A group of students was demonstrating at a lunch counter in Grant's Department store four blocks south of Dad's office at Gulf Life. Instead of serving them, the manager closed the store and chased the students outside, at which point, according to witnesses, between 150 and 200 armed white men charged them. Merchants nearby locked their doors to prevent the panicked students from seeking refuge and then watched from the display windows as the attackers brutally beat down every black body they saw.

In an article in *The Florida Historical Quarterly*, Abel Bartley describes what happened next: "At noon, a few African Americans gathered downtown for a scheduled demonstration. The group grew to about three thousand peaceful protesters, joined by a few black gang members for protection. The demonstrators stood in the same location where the Klan had stood just a few hours earlier. The Klansmen taunted, then attacked them. Jacksonville police officers were conspicuously absent. White people walking by watched with obvious satisfaction as Klansmen pummeled unarmed people. A Catholic priest asserted that if Christ walked the streets of Jacksonville, he'd be horrified."

Calvin Lang, who was walking home after visiting his mother at her job in a downtown store, vividly remembered seeing whites chase a young man down the street and hit him in the back of the head with a baseball bat. At least fifty people suffered severe head injuries. Police arrested sixty-two people on charges of disorderly conduct. Forty-eight of them were black.

I have no idea what Dad was doing during this madness. Was he at the office or out on a call or locked in a shed somewhere? Or was he one of the white people strolling by and "looking on with satisfaction?" I can't imagine him being that cold, and yet, how could a man who spun stories out of the most trivial of life events not ever have spoken about something so momentous, so earth-shaking? It all took place just a few blocks from where he worked, and the wannabe Confederates with their ax handles must have marched right past the entrance to Gulf Life. His mother worked in the store where they'd been sold. Being a Saturday, perhaps Dad wasn't even at work that day, but he must have seen the dozens of demonstrations in the streets around him during the weeks before that explosion. He might even have been having a doughnut and coffee at the Kress lunch counter when the students staged their sit-in. Was he one of the sympathetic whites or one of the ones who felt demonstrators got what they deserved?

The Florida State Census turns up a name of a woman living in Jacksonville at the time that is eerily familiar, Queen Stubbs. This was the name of one of the black children living near Memaw when she was a girl, granddaughter of one of her father's sharecroppers and one of the kids she may have been playing with the day her mother beat her with the razor strop, one of the people that may have hidden in Miss Linnie's cane field the night the white mobs burned down black homes and churches. Of course, I have no way of knowing if this is the same person. The official information is meager, tantalizing. Both Queens were born in Georgia in 1918. How many women with that name could there be with the same data? Perhaps the little girl in Autreyville had fled with her family to Florida after the lynch mob rampaged through the black community. Lynching often served as a kind of forced population transfer, an ethnic cleansing.

The Queen Stubbs of Jacksonville lived on Evergreen Avenue in Eastside, where a mural to Ax Handle Saturday adorns the wall of the Eastside Brotherhood Club a few blocks from her white clapboard house, now a ruin, all boarded up and falling apart among a yard full of palmettos and pink azaleas. In the center of the mural is the image from an iconic photo taken that Saturday of Charlie Griffin, a young man wearing a look of disbelief and a shirt splattered with blood. It's all guesswork, all imagination, but I wonder if some relative of Queen Stubbs or perhaps Queen herself was there that day to face the mob and their bludgeons in Hemming Park, a mob like the one from which she'd hidden in the Hamner field in Autreyville? Or if perhaps she and Nell came eye to eye again after forty years at the Sears lunch counter? Or if maybe she'd had a son, and he'd tried to sit next to Nell's son at the Kress?

It seems unfair to my father to speculate like this. Yet he was there in the city, newly arrived from rural Georgia when all this violence raged in the streets. If I knew him at all, I would guess he probably felt some sympathy toward the young students and their cause yet mired in a lifetime of Wiregrass culture with its centuries-old views on race, disapproved of their civil disobedience and anything he considered radical, or at least preferred to watch it from a distance. He may have simply avoided meals on days a sit-in was taking place or shook his head disapprovingly at the photo of the bloodied Griffin in the newspaper but never once thought about taking action to help either side.

I don't know. What I do know is that the year of the lunch counter protest was also the year he married his first wife, a union I am almost certain helped launch him down that calamitous path toward suicide and most likely, the honest answer to Delal's father's question about what my father was doing during the Civil Rights Movement would simply be that he was trying to negotiate the new personal hell he had fallen into.

***

One of my cousin Karin's strongest memories of my father connects to food. She would be in her room at the back of the trailer that sat on the side of my uncle's house, doing her homework or talking on the phone when she'd hear footfalls in the dry leaves outside her window. The rhythmic crunching would end in a soft knock on the glass, and my father's sardonic basso voice would say, "Hey Bird-legs, we've got steak and spaghetti for *soooopper* tonight if you wanna dine down the road with me and the Madame."

Karin adored steak and spaghetti, pronounced, of course, as if one word. It was my father's signature dish, his claim to fame, and even now, nearly twenty-five years after his death, my cousins and aunt pester me to make it for them whenever I'm in town. The recipe appears in no tome of Southern cuisine, no magazine or Baptist church cookbook. Basically, on one side of your plate is a mound of pasta coated in a peppery tomato sauce, a rich red ragu that slow cooks all day. On the other side is a tender piece of seared round steak smothered in mushroom gravy. Most of us liked to drizzle the gravy over the noodles, too, then sprinkle the whole thing with Parmesan cheese. Only Memaw, of course, tried to break the spell of amity this magical meal created, when disparate members of the family who normally couldn't stand the sound of one another's names might suddenly find themselves gathered around the dining table salivating over the same pot. She'd look at each of us one by one, then deliver her infamous chuckle and say, "What a shame to do that to perfectly good meat."

I worked with Dad on days he prepared steak and spaghetti, serving as a kind of sous chef and learning the various steps and secrets as we went. Fry the salt pork until you get an even layer of grease at the bottom of your pot, then add in the garlic until the scent fills the kitchen. Stir-fry the tomato paste a bit in the oil to bring out the flavor and add your heat toward the end, just one pepper would do, a Bahamian chili we'd pluck from the garden in the backyard.

"Where did you come up with this recipe?" I asked him once. "No one else has ever heard of it."

"Like most of the dishes I make, I learned it from Miss Bertha when I lived in Jacksonville. Perhaps the greatest cook I ever knew."

"And who was Bertha? Your girlfriend?"

"My mother-in-law. The mother of my first wife, Janine."

Janine. Dad had mentioned her once or twice, most extensively and candidly on a father-son trip to Jacksonville Beach around the time I was crossing over into puberty. He had finagled Memaw's car away from her somehow, and we were driving slowly along the sand while to my great embarrassment, he began scoping out the women sunbathing on the sand. I remember the water was a dark cobalt blue, very different from the bright green of the Gulf beaches I was used to.

"How about that one, Jeffrey?" he said, and pointed with his chin to a woman in a white bikini. I caught a glimpse of a brown leg, knee up with a book propped on the bare thigh. She glanced up as we passed, squinted in the sunlight.

"Dad! Jesus Christ."

"Don't be embarrassed, son. It's natural. I bet you're thinking a lot about girls now."

I refused to comment. There was one in my church youth group I had fallen hard for on a trip to the now defunct amusement park, Circus World, but I wasn't ready to go public.

"Check out that one there in the red," he went on. "She's not got much going up top, but I've always preferred what's down below anyway."

Please stop, I thought. Didn't he know that the last thing a teen boy wanted to hear from his parents was their sexual fetishes?

"That's how my first wife was," he continued. "Kind of deficient in the titty department but with a very shapely derriere." He paused, laughed a bit. "Am I embarrassing you?"

"No," I lied. Did he actually say "titty?"

"Well, since we're on the subject, let me give you some advice. Never marry for looks."

"You gotta feel a physical attraction," I argued, thinking of my Circus World sweetheart.

"Listen to me, son. Don't choose a girlfriend that identifies too intensely with being pretty. You'll regret it for the rest of your life. That's why I got married the first time. Oh, I was young and stupid, and she was a good-looking little thing. She knew it, too, because her dear daddy told her every chance he got, so she naturally expected me to do the same, to constantly fawn on her and shower her with gifts and gush praise over every flick of her pinky. When I didn't, well…" He reached down and pushed the car lighter in with a click, then put a cigarette in his mouth. "She found someone who did."

"Tell me about her."

Dad married Janine in March 1960, just after his twenty-third birthday and a few months before the NAACP launched its campaign against the city's lunch counters. His new wife was not yet nineteen and had just graduated high school where she was the star of her senior class, prom queen, homecoming queen, a fun and carefree party girl pursued by every young man in the city and caught by none until she started working at the Sears cosmetics counter and met my grandmother. Memaw thought Janine the perfect match for her son—she told me this herself when I was a teenager. Janine's was an old Florida family, she explained. She had both breeding and money.

"Basically," Dad said, "your memaw engineered that whole fiasco."

They had a daughter a year after the wedding, Jennie, my half-sister whom I had never met or spoken to because Dad had lost contact with her after the divorce. He kept a school picture of her in his room, propped up in the corner of a frame holding a much larger photograph of me. She must have been around ten in the photo, a dark-haired waif with big brown eyes and the kind of gritted teeth smile parents forced you to perform in formal pictures. I would stare at her visage and marvel that she remained so uncompromisingly a stranger, that we looked nothing alike, this supposed blood relative of mine. The whole display had the air of a shrine, a memorial to the dead; it was like one of the pictures hung up in laundromats of missing children. And why this absolute sundering of ties? Dad, a man who fought to have me visit every single vacation and weekend that was available, maintained no contact with his first child, no phone calls or letters or Christmas cards, nothing. I'm not sure he even knew where she was. *There was something extremely fishy about this*, I thought, *something he was holding back*. On this trip to Jacksonville Beach, since he was spilling everything else, I decided to ask.

"What happened with Jennie? Why don't you ever talk to her?"

"She wrote me a while back," he said. "Around her sixteenth birthday, I think. Her mother had remarried, and the new guy wanted to adopt Jennie and become her legal father. She asked me to sign some papers to make it final."

"Who? Her mother?"

"No. Jennie herself."

I was shocked. "And you signed them?"

"If my own daughter had no objections, then why should I?"

"But how could you possibly know how she felt? How could you just let her go?"

"She wanted me to."

And with that, he clammed up for a long while, for years.

***

It's Aunt Nancy, of course, who's willing to tell stories about Janine. I start asking as soon as we get back from Jacksonville Beach.

"Oh, she was a real piece of work," Nancy says. "Daddy's little princess and spoiled rotten. She had her eye on Gene for a while. Yeah! They came over once, we were in the living room, and suddenly she disappears with a shopping bag and pops back in a few minutes later wearing a white bikini, turning around and around like she was on the runway and sticking her bony ass in Gene's face. 'What y'all think?' she says and puts her hand on her hip, fluttering those doe eyes of hers. Well, I thought she looked like she was auditioning for a porno, and

Gene said, 'Well, that's real nice, Janine, but don't you know these white swimsuits are see-through when they get wet?' And what does she do but trot her fanny into the bathroom, hop in the shower, then skip back to where we are, her big old brown eyes wide with surprise looking down at her nipples poking out of that white suit. 'Why, you're right!' she squeals. 'You can see it *all!* And your daddy sitting right there! Yeah! That's how she was. I wanted to take her head off that night. She'd better keep her hands off my man, I thought, and all that sort of bullshit, though now I wish I'd just sent the two of them off somewhere with a suitcase and a bag lunch. Would have been better for both me and Bob."

"Did Dad drink back then?" I asked, wondering if incidents like this might have led to his alcoholism or if it were already a problem.

"Not like later," she answered. "Oh, we all drank a little; we were young and liked to party. Oh boy, did we party! One night, we'd been having some champagne and your daddy had knocked back more than his fair share and was snoozing in front of the fireplace, laid out there on the carpet and snoring like a buzz saw. She came in wearing this little sailor's hat of hers cocked to the side, a full glass of champagne in her hand, and then she grinned at me like she'd just thought of the cleverest thing in the world. 'Wanna see something funny?' she says. I knew her well enough by then to brace for the worst, and sure enough, she pranced over to where your daddy lay, giggled like a naughty child, and then poured that entire glass of champagne in his face. Well, I never saw your daddy hit nobody. Normally, he wouldn't swat a bee if it bit him in the butt, but he came rising up just as fast as lightning and socked her in the jaw. I think it just shocked him, you know? She ran upstairs a'boohooing and locked herself in the bedroom.

"It wasn't a few weeks later that she and I were in their kitchen washing dishes when suddenly she stopped, flashed me that grin of hers and said, 'Hear that?' 'Hear what?' I said. 'Oh, I just love that sound!' she said. And sure enough, I heard a motorcycle revving from somewhere out by the driveway. 'That's my new boyfriend, Tommy,' she said. 'Your boyfriend?' I said, and she just nodded like it was the most natural thing in the world. 'He's going to take Jennie and me away. We're going up to Valdosta and getting married. He comes by every night after work and lets me know he's out there thinking of me.' I thought she'd gone completely off her rocker. She made up all kinds of cockamamie stories, and half the time you couldn't believe a word out of her mouth, so I didn't say nothing to anyone. Well, I'll be damned if not a month later your father comes home from work to find the whole house empty except for his red armchair, and so there he sat, all by himself in the empty living room and got stinking drunk. Yeah! She'd cleaned out their bank account, took Jennie, the furniture, and everything else. Didn't even leave a note."

***

I am not being completely genuine here. Aunt Nancy did not spill all this information in one go. Rather, fragments of these stories were repeated piece-meal from the time she felt I was old enough to hear them (say eight or nine) until most recently last summer, when I asked her once more for a refresher on Dad and Janine's relationship so I could be sure of the details before writing them here. These scenes from my father's marriage waft back and forth in the family air like electricity, an explosive part of the atmosphere we breathe. It's like Delal's cousin Murat said of the Dersim massacres, "When you are surrounded by these stories, they become part of what you are." Only, in our case, we did not collectively remember an extinction level event of a whole people, but of a single nobody from rural nowhere.

When Dad told me about his final days with Janine, however, it was all in one go, at a specific time and place. We were on our way home from a trip to Gold Head Branch State Park, where we'd hiked the spring-fed ravine then swum in the lake. I remember the late-afternoon sunlight and my sunburn and the wall of pine trees racing by in a green blur on either side of us. Memaw had given us a curfew. We had to have the car back before dark, and the sun was starting to set.

"When Jennie was born," he said, "we lived on Citrus Lane in the Highlands. That was a fancy neighborhood back then. I couldn't really afford it, but Janine and her daddy wouldn't have anything less. All the houses looked alike, with perfect lawns and two cars in the driveway. I went to work with my shirt and tie like every other chump on the block, and somehow it made me feel like I had made it, to be part of something so clean and respectable. We bought an expensive couch, I remember, with a horsey pattern she just loved, and had a cabinet with all the fine china displayed. It was that kind of life.

"One Saturday, I was home puttering about in the yard. Janine had taken Jennie to her parents for the afternoon, and I was alone. A group of neighbors came up the driveway and asked if they could speak with me for a minute. I invited them inside, served them all a tall glass of iced tea, and asked what they wanted. I remember thinking it was odd because there were about five of them, all women, each from a different house, and they acted like they had been selected as representatives, as if they were a delegation. I wondered if we had committed some suburban sin, not watered our lawn, or bought the wrong breed of dog.

"'We all have sons,' one of the women began after the standard pleasantries were out of the way, 'at the high school, and they have been coming here after classes to babysit your daughter.'

"'Occasionally,' a second woman continued. 'They even skip school to do it.'

"'Well, where's Janine going?' I asked, getting pretty pissed off. I was thinking mainly of Jennie being left alone with high school boys, of how irresponsible that was.

"'Well, that's just it,' the same woman said. 'She doesn't go anywhere.'

"There was one woman who had been sitting nervously at the edge of the couch the whole time, not watching me like the others, but staring fiercely down at the carpet. At some point, she looked straight at me, and with this high-pitched kind of desperation said, 'My son says he's going to kill himself. He says she promised to run away with him, but apparently it was all a joke, and she told him she doesn't want him to come over anymore, so he's locked himself in his room and is talking about suicide. You tell her to stop. You make her stop!'

"'If you move,' the first woman says, 'get her out of the neighborhood, then none of us will press charges. No one needs to know.' And so, we moved. And no one knew."

"She was having sex with those boys?" I asked. "With Jennie in the house?"

"That's what it sounded like."

"Jesus. How old was Jennie?"

"Just turned three," he answered.

And so in 1964, when Martin Luther King, Jr. came to St. Augustine, forty minutes south of Jacksonville, for a conference with local Civil Rights leaders and was arrested at the Monson Motel where he had tried to eat at the all-white motel restaurant, when white and black protesters at the same motel jumped into the all-white pool, and the owner poured acid into the water to drive them out, when unknown gunmen fired on the house where King stayed after the address was leaked to north Florida's white extremist groups, when demonstrations the reverend held in the city led to the passage of the Civil Rights Act, my father was looking for a new house so his wife could avoid prosecution for statutory rape.

I said nothing for a long time after that, just watched the road roll out ahead of us, propelling us toward Memaw's house. I wanted to ask him if this was when he started drinking, but somehow that felt like I would be going too far. The story wasn't even over. I wanted to know if he ever tried getting custody of his daughter, and if he hadn't, how he could possibly have left a child in the care of such a person. I decided to risk crossing the line.

"I had no choice," he said. "Janine disappeared one day and took Jennie with her. She left nothing in the house but an old recliner, and for a long time, I had no idea where either of them were until the divorce papers arrived in the mail. She was getting remarried and needed me to sign off so that she could do it legally. She said her new husband was going to adopt Jennie."

"But you said she sent you papers when she was sixteen."

"Tommy didn't last long enough. I guess the one after him did the trick, though."

After that, he refused to talk anymore about it. I had so many questions. What about his in-laws? He had been close enough to his wife's mother to learn all her recipes. She was the source of the fabled steak and spaghetti, after all. Wouldn't she have helped him keep in touch with his daughter, given him an address at least, a place to send child support? Or couldn't he have gone to court? My mother said Janine had called shortly after I was born wanting money for a band uniform or something along those lines, some expense connected to school. Dad must have known where she was then or at least could have found out easily enough, with a little effort could have contacted her, phoned her, visited her. Later, I would bring up the subject again, and he would always remind me that at sixteen Jennie asked him to sign his fatherhood away. She didn't want him, so why bother? And though I never said it, all I could think was that she must have been pretty sure *he* didn't want *her* by that time, after all that absence.

***

Throughout the writing of this memoir, I have been plagued by these pangs of doubt that my dad's story, his suicide and all that led up to it, is not worth exploring so publicly. It certainly isn't unique. As a middle school teacher, I hear at least once a year of some devastating tragedy in the lives of one of our students. One thirteen-year-old girl's father gets cancer and her mother ships her off to a boarding school in Canada to avoid breaking the news. When he dies a few months later, the daughter finds out in a phone call from a friend, and she must deal with the news all alone in Toronto. My sister, Michele, works with special-needs students in Lakeland, one of whom was permanently brain damaged after being slung against a wall by his mother as a toddler. Another student is a Mayan immigrant from Guatemala who spent his childhood in a refugee camp for victims of that country's genocide. In Turkey, I am surrounded by Kurdish friends and family who have been tormented, abused, and persecuted their entire lives in their own civil rights struggle. People move on. You would never know there was anything amiss in the past unless you went poking around. So why do it? Why drag it back to the surface? Do my father's woes make a mark on the world?

A few years before his death, Jennie contacted him. It started out as letters, then, once they'd mutually decided they were ready, she called him out of the blue one night at Memaw's house in Keystone. I don't remember how this little reunion came about, but I have a feeling Memaw helped set it up. I don't know, either, how those first conversations went. Dad was always understated. When he announced he had spoken with his long-lost daughter after nearly three decades of painful estrangement, he did it with his characteristic reserve.

"Well, I talked to your sister."

"Michele? Why?"

"No. Jennie."

"You spoke with *Jennie?*"

It turns out his absence did indeed have a profound impact on her life. She told him horror story after horror story in the same laconic, emotionless tones he used to tell his own.

She had dreamed often as a child of meeting her real dad, she said, fantasized about him coming to whisk her away from the chaos of her mother's eccentric parenting and her occasionally abusive boyfriends. As a child, she'd been left home alone for days.

One night, when she was sixteen, Jennie's boyfriend had asked to sleep over because he was afraid to go home to his own abusive father. Jennie set him up on the couch and then retired to her room to sleep. She woke up in the middle of the night at some sudden noise and looked toward her bedroom door where she saw her mother in a see-through negligee storming angrily down the hall. A few minutes later, her boyfriend was sitting on the edge of her bed and saying he had to go. "I don't like telling you this," he said, "but I woke up to your mother looming over me. She wanted me to fuck her and got really mad when I said no. She said I had to leave."

Jennie had gotten married young to escape all this, to an abusive man who ruthlessly beat both her and her son, Charlie, for the least little infraction. "I think I was looking for a father figure," she explained. "Someone strong, and that's what I thought was strong."

She had always felt a little lost, her identity smudged, a little orphaned and blurred.

I listen to Dad tell these stories Jennie told him, and my stomach constricts. I wonder what he feels being so much closer emotionally, so much to blame? If he had exerted just a little more effort, any effort at all, even, he could have made a profound difference in his abandoned daughter's life. He could have changed everything, absolutely everything. He must have known that. That he didn't try makes me think Janine was not the trigger of his downward spiral, but just someone who helped speed him on his way. Any other man would have fought to protect his daughter, but maybe he already had something in him that determined how he dealt with this crisis, that chose inertia instead of rage, that assumed defeat before he even started to fight, that surrendered to self-pity instead of rising to battle, to paternal action, to life; something, perhaps, buried in his very genes.

In our genes.

NINE

It's Halloween in Istanbul. In Taksim Square, a couple friends and I take a booth at the James Joyce Pub after work. Stephen and Ned are fellow Americans and teachers at the private school where I work. It's a Friday, and we're all exhausted from a week of trying to educate wild teenagers, and so we're unwinding over beers, the effects of which soon set off a boozy nostalgia for home. In the spirit of the season, we fall into telling ghost stories, running the gamut from demon possession (Stephen and I are both from the South) to Sasquatch (Ned is from Seattle), and I recount what I know of the Skunk Ape, the malodorous bigfoot that supposedly stalks the forests of Florida. A friend's aunt used to terrify us with tales of the creature whenever we camped on her property along the Suwannee River, I tell them.

"It was a pale thing, she said, much taller than a man with long, thin arms and flat hands like flippers. She'd seen it descending into the springs one twilight where we'd pitched our tent!"

From the terrace, we have a view of Istanbul's famous Bosporus as it empties into the Marmara Sea. A red freighter flying the Sierra Leone flag passes beneath, loaded with crates. In the sinking autumn sun, the converging waters are a deep navy blue, the sky a lighter shade with wispy clouds. Jumbled rows of old buildings like pastel dominoes line the hill that plunges toward the coast, pink and yellow and pale green. *How far from Florida you are*, I think to myself.

"Get this," Ned says. "My father-in-law claims a jinn haunts their family." He brushes his blonde bangs from his eyes and leans in as if imparting a closely-guarded secret. "My wife, Oya, had a strange dream once, and when her dad heard it, he said he knew exactly what it meant because everyone in the family had that same dream. The family jinn puts it in their heads." At this, he leans back and guffaws. "Can you believe it?"

"It haunts the whole family?" I ask.

"I guess so," Ned says, still chuckling.

"Does it get passed on? You know, like from generation to generation? Will it haunt your kids?"

"That I don't know. I'll have to ask him."

"What sets off a haunting? Like, did one of your father-in-law's ancestors do something to piss it off?"

"Someone's serious all of a sudden," Ned says, raising his eyebrows playfully in my direction.

"What was the dream?" Stephen asks. He's been listening quietly the whole time, calmly smoking beneath the framed black and white of nineteenth century Dublin.

"I don't remember that either. Oya can tell you. Her dad even knows the jinn's name, but I'm not supposed to say it out loud because it might attract her to us." He laughs again.

"That's what they say about demons back home," Stephen says.

"It's a her?" I ask.

"Yeah. It's a woman apparently."

Few people have ghost stories in Turkey, but a lot of people have jinn stories. When I first moved to Istanbul, I taught English conversation to adults and one of my students claimed she had come home one night to find her parents and two little brothers sitting in a line on the couch watching TV. When she appeared in the doorway, they turned in unison and said, "Welcome." She ate a quick snack, bid them good night, then went upstairs only to discover the same people asleep in their rooms. Spooked, she crept back down to the first floor, thinking she must have made a mistake. Maybe they were playing a joke on her, or maybe she was seeing things. When she reached the living room, they still sat in front of the TV, but she noticed that none of them wore any slippers or socks (a must in any Turkish home) and that their feet were pointing backward.

This is typical of jinn stories. They will mimic the image of a loved one, but one detail will be off in a peculiar way—body parts are missing, misshapen or displaced, like they don't know how to piece a human together properly. It's the same idea as the skunk ape's flipper-like hands. Typically, only religious people see jinn, as the concept comes from the fifteenth sura of the Quran where God explains that as Adam and Eve were created from the dried clay of smooth black mud, the first jinn were created from "a smokeless flame."

Delal arrives as we tell these stories and orders a beer. When she hears what we're talking about, she rolls her eyes.

"Can you contribute a crazy jinn story?" Stephen prods.

"When I was about twelve," she says, "my religion teacher gave a lesson on jinn, and though it sounded stupid, it made me curious. I really wanted to see one. So, one day at the house, when no one else was around, I wrote the letters of the alphabet on a piece of paper and cut them out. Then, I arranged them all in a circle, put a cup in the middle, and tried to call up a jinn. I must have waited for hours, but nothing appeared. I was pretty disappointed. But it confirmed one thing. It's all bullshit."

"Interesting," Ned says. "It sounds just like a Ouija board. I didn't know that was a thing here."

"I used to play with them when I was little," I tell them. "My dad's mother needed my help to summon her ex-husband. I guess you'd call him my step-grandfather. I must have been like seven."

"Your grandma used you to call spirits?" Stephen says incredulously. "That's bizarre."

"She was bizarre, all right." I hesitate. "A part of me believes it, though." Everyone casts a skeptical glance my way. "I mean, we hear these stories here. I heard them in Japan, too. If people tell them in such radically different cultures, maybe there's something to it."

Delal rolls her eyes.

"Something happened once to me, personally," I insist. "Something that really made me wonder if it could all be real. It has to do with my dad."

***

While rummaging through a box at my mother's, I rediscover the last picture I ever took of Dad. I struggle hard to feel something, some profound stirring of recognition, grief, or sorrow, but it's so long ago. Plus, it's a shitty photograph, snapped with an automatic Minolta I'd bought in Japan. Dad is on the back porch of Memaw's house in Keystone, his huge body completely eclipsing the chair he's flopped himself into. His hair is long and unkempt, maybe an attempt to hide the monk's spot on the back of his scalp, and he's wearing a red-checked button-down over his ballooning paunch. "The baby's almost due," he'd quipped. His long legs are crossed in front of him, the pants legs coming up short as always, revealing his pale shins. Next to him stands my best friend from Japan, Kuniko, in a rainbow-colored tie-dye shirt. She's holding a bottle of pepper sauce my father has just gifted her, though she hated spicy foods. "Those peppers came right out of my garden," he'd told her. "Try it on zipper peas or in a bowl of greens." Kuniko and her family, the Tsuchiyas, had basically adopted me back in Tokyo. I'd gone everywhere with her, her husband,

and their four children, and now it was my turn to host them in America.

I clearly hadn't given the first thought to lighting when taking the shot. Behind the two of them is a blaze of summer green so bright it casts both their figures in shadow, and the whole image is milky from the glare. I can barely make out Dad's bushy moustache, but the far edges of his face reflect the sunlight; he's lit like the nightside of a planet.

"So, this was goodbye," I think.

I didn't even spend half a day with him that last summer. It was my first time home since going to Japan, my first time seeing Dad since the fiasco of my college graduation, and after two long years, he was eager to have me visit. He'd begged me on the phone to stay a couple days, at least, so we could catch up. Undoubtedly, he wanted long night-talks on the back porch where I would regale him with stories of the Far East. But I had other plans. Kuniko and her two sons had come back with me; Eiichiro was sixteen and his brother Dai was twelve, and both looked up to me as a kind of big brother. I was going to make myself worthy of the title by unveiling the wonders of the world I came from. Or at least that was the vision.

An aside: while in the States, my relatives had trouble pronouncing the three Japanese names, and so Kuniko told people to call her Kuku to make it easier. For Eiichiro, we used an old nickname coined one evening after he burst screaming from the toilet, fleeing from a cockroach he'd seen crawling up the wall. Playing off the last syllable of his first name, I'd dubbed him "Roach." Dai's name was the easiest of the three. Dad got a kick out of this when I introduced them. "What a family!" he'd crowed, ushering them into the living room. "Coo Coo, Roach, and Die."

Anyway, it was everyone's first time overseas and we were embarking on a quintessential road trip, a sweeping grand tour of the US. I didn't have time to dilly dally among the dysfunction in Keystone, as the itinerary I had created required us to journey to the Grand Canyon and back in just one week, popping by New Orleans and Memphis on the way. I would have time to hang out with my father later, I figured, but the rental car had to be back in seven days, and the Southwest urgently beckoned. Frankly, Dad was low on my priority list. I promised him that I would return once my Japanese friends had flown home. I had a week after they left before I had to go back, too.

The road trip was fun, an American classic: all-night jazz on Bourbon Street, Montezuma's Revenge from tacos in Ciudad Juarez, a hike among the Navajo ruins of Canyon De Chelly. We went from breathtaking landscape to breathtaking landscape and spent nights at cheap, bug-infested motels, paying for two and sneaking in the rest.

I didn't keep my promise to Dad.

Guilt gnawed at me on the plane back to Tokyo. I knew I was my father's only outlet, the only person he really talked to, the only part of his life not mired in the miserable inertia of that isolated house with his unstable mother, and I'd abandoned him. So, to make up for it, I concocted my plan to pluck him out of Wiregrass Country and bring him to the opposite edge of the Pacific. Why not? I'd done it two years before with my mother. I'd bought her a plane ticket to Japan for Christmas and together we'd traveled to Kyoto and Nara, climbed the hill through the Buddhist cemetery at the majestic Kiyomizu Temple, and watched the crowds in Shibuya cross the "scramble" intersection from a coffee shop high above the street. (This last is what sticks in my mother's memory the most.) Kuniko and the family had invited us over for New Year's dinner where Mom tried sushi and sake for the first time in her life. Why not treat Dad to the same adventure? It would not only more than make up for my criminal negligence but would do him good to get out of his tiny fishbowl. It might even be life changing.

God, I concocted such plans! An itinerary devoted to him. I'd fly him over for Christmas when I had plenty of vacation time, and we'd embark on a whirlwind tour of all the historic sites, starting with the Imperial War Museum in downtown Tokyo where an original kamikaze plane was on display. Then we'd take the shinkansen to Hiroshima (he had a fascination with bullet trains), and we'd visit the atomic bomb dome and peace museum. Being the World War II nut that he was, all of this would blow his mind. On the way back, we could stop by Kyoto, the twelve-hundred-year-old city, and I'd show him the same sites I had shown Mom.

And the food! We'd have something different every night. He might not go for sushi at first—Mom hadn't, either—but like her, he would learn to crave it. He would love *yakiniku*, grilled strips of spicy Korean barbecued beef, and I'd take him to the best venue I knew, a hole-in-the-wall built under the train tracks where we'd also order *ishiyaki bibimbap*, the spicy mix of vegetables, beef, and rice cooked against the hot iron wall of the bowl it came in. We'd try *okonomiyaki* and *tonkatsu*, *tempura* and *tonkotsu ramen*. There wouldn't be time to get it all in. A man as "addicted to his gullet" as Dad would think he'd died and gone to heaven. He would never be the same. It would be his first plane flight, his first subway, his first skyscraper, his first foreign country. Only Mom put a damper on my spirits when I revealed my plans to her in our weekly phone call.

"What if he won't leave?" she asked.

"What do you mean 'won't leave?'"

"Do you think once he's free of your memaw he's going to want to go back to Keystone? You'll be paying for everything. It's the perfect life for him."

"He'll have to go," I reasoned. "He won't have a resident's visa."

"Or if he gets drunk and won't leave the house when it's time to go to the airport?"

"He'd never do that," I said, even as I realized it was the most likely ending to this whole adventure.

But Dad surprised me. He was so enthusiastic about the idea of traveling to Japan that he started working again after a hiatus of nearly ten years, which erased any fears about him becoming financially dependent on me in Japan. The job wasn't much, a part-time gig as a Winn Dixie bagboy in Starke, but he kept at it even though it was murder on his pride.

"I'm the only one there not sixteen, mentally disabled, or living at a halfway house," he'd grumbled.

He was determined to raise money for the trip, he said, because he wanted to pay for things himself.

"Plus, if I keep at it after I get back," he added, "I'll save up for a car, and once I have my own wheels, I'll be able to find something more my speed." *My God*, I thought. *Already it was happening.* Just the possibility of this trip was working a change. I'd set something in motion, a powerful alchemy. I had that same fluttering of hope deep in my stomach I used to get when I found out he was racing his sailboat. *This could break the cycle,* I thought. No more Memaw, no more booze, a whole different outlook on the world.

I went to Kuniko's house for dinner and told everyone my dad was coming to Japan. The whole family was thrilled. When Kuniko found out he was working again, she grew as excited as I was. I'd told her my father's entire sordid history of joblessness and alcoholism, so she knew what was at stake.

"Maybe this is what gets him out of that pattern!" she said, echoing my own thoughts, and we started to make plans together. She'd take a day or two off work, and we'd all go to the Tsukiji fish market at five in the morning where every sushi chef in the Tokyo region came to buy their supply for the day. It was quite a spectacle, she assured me. Then we'd take him to Hakone where we'd cook eggs in the volcanic springs and boat across the lake for a brilliant panorama of Mt. Fuji. The to-do list and excitement grew exponentially.

We hit the first snag after Dad talked Memaw into driving him to the post office to apply for his passport. He dutifully submitted his application along with money from the first paycheck he received from Winn Dixie. A few weeks later, the answer came back: Rejected. The birth years listed on his driver's license and on his birth certificate didn't match. Apparently, Memaw had not had him registered immediately after he was born but had waited a few years to get his official documentation. The hospital officials had misprinted his birthdate as the date she picked it up, and no one had ever bothered to have it adjusted, figuring it wasn't a big deal. What did any of these clerical errors mean in the Georgia backcountry anyway?

"It's not a problem," he assured me over the phone. "All I have to do is call the Tifton hospital and have them issue a new birth certificate."

"How long will that take?"

"However long the mail takes, Jeffrey. I have to send a formal request, and they have to rummage around in their files and then send me back what I need."

I did a few mental calculations. "About six working days."

"I wouldn't count on it being that quick. This is the great American bureaucracy we're talking about."

"Just let me know," I told him. "I have to buy the tickets soon to have you here for Christmas."

This must have been in September or early October. Two weeks later, we hit the second snag. As it turned out, Tifton's hospital didn't have the birth records of anyone before the 1940s. They'd thrown them all out in a document purge when they'd switched to a digital system. He'd have to apply for a new certificate through the federal government, and for that, he had to gather a lot of paperwork. This would have to be notarized; that would have to be sent away to D.C.

"I'll have to take a trip up to the Social Security Agency in Atlanta, too," he said. "And right now, your memaw doesn't seem interested in making the drive. She says she's too old."

"But you can drive."

"That's what I said, but she says she doesn't trust me. Don't worry. Just give me time to work on her. I'll sweeten the deal with a visit to Aunt Dorothy's."

"Do you think you can have it done by the holidays?" I asked. "That's when I have my longest vacation." My voice had gotten childishly whiny. "I've already started making reservations." I had cooked up so many fantasies in my head about Bob Gibbs' transformative Christmas in Japan that I was having a hard time letting it go. Didn't he get it? This was going to be a turning point for him, for our whole family.

"I just don't think it can possibly work out that quickly."

"But you'll try, won't you?" I persisted. "You can put a rush on your passport, you know, when you order it."

"Jeffrey," he said, "I don't have proof enough that I was born to satisfy these people. On paper, I don't even exist. I never have."

A week later, just after Thanksgiving, he vanished. He'd lost his job because he had come in drunk one day soon after our last phone conversation. He and Memaw had been bickering more than usual, and he'd started sneaking booze from somewhere and hiding it around the house. There was a knot in an oak tree in the backyard, a nook in the attic, medicine bottles in the bathroom cabinet. She'd issued her go-to ultimatum: stop drinking or get out. When he got plastered the following night, she packed him a suitcase and set it by the door, but as usual, he wouldn't budge from his armchair. (How often armchairs punctuate some tragedy in his life!) She summoned Uncle Gene first, and the police second, both charged with dragging Dad away.

"He spent a night or two in jail," she told me. "Then someone bailed him out. I think Clark. I have no idea where he went after that."

I don't know what precipitated this debacle. I vaguely know that at some point Memaw told me to quit pressuring him about Japan. She either grabbed the phone from him one night while I was talking or called me herself. I don't remember the conversation, but I know it happened in the way I described a while back, as an impersonal fact independent of memory. And I know I suspected her of sabotage, of deliberately throwing a monkey wrench into the works just to prove who was ultimately in control. "You think you're ever going to get on that plane?" she'd say to him out of the blue.

I do remember being angry and frustrated that he'd lost his job. It had all been going so well, and now it would be next to impossible to get him a passport. Everything was unraveling, slipping apart. I'd have to find him first, then fix his and Memaw's relationship enough for him to persuade her to drive up to Atlanta or wherever the hell he had to go. In the back of my mind, I knew the whole thing was over, but I didn't quite want to face it, not yet. I stubbornly kept phoning my grandmother, asking her if he was back or if she knew where he was.

"Still haven't heard," she'd say.

Trying to bring Dad to Japan was like trying to catch that gar a long time ago on Santa Fe—the resistance, the mystery of that black lake surface in the middle of the night, the strength of the unseen that would not yield. I'd labored hard to pull him out of Wiregrass Country, but the Wiregrass Country had pulled back, and the struggle ended like the snap of a fishing line, with the monster charging back toward the bottomless dark.

***

We built the Ouija board one night in February out of sheer boredom.

It was late winter in Tokyo, and there were three of us huddled in my friend's living room, sitting cross-legged on the tatami bamboo flooring. There was no central heating in our apartments, and so we used huge kerosene-powered contraptions that burned like rocket engines to blast away the chill. Night had already fallen, and we were exchanging ghost stories over the "fire" while drinking instant cocoa someone had brought from the States, complete with tiny fake marshmallows. Julie, another Floridian who came to Japan the same year I did, was telling us about a time that she and her friends had played with a Ouija board in high school.

"We were at my house, and everyone wanted to try it. I had my own board, but for some reason I couldn't find it, so one of my friends taught us how to make one. We cut up little squares of paper, wrote a letter on each one and arranged them in a circle. We also made a paper for 'goodbye.' That was very important, my friend said, to keep the spirit from lingering."

"Bullshit," said Leslie, a fellow English teacher who had arrived in Japan a few years after Julie and me.

"*Anyway*," Julie said, ignoring her. "We used an upturned saucer as the planchette. We started asking it questions, and at first, it responded like it always did, with nonsense words and random letters. Then eventually it got really strong and began racing around the table. I asked it where the original board was, and we heard this loud crash in my sister's room."

"Which was just your sister, of course, falling out of bed."

"Nobody was home but us. We huddled there for the longest time, listening for something else to happen, like footsteps or voices or I don't know; we were terrified. Then we all went together to my sister's room and opened the closet. My Ouija board sat on the floor, facing up, you know, like it was trying to show itself. Everything else had fallen around it. It had been sitting under all these boardgames at the top of the closet. My sister had these things called Fashion Plates at the time, stencils for designing Barbie clothes, and it looked like they had exploded everywhere, not like they had simply fallen but like they'd been flung—and hard."

"It was just a coincidence," Leslie says. "It probably didn't even fall when you asked. You're just remembering it that way because you want to believe so badly."

"Ouija boards work," I chimed in. "I used to play them with my grandmother all the time when I was a kid."

"That's fucked up," Leslie said. "And doesn't mean it's not bullshit."

"Let's make one," Julie said then. "And we'll prove it works."

And so, we cut pieces of paper, wrote the letters of the alphabet on them, and placed them in a circle on the kitchen table as Julie had explained. We added papers for "yes," "no," and "goodbye." I was playing along but couldn't stop smirking. As much as I liked getting into the ghost story mood, I also thought the Ouija board was nonsense. Dad used to watch Memaw and us kids with a skeptical scowl as we followed the circling planchette.

"Running another seance?" he'd ask sarcastically.

"You can't deny it's moving," I'd insist. As a seven-year-old, I was a believer.

"You're doing it unconsciously," he'd answer. "It's called the ideomotor effect."

"What's that?"

"Your brain is responding unconsciously to suggestion, like hypnotism. Whatever is spelled out on that thing is coming out of your own head. *I-de-o-motor*; idea motion. Not important, but nice to know."

Julie took a small saucer out of the cupboard and placed it face down in the middle of the letters. She laid her pointer finger and middle finger lightly on the surface, and I did the same from the opposite side. Leslie was snickering.

"You guys are morons."

"It'll move," I assured her. "Why it does, I don't know. My father used to say we moved it without knowing it. Your brain gets the suggestion that there's a ghost in the room, then your hands subconsciously start pushing the planchette. The answers are really coming from us, but I don't know if it will work with a dish."

"It always works with me," Julie said.

"My dad's probably right. I don't know, though. I used to play with friends in high school, and I would always ask about this girl I liked. 'Will Samantha

and I ever get together?,' I'd say, and it always answered 'no.' I figure if I were the one pushing it subconsciously, then *subconsciously* I would push it toward a nice, solid 'yes.'"

"Maybe you're just a loser with no confidence," Leslie quipped.

"Maybe you're an asshole."

"Is there a spirit in the room?" Julie asked aloud, and Leslie rolled her eyes. After a minute, the dish started to slide gently right and left.

"You're doing that," Leslie said.

"Not that I'm aware of," I said.

Julie repeated the question, "Is there a spirit in the room?" The dish slid decisively toward 'yes.'

"What's your name?" she asked.

The dish moved to R, then S, then skipped to V.

"This is exactly what I remember," I said. "Whatever you ask, it just spells nonsense."

"I still say you're moving it," Leslie said.

"You have to let it gather strength," Julie said. "It takes a little time."

"So, you're a medium now?"

"Just wait," Julie said, then repeated, "What's your name?"

At first, nothing happened. We heard the howl of the wind outside and the rumbling of the heater. I looked at Julie and shrugged. Then the saucer started to circle, first in small loops, but gradually in ever wider and faster ones until it finally stopped on B. It lingered a second before jerking across the table to L, then O.

"There," said Julie. "Now it's spelling a real word."

It slid to O again, then D, Y, and when it reached M, I jerked my hand away.

"You're making it spell Bloody Mary," I said.

"No, I'm not." Julie protested. "I swear."

"I told you how when I was a kid that story scared the shit out of me, so you're making it say that name."

"I swear I'm not."

Leslie shook her head. "You two are putting on a good show."

"It's not a show," Julie said.

"Then prove it," Leslie said. "Ask it my middle name."

"Okay. Jeff, put your hand back on."

I placed my fingers on the dish, and it immediately started circling slowly again.

"You're doing this," I said, echoing Leslie now, though inwardly I was thinking the Bloody Mary thing fit Dad's theory perfectly. We'd been telling ghost stories, and if ever a name was going to pop out of my subconscious when ghost stories came up, it would be that of the spook that had given me nightmares since elementary school. A third grade classmate had claimed Mary haunted the grove between our school and the junior high. I couldn't even look at those orange trees without shuddering. And if you turned twelve circles in a mirror and said "Bloody Mary" every time you faced the glass, she'd appear that night at the foot of your bed and chop off your head.

"What's Leslie's middle name?" Julie asked.

The dish zipped rapidly back and forth between letters, spelling out "Maria." I burst out laughing. Leslie was pale, blonde, and heavily freckled. I knew no one WASPier than she. There was no way in the world she had a Latin, Catholic middle name like "Maria."

"Well, that's an epic failure," I said.

"You knew," Leslie said.

"Knew what?" Julie asked.

"That's my middle name."

"No, it is not," I said.

Leslie took out her driver's license and placed it face up on the table. Leslie Marie Jepson, Orlando, Florida.

"It's Marie, not Maria," I said.

"That makes it even creepier," Julie said. "You know what I mean? Like it had a little trouble seeing clearly into our world from another."

I was deeply spooked at this point. If I'd had to subconsciously guess what the translucently-white Leslie's middle name was, Maria would never have been what came out. I was sure the same was true of Julie, too. She looked equally surprised.

"Maybe one of us knew, and it was just dormant information?" I offered.

But I didn't think we were the ones moving the dish anymore. I decided to ask where my father was. The dish flew around the table and spelled the phrase, "EATING GRASS."

"I don't understand," I said, and asked again. It spelled the same thing, "EATING GRASS." When it reached the end, it didn't wait for another question and instead immediately began repeating the phrase. E...A...T...

"We're back to nonsense again," I announced. "Let's go with something more classic. What's my future? Where will I be in ten years?"

EATING GRASS. HA HA.

"That's weird," Julie said. "What does that even mean?"

"It means dead," Leslie said. "Duh. That's obvious enough. If you are buried in the ground and facing up, you're eating grass."

Now I was sure the movement of the dish had nothing to do with us. If it had, why wouldn't we know the idiom it supposedly pulled out of our own minds? Why would we need the interpretation of someone who didn't believe in the first place?

EATING GRASS.

My father and I.

Two months later, I got the call from my sister telling me he was dead.

I am not one to believe in ghosts or prophetic dreams or much of anything supernatural, but when it comes to this stupid night with the Ouija board, I lose all rationality. I have this guilty feeling that I called something down on Dad that night in Tokyo. I realize it's typical for the loved ones of a suicide to blame themselves. "It's not your fault!" urge the books and websites. "There was nothing you could have done!" And so usually I cut myself some slack. But sometimes I think I tapped into something that night. Maybe I had even contacted a spirit that already hovered over my father and our family—a curse, a possession, or whatever you want to call the dark power that carried doom from one generation to the next and might even now be bearing down on me.

TEN

On the second day of our Georgia tour, Lisa drives Delal and me to the cemetery in Omega where both my father and her grandmother, Aunt Dorothy, are buried. Dad's headstone is at the back, on the border marked by a barbed-wire fence and a line of dead trees separating the graveyard from a sea of dark-green cotton fields. Industrial sprinklers jet water over the plants in white bursts like comet tails; their rhythmic swishing is the only sound.

The marker lies at the foot of a live oak I planted when I buried him, mixing his ashes with the Wiregrass soil and peat I'd bought from the nursery. My idea was that he would seep into the tree's roots and pass up into each branch and twig, cell by cell. The atoms that once made up his body would circulate through the xylem and phloem as they became stitched into the chemical substructure of the wood and bark and leaf. I had visions of it growing to gigantic proportions, a sprawling Southern oak worthy of a postcard. It would produce acorns, each a seed with a bit of him inside that I would then plant all over the planet, wherever I traveled. From an isolated and anonymous life, from a violent and premature death would emerge a graceful opening up into the world.

Then the groundskeepers cut his oak down.

The first time I took Delal to see it was the year before we were married. The trunk was still thin, but the tree itself was tall, at least eight feet. There were acorns, and I collected them to plant in Istanbul. On our next visit, the tree was a butchered stump. The main trunk had been chopped off just above the soil's surface. I was devastated, but it was a resigned sort of devastation. These were the kind of disappointments he and I had always weathered. *It had been a dumb idea anyway,* I thought to myself.

"But look," Delal had said. "It's already coming back." New branches grew thick and bushy from the sides of the butchered base.

Now, as we pull into the cemetery and start bouncing down the clay road, I am steeling myself for what we might find. The whole thing could be gone, roots and all. I hadn't asked anyone's permission when I planted it, hadn't let a single person know. For everyone but me, it was just a nuisance, little better than a weed.

"Do you remember where it is?" Lisa asks.

"In the back," I say. "I usually look for the tree, but that might not work this time."

"Why not?"

I tell Lisa the story of planting the oak and its subsequent cutting.

"I do remember something about that. The Patrick family were pretty upset with you for just sticking a grave there without asking."

I had placed Dad at the foot of his father, my grandfather, Robert Lenward Gibbs Senior, who himself lay buried in the same plot as *his* mother, Hattie Patrick, along with many of her brothers and sisters. It was a choice I'd made for two reasons. First, I knew Dad had loved his grandmother, Miss Hattie. When he spoke of her, it was as if talking about an idealized mother; she seemed the sole relative not mixed up in the family rancor and animosity. Second, there's a continuity between Dad and his own father. They were both outcasts, both lost, both tormented by alcohol, joblessness, and loneliness. They seemed to belong together now, in death.

But I hadn't paid anyone for the land, hadn't considered that it might be a family plot, parceled up and owned by relatives I had never met. I hadn't cared. I just showed up one day, dug a hole where I wanted, and dumped Dad's ashes in it. At the time, I thought the whole family from Uncle Gene to the twentieth cousin could go to hell. Plus, I blamed bureaucracy for killing him in the first place, or at least, for striking the final blow. I figured if all that red-tape madness with his passport and birth certificate had gone more smoothly, he never would have sought out that train. "On paper," he'd told me, "I don't really exist. I never have." In the end, he'd simply made the reality fit the official data. I thought, *If someone wants me to launch into another cycle of licenses and permits and paperwork in order to put his wandering soul to rest, then I am going to teach them a thing or two.* Humanity would trump cold officialdom. And if it ruffled a few cousins' feathers, then that was all the better; one of their own taking his life should make an impact. Such a day should not pass quietly into the next and be forgotten like everything else. I wanted to stir up trouble. I wanted to break things.

Twenty-five years later, however, I see the disadvantages of this approach.

"I understand why they were pissed," I tell Lisa. "I just wanted to put him close to his daddy. I wasn't thinking of much else. Of much of anything really."

"Totally understandable," Lisa answers. "Still, the Patricks were hopping mad. It was a scandal up here for a bit, but Grandmama managed to calm everybody down."

"I think Memaw told me that. I always wanted to thank Aunt Dorothy, but…"

But I barely even knew her, I finish privately.

"I've never been to Bob's grave," Cousin Clark says. "Where did you say it was now?"

My eyes are scanning the fence for the shrub I last saw five years ago, but I can't find it. *They've done it,* I think. *They've finally just torn it right out of the ground.*

"Isn't that it?" Delal asks. She points to a large tree at least twenty feet tall.

"That can't be it, honey," I say. "It's too big."

"But that's the place," she insists. "There's the spigot where we refilled our bottles."

"That *is* the Patrick plot," Clark says.

Then I see the familiar stone border around the cluster of headstones, but the tree is too big. It could never have grown back so quickly and so tall, taller than it had been when it was cut down. I clamber out of the truck, my heart's racing. I need proof. When I read his name in the gray granite stone at the base, I let out a peal of laughter and tears pool in my eyes.

"Dad!" I say, with all the ease now I was never able to muster when he was alive.

"Sometimes they'll grow faster if you trim them back a bit," Lisa says.

The tree is huge like I always hoped it would be, with a prolific sprawl of branches arcing skyward. It casts a patch of blue shade over the grass and over the graves of Dad's father and grandmother, over his great aunts and uncles. You could have a picnic in that shade, spread a blanket wide and sprawl out, take refuge from the pounding summer sun. Where there was once just a single trunk, there's now a wide base from which grow eight separate trunks, each thicker than my thigh. Delal immediately fills an empty Gatorade bottle with water from the faucet and begins to wash Dad's headstone, wiping away the dirt that's crusted in the grooves and pulling away the crabgrass that has spread over the surface. It's what she does with her own family's graves back in Kurdistan.

My ritual is different. I have two pennies. One I place face up on my dad's headstone, the other on his father's. Many years before, I had come to this cemetery with Dad to pay respects to my grandfather. As I explained before, I had never met the man. I knew nothing about him. All I had were a few scraps of stories I'd picked up from Dad and Aunt Nancy, fragments of fragments. No one wanted to talk about Pepaw. Maybe there hadn't been much to say. I knew he was a drunk, that he could disappear for months or even years. For the longest time, there'd been no pictures of him either, no record of any kind. He was like one of the mysteries I loved to read about, a Bermuda Triangle, a UFO, a ghost no one quite believed in. I began to ask obsessively about him. There was an answer there somewhere to the way the family was now.

Then one day, when I was about sixteen, a photograph finally turned up.

"I thought you might like this," Memaw had told me casually and handed me a wallet-sized picture taken in a carnival photo booth. It was faded and ripped at the corner, fished out of God-knows-what box pushed into the back of God-knows-what closet. It revealed a handsome, beaming youth holding a baby Uncle Gene. The young Pepaw pressed his rough cheek to the crying infant and grinned into the camera. He couldn't have been more than twenty-five years old. He had curly, coal-black hair, sun-bronzed skin and eyes that crinkled at the corners like an elf's. I knew his eyes were blue from Memaw—the one thing she admitted about him was how good-looking he had been—but in the black and white photo, the irises looked silver, luminous. He was wearing a white cap rakishly askew on his head. I had assumed it was a sailor's hat, but Memaw informed me it was part of a service station uniform. He had pumped gas as a youth. Or worked as a mechanic. I can't remember which. The name "Buddy Gibbs" was written in pencil on the bottom. He looked like a wizard, or a gifted conman.

"How did you two meet?" I asked.

"Oh, it was at a house gathering in Omega. I set my sights on him immediately. He had those bright blue eyes. And he was built! We weren't even twenty years old, I guess. He started making eyes right back at me, and so I sat on the arm of his chair, just a'giggling and chatting. It was storming outside, and the lights suddenly went out, the whole place so pitch black you couldn't see your hand in front of your face. When the electricity switched back on, I saw this other girl, Lucille, crawling toward his chair on her hands and knees with this wild look in her eyes. They'd been 'courting' for a while at the time, I think, and there she was on the floor like a dog in heat, and she didn't even care I was there! Oh boy, I was jealous, I felt these sharp little tingles on the surface of my skin, like somebody was sticking me with pins, and I made a promise that that man was going to be mine."

I'd had Lenward's picture with me on that first visit to the grave with Dad years before his death. As we were about to leave, I placed a penny on the foot of Pepaw's gravestone. I'd tried to do it on the sly—I was somewhat shy about anyone knowing the way I had fixated on my grandfather. Dad noticed, however, reached down, and flipped the penny over.

"Put it heads up, son," he said, then added in a gentler voice, one I had never heard him use before. "That man needs all the luck he can get."

I don't know where the photo is now. It stayed with me in Japan, through my moves to Tucson, Texas, and Boston. It got lost somewhere in the transition to Istanbul, probably at the bottom of a box in one of the various places I've stored my belongings. But it's one of the few things I can call to mind perfectly. Other memories flicker and jump away when I try to look directly on them, but the memory of that photo holds still, luminous against a background of black, every detail crisp and sharp, like a hexed Tarot card, the Magician with his wand held in the air and the snake around his waist, eating its own tail. If there were any malign spirits hovering over my family line, they were certainly with Pepaw.

***

The first thing I learned about my grandfather was that he had been in and out of jail.

"Where did y'all come up with my name?" I asked Dad once.

"I got Wade from a character in one of my favorite cowboy movies."

"And Jeffrey?"

"I just liked it. Your mama's big idea was to name you Jean Paul."

I laughed. "That sounds too French for Lakeland."

"It was either that or Robert Lenward the Third."

"I was almost a third?"

"Your mother thought that if we continued the tradition, it would sound regal."

Suddenly, so did I. This must have been when I was about to enter middle school because I remember having to fill out a bunch of forms and being presented with a box where I might place a check if I were a junior or a third, which struck me as a distinguished thing to be. What if I had my name legally changed?

"Why didn't you go with that?" I asked.

Dad sighed. "To protect you."

"From what?"

"Well, son, it's not always a good thing to carry on a legacy. When I was a young man in Jacksonville, cruising with my girl one night, the cops pulled me over looking for a Robert Lenward Gibbs who had done something or other earlier that evening. They took one look at my license and figured they had their man. With my date watching, they handcuffed me, shoved me into the back of the squad car, and hauled me off to jail. I spent a couple of nights there before they figured out they had the wrong Robert Lenward. I hadn't even known Lenward was in town. So, you see, I wasn't about to visit the same torment on my son."

"But why would you? You've never been arrested."

He shook his head and let out a caustic laugh as if to say, "There's a lot you don't know."

"Trust me. It was the right thing to do. I cut the link and deliberately faced you toward the future."

The way he said that, "cut the link," makes me wonder if Dad believed in a curse as well. He told me this story of my naming many times over the years as if it were something that weighed heavily on his mind. My mom, on the other hand, doesn't remember wanting to name me after my father at all. Perhaps for her, it was just a passing whim that she quickly forgot when she hit on Jean Paul, because she definitely recalls wanting to call me that and still gets misty-eyed when she talks about it. "It would have been such a pretty name!" For Dad, however, the suggestion of giving me his own name got snagged on the thorns of old memories. So much so, that as a young father of thirty-four, the idea felt like a calling down of doom on his newborn son. He was already anticipating screwing everything up. Clearly, it aggravated some kind of trauma.

"Robert" was a family name on the side of Pepaw's mother, Hattie Patrick. Her father had been a Robert, as well as her uncle, her great-grandfather, and several of her great-uncles. In fact, a Robert has been in the Patrick line for at least twelve generations, which is as far as I have been able to trace. The name goes all the way back to our ancestors in Scotland who probably used it as a tribute to Robert the Bruce, the old Scottish King whose heart was buried in Melrose Abbey, the "Melrose" for which Florida's town was named. People referred to my grandfather by his middle name, Lenward, which was another family heirloom sported by another of Miss Hattie's brothers. Did this chain of Roberts and Lenwards, these words, carry some kind of curse? My father clearly sensed something pernicious flowing down toward him through his paternal line. Many of the answers to why he was on the tracks that morning lay not just with Memaw, but with Robert Lenward the First.

***

Memaw's gift of Lenward's picture unlocked some of my father's closed doors.

"He was a handsome man," he said with a strange mix of pride and despair when I showed him the photo.

"You look a lot like him," I said.

"So do you."

In the beginning, all the stories he told about his father made Pepaw seem like some kind of comic hobo clown. But a word before I start retelling them. I cannot swear to their factual accuracy. If I think too long on the exact words Dad used or the place and time I heard the particular story, the images jump around, blurring with the motion, and I can't be entirely sure I've got any of it right. What I can do now, the only thing, is relate how these stories settled into my imagination where they've become like classic films I have watched and rewatched so many times I've memorized them. I know well enough my father's speech patterns and diction. If I just let go a little and don't try to hold on too tightly to the details, the stories flow.

"It was just after the Depression," Dad told me once. "And things were still rough, financially speaking. Hardly ever had any meat on the table. Then one day, your pepaw just up and vanished. He'd got to drinking again and ran off to where he could get smashed out of his mind in peace without a wife and kids nagging him. Of course, without his paycheck, we had no money coming in and went from barely getting by to dirt poor. He did this pretty frequently, and your memaw was tired of it, I guess, because she decided to move while he was AWOL. She figured he'd never be able to track us down. And he didn't for a while. We went to Jacksonville, she found her a job, but within a few months, he turned up at the front door. He'd built us a house, he said, with his own two hands. No one asked how he'd found us, or if they did, I can't remember, but off we moved to this new place. He'd gotten work as a carpenter, and everything was hunky dory for a spell. Our house was where the St. John's meets the Trout River. This was toward the end of World War II, and I remember going down to the shore and watching those gigantic aircraft carriers heading out toward the ocean from the naval base. They were big as continents, just these colossal mountains of metal floating on the currents. I'd never seen anything like them. I also remember how at night you could hear the lions roaring from the zoo on the other side of the river. I'd lay in bed and drift off to sleep to the bellowing of those big cats."

The house still stands on Wilder Street in Jacksonville, just a few blocks south of the Trout River. It's a single-family clapboard home painted dark green. Through the modern miracle of the internet, I find out through Zillow that it was built in 1944, which puts an age on Dad when all this happened. He was just seven years old.

"Within a year, Lenward was gone again—just stopped coming home. He'd run off with his paycheck, I guess, blowing every penny on an extended bender. Or maybe he was in jail. In any case, we were on our own once more. Who knew if he'd ever come back, or if we even wanted him to? This went on for months, and things finally got so desperate that your memaw was looking to move again. She'd had to go back to work but couldn't handle everything on her piddly salary alone.

"Now, the railroad tracks passed right behind our backyard, so close that a train would shake the fire out of our little house. One morning before the sun had even come up, I heard the morning freight coming like it always did about that time, only there was a voice, too, someone calling my and Gene's names. I thought I was hallucinating. We dashed outside in our pajamas to find Lenward standing at the door of a freight car. He was tossing food into the yard, big ol' frozen turkeys, one after the other, just as fast as he could. I can still hear the thump as they hit the ground. 'Hurry up, boys,' he said. 'Before the security men catch wind of what we're doing.' We'd been without meat for so long, all I could think of was how good those damn birds were going to taste. We filled the deep freeze with them. That was his apology, I guess, his ticket back home.

"That time he stayed with us a long while. One day, he called me into the storage shed because he wanted to show me something. He was all excited, just a'jumping and a'jittering, talking a mile a minute. 'You'll understand this,' he told me, 'in a way Gene or your mama never could.' I knew he'd been screwing around out there pretty much all day long for at least a few weeks—instead of going to a real job, of course, as your memaw was always pointing out. So, I followed him out to the shed to find this contraption he'd made that looked like he'd taken every loose bit of metal and wood he could lay his hands on and cobbled it together with wire and nails and bits of string. It was hooked up to a bicycle and he climbed up on that thing and started pedaling. A light burned here; a chain clanked there. He hopped off and bent down, squinting at the gearbox. 'Not quite there yet,' he said. 'What's not there?' I asked. He just laughed, 'Why Bobsy, this here's a perpetual motion machine. Just you wait. Once I get a patent on this baby, we'll open up our own company and sell her from coast to coast. We're going to be richer than Andrew Carnegie!'"

Lenward vanished again before he could wow the world by breaking the fundamental laws of physics, and Memaw tried another move. He found them just like he had before, appearing at their new house almost a year later with a burlap sack full of nuts he claimed were a French delicacy called "aqories." "Spelled with a q and a bunch of silent letters," he'd explained.

"Hell," Dad said. "Sounded French enough to us."

He called his sons into the backyard, where he was roasting the 'aqories' over a hastily-built fire. Memaw was furious and kept trying to halt the entire culinary experiment, but Lenward assaulted them with a dazzling fusillade of speech, distracting his sons and wife with stories and jokes until he was satisfied the aqories were ready. Then he set the whole clan around the kitchen table and made them eat a handful of these gourmet nuts, saying if they didn't like them, it was because their palates weren't refined enough. "I've been to Paris," he told them with a wink of those bewitching silver-blues. "I know what I'm talking about." And who the hell knew? Maybe he had found his way to the City of Lights and, dwelling on thoughts of his dear family, brought back this rare dainty he wanted to share.

"We'd been eating so crappily I was really looking forward to trying something special," Dad confessed. "I mean, he had me convinced. He had that kind of power. But son, it was the bitterest, nastiest thing I'd ever put in my mouth. And I realized what I had known from the moment he showed us the damn things. These fancy French 'aqories' were nothing but your goddamn run-of-the-mill acorns."

I laughed. "Sounds like he was trying, though. You know, to kind of make things seem magical during hard times."

"That's for sure. Though your Uncle Gene never fell for it much."

"I wish I had met him."

"You did. When you were just a baby, we took you up to Omega. I wanted to introduce you to your great-grandmother, Miss Hattie. Your pepaw was there, too."

"What did he think of me?" I'd been practicing my grin in the mirror, imitating the picture of him, trying to see the wizard hobo's face in my own.

"He thought you were the greatest thing since TV dinners. He asked your mama to let him hold you, and he didn't want to let you go."

A blush rose to my cheeks.

"He made your mama nervous, though," he added with a grin of his own.

"How?"

"By almost getting us shot. It's 1972, you're barely one year old, and your pepaw is living by himself in a little apartment. We are at Miss Hattie's, and he shows up unannounced, shouting out in the yard. 'Is that my new grandson in there?' He says he has some places he wants to show us, so we all hop in the car and he's hollering directions. He's as excited as can be, talking a mile a minute. He takes us up one country road and down another, pointing little things out. After about an hour of this, we are all pretty hungry and I'm talking, *mean* hungry, your mother and sister and brother, too. 'I know just where to go,' he says. Meanwhile, everybody's grumbling from the backseat, or maybe it's their empty bellies growling, I don't know, but we finally find the place he's looking for, a farmhouse set back off the road with a big vegetable garden out front. 'Stop!' he says. 'Park at the edge of the road.' He tells your brother and sister to go in the garden and pick everything they can get their hands on. 'We want variety,' he says. 'But whose house is this?' your mother asks. 'Oh, an old buddy of mine's,' he says. 'He told me to swing by any time and take whatever I want.' So, they all start picking corn and cabbages and okra and cucumbers. About that time, a woman appears on the front porch and she's carrying a .22, not pointing it at us or anything, not yet, but she's got it in her hands, and it's not quite pointed at the ground, neither. 'Who the hell are y'all?' she shouts. 'And what are you doing on my property?'

"Your brother and sister stop dead-still right where they are, their eyes looking to me bright with panic. They've each got an armful of produce. Your mama is poking me, 'Bob, she's going to kill us all!' Your pepaw tells everybody to resume what they were doing, and they all look from him to the woman on the porch and then back to me. Lenward, for his part, keeps picking as if he sees nothing awry.

"'I said, get off my property!' the woman on the porch repeats and shifts the muzzle of that gun just a bit more in our direction.

"Your pepaw stands, takes off his hat, and laughs. 'It's just me. Lenward. Don't you know me?'

"'Lenward?' she says, squinting. 'Why, it's been years!'

"Soon, they are grinning and hugging one another. She calls us all inside and starts cooking the vegetables we were just about to steal."

"Whose house was it?" I asked.

"You know," Dad said, "I still haven't the foggiest idea."

My mother, sister, and brother recall none of this. My mother describes what little she remembers of him on one of our weekly phone calls from

Istanbul. She recounts how Pepaw rode around in the car with them and how every single person they passed, whether on foot or in another car, waved and shouted his name.

"That man knew everybody!"

The talkative performer Dad described she recognizes not at all.

"He was quieter than your daddy. I remember I was alone in the front yard when he came over to Miss Hattie's house—that's where we were staying. You were in your playpen, and he scooped you out and plopped down in a lawn chair next to me. I had no idea what to say to the man. We sat there in silence for the longest time, and I kept looking at the door, hoping someone would come out and save me. He did chatter a bit at you, though—but it was in a real low voice I couldn't even hear."

His death came soon after that visit.

"He was working construction," Dad told me. "They say he was walking somewhere, on his way to get something from the shed, and he started moving in a circle. The other guys asked him what he was doing, and he just turned in tighter and tighter arcs until he fell down in the middle. It was a brain tumor."

That image has always stuck with me. It seemed appropriately cinematic somehow, the ever-tightening orbits around a center that finally sucked him in.

***

I have started to wonder how accurate these tales of Lenward's romantic eccentricities are. Maybe Dad made a few things up, or maybe I have distorted what he told me. How can no one in my family remember the Brer Rabbit-like thievery in the garden? At times, Pepaw seems as mysterious and unknowable as he was when I was a child. But there were other stories, too, not so romantic, stories when he wasn't so charming or sober. They are the ones that make me think of generational curses, of being haunted by demons and jinn and bad genes, stories that make me think my dad was in many ways an echo of his own father, that make me lay the responsibility for Robert Gibbs' wrecked life at the elder Robert's feet.

The first of these disturbing memories I heard from Aunt Nancy when I was about twelve. Karin and I were in the kitchen one night, eating a bowl of cobbler and ice cream. I asked Aunt Nancy if she remembered much about Pepaw, knowing she usually had a few good tales stored up of matters everyone else preferred to forget, however much she might add embellishments.

"Lenward was handsome," she said immediately. "He may have been as short as a sawed-off stump, but, Lord, he was good-looking. Bob and Gene get their height from the Patricks, I guess. Their Uncle Trummie was as tall as a redwood and with ears he could fly with, but they get their black hair and olive skin from their daddy. Oh, I just love that olive skin! It's what made me giddy over Gene in the first place, though he was a devil on the inside. Who knew? Like one of them candy bars they're always advertising on the television, chocolate on the outside and something else in the middle. Well, I got the something else. Lenward had those bright blue eyes, too. He was real athletic, with wide shoulders; he played both basketball and football. He was a carpenter, whenever he had a job at least. He'd get off work on a Friday payday and go in the woods with a jug of moonshine, and you wouldn't see him till Sunday night. The first time your memaw laid eyes on him he was drunk as a skunk sitting on a curb in the middle of town. Yeah! Oh, she can make out like she was a damsel in distress her whole marriage, but she knew what she was getting into from the get-go. The ingredients were written right there on the package.

"I remember when I met Lenward. Our first howdy-do wasn't all kisses and roses, I can tell you that. Your memaw had moved to Jacksonville, right down the street from Mother. I was cleaning the house for her and was using this broke-down vacuum cleaner that wasn't good for nothing but rearranging the dirt. Gene was too cheap to get a new one. Pepaw came in, lit three sheets to the wind, and tried to open the freezer door. For some reason, it wouldn't give, and so he put his fist through it. Yeah! That was my first glimpse of my daddy-in-law. Nice to meet you, Pepaw! We inherited that damn fridge when Nell got herself a brand-new Maytag, and I had to use the secondhand piece of junk for years, smashed-up freezer and all. But when he wasn't drunk, Lenward was as meek as a kitten, just like Bob. They both had to drink to get the gumption up. Back when they lived in Highlands, the fancy neighborhood in Jacksonville, he came home one night smashed out of his mind and dead-set on killing Nell. He was going to tear her every which way to Sunday. So, she locked herself in the bedroom and called me to come help. Well, I hauled buggy down there, didn't know she was a crazy bitch back then. When I arrived, he'd already kicked a hole in the damn door trying to get at her. So, I took her home to hide at our house. Yeah! I was always having to do things like that."

"Dad told me Memaw would sometimes move whenever he was out on a bender," I said, "trying to get away from him."

Aunt Nancy raised a skeptical eyebrow. "Your memaw loved to get him riled up. Oh, she lived for it. The reason he was trying to kill her that night was she'd burned everything he owned in the backyard the day before. Yeah! Took all his clothes and whatever else she could lay her hands on, claiming it was all infested with bedbugs, had Bob or Gene dig a little pit, and then lit the match. Well, he knew she was lying. There weren't any bedbugs. He never started any of the knockdown drag-outs they had. He followed her around like a hound dog waiting for a treat. She bought him a one-way ticket back to his mama in Omega after that little incident, put his butt on the bus, and told him not to come back."

Aunt Nancy's version of his death is different from Dad's and sounds more plausible. Neither of them had been there, but Dad had always been less connected to his Georgia family than Gene, so Aunt Nancy naturally had more details.

"Cancer took Lenward down in the end," she explained. "He was living in a little apartment in Tifton and had a brain tumor. He figured it out because he'd be going to the kitchen and end up in the bathroom, and he wasn't even drinking. Normally, if he could walk in a straight line, it was a good day. Turns out he had a tumor on his heart, too. It had spread down from his brain, and I remember them saying it was like a baby feeding off the mother, the one in his brain nurturing the one in his heart. They put him in a nursing home with Miss Hattie, right there in Tifton, and that's where he died, next to his momma. She went soon after."

Like I've said before, many of Aunt Nancy's stories turn out not to be entirely true. Her account of the moment Memaw first set eyes on Lenward, for instance, differed greatly from the story Memaw herself told me, but there is an undeniable poetry to her version of his death. She knows how to arrange the symbols. The tumor in his brain feeding the one in his heart. You could have said the same thing about my father.

The phone directory in the Tifton Public Library's historical archives gives Lenward's address in 1974, the year of his death, as the Wilton Arms Hotel, an old brick building from the turn of the century that was falling into disrepair. Like my own father, he had spent his last days living in a cheap hotel room, most likely financed by his mother. It was another echo between them, another way their lives rhymed.

Clearly, there was a lot more to Pepaw than the comic stories my father related, the violence, the way Memaw kept moving them from place to place to get away. Why not just get a divorce? Why the dramatic escapes to new cities and new houses? What was it like to grow up like that? I asked my father if Aunt

Nancy's stories were true. I wanted to know if Lenward had ever hit Memaw. Could years and years of abuse be why she was so strange?

"When I was older," he began cautiously, "and he was living with us again, I would come home and find her crying. She'd tell me he had gotten drunk and beat her, and so either I'd go hunt him down and knock the shit out of him at whatever bar he'd scuttled off to, or else he'd still be in the house, and I'd knock the shit out of him there. This went on for a while. One night I came home, and he was in that old recliner of his, almost passed out in front of the TV. His eyelids were heavy, half closed, and he couldn't lift a finger or form a sentence to save his life. She came out of the kitchen, crying. 'He beat me! He beat me again! You've got to do something!' So, I pulled him out of that chair, like I always did, and gave him a good sock in the mouth, and he's just limp, you know? A short little guy and already by that time, I was at least a foot taller than he was, if not more. Well, I was whaling on him and then, for some reason, I looked up, and I saw her standing there in the doorway that led to the hall, with her hands on her hips just a'smiling, as pleased as she could be. I've never forgotten that smile. I felt like I woke up to something, like I saw what had been going on the whole time. I thought I'd been such a good son, protecting my dear mama. Now I wasn't sure of anything, just that my father's face was covered in blood and hers in glee, and it was all because of me."

I sit back after writing that last sentence and breathe a little. I think of my mother's mantra about remembering "nice things," and I wonder what the hell I am doing dragging all of these terrible things back into the light. When Dad first told me about beating his father, it didn't horrify me as much as it did just now. I guess it was such a part of the way things were then, drunk daddies and crazy Nells. Now, at a distance, I see the obvious missing background to the little glimpses of his past he was willing to tell me, years and years of madness from both father and mother until he finally left home when Memaw set him up with his first wife, another destructive person who helped duplicate the abuse of his childhood.

***

I have one artifact belonging to Lenward himself, one fragment of his voice captured on a page from the senior yearbook of Memaw's second youngest sister, Aunt Carolyn. It's only a photo of what he wrote, emailed to me by a cousin after I asked if she had any old pictures of my grandparents. The yearbook is dated

1932, when Pepaw and Memaw were still dating. It's filled with page after page of limericks and jokes from a host of friends and relatives. Aunt Dorothy, for example, inscribes a sports chant diagonally across the page, boasting of the girls' varsity basketball championship. For her part, Memaw, only nineteen at the time, writes, "In your slide down the banister of life, may you never hit a splinter." It's signed "Miss Ruby Vernell Hamner."

Next to all this wit and sports braggadocio, Pepaw's contribution is self-deprecating and apologetic, perhaps too much so. In an angular, almost feminine cursive he writes: "Very dum on Tuesdays, not bright on any other day, always think of dumbskull when your mind is about for Buddie. Robert Lenward Gibbs."

***

I could summarize my grandfather's life like this: Robert Lenward Gibbs was a handsome, charismatic man who was also an alcoholic. Whenever he drank, he'd lose whatever work he'd managed to procure and disappear. His wife would move away with her sons, find a job of her own, and try to support the family. He would come back with a few wild ideas about how to get rich by patenting this invention or that and then end up drunk in the recliner in front of the television. This happened over and over again, until everyone simply stopped trying. He was never a real father, never managed to support his family emotionally or financially or physically or spiritually. He probably silently hated himself. When he died, he was living in a cheap hotel near his mother and had been depending on her for several years.

Of course, this summary applied to my own father as well, without changing a word. He must have been acutely aware of this, how the pieces of his own life were slowly coming together as he got older to form a duplicate of his dad's, the very man he'd spent his childhood resenting and running from and beating half to death. I think back on everything that led up to Memaw's attempt to kidnap me as a toddler, how Dad threw my mother from the kitchen, how my brother came at him with a bat, the shattered lightbulb. Things were coming full circle. He was physically attacking his wife. Her son was coming to her aid. His face was bleeding as his father's had. He must have seen the storm gathering. Did he look at me and wonder if the same darkness would swallow me? By then, running to his mother was like fulfilling a prophecy. It was what fate required of him to repeat of the first Robert Lenward's life. This was the curse; this was the way whatever spirit loomed over my family worked. Had I spoken to this thing that night over the Ouija board in Japan? Or was all that just crackpot fantasy, the ideomotor effect revealing what I knew with my subconscious? Do I have some similar doom in store? It had said my father was eating grass and that I would eat grass as well.

This is what's on my mind In Istanbul after the Halloween conversation with Stephen and Ned at the pub. Ned's wife has a spirit attached to her family, which means others believe this sort of thing, too. Maybe it's a worldwide belief, transcending culture, and there's some universal truth to all these tales and legends, something people in this centuries-old country know that we've forgotten or dismissed.

I make a list of questions for Ned to ask his father-in-law about the jinn that haunts them. It takes about a week, but he meets me in the hallway outside my classroom one day with a few pages of notes.

"Well, it took a while," he announces, "but I finally got the story out of my father-in-law. I asked the questions you gave me, but he kept going off on tangents about sin and the Quran. After, like, thirty minutes I'd have to re-ask only to get a similar runaround. It was exhausting."

"So, what did you find out?" I press.

He reads from a notebook.

"So, the jinn's name is Esma, and she is taller and thinner than a human being, with long arms and splayed feet. He also says she has 'slanted eyes.'"

"Uh oh. You just said her name."

"I know."

"I thought that was a no-no."

"Well," Ned says, raising a professorial finger. "Here is where I was mistaken. It seems Esma is a good jinn. You see, there are good ones and evil ones, just like there are with people, and a whole group of them have apparently converted to Islam and taken Muslim names. Esma only appears when a child is in danger. He told a story about how his sister was breastfeeding one day and fell asleep on top of the baby. She nearly smothered it, but something kicked her in the back, and she woke up. When she turned around, she saw Esma standing there staring at her. So, when Oya saw the jinn in her dream, everyone thought that it was trying to warn her about Julia, not that it was going to do something to her. Now, as to your first question about how she became tied to the family, he says his father somehow invited it from the spirit world and that it was working for him."

"So, it moves through the generations!"

"Yes. And it only follows his father's direct descendants and will do so until the last one is dead."

"So, it will follow *your* daughter, too."

"I suppose. He also says that everyone gets a jinn at birth, kind of like a guardian angel. He hears him whisper things in his head whenever he's trying to solve puzzles, for example. I don't know where he gets all this stuff, by the way, if it's based on folklore, the Quran, or if he's just making it up on the fly. He's a bit eccentric." Ned turns a page in his notebook. "About the evil jinn, he says that they can possess you or curse you, bringing all sorts of trauma and bad luck. You usually invite them by committing a great sin, like rape or murder."

My mind goes immediately to John Henry Williams. It makes so much sense, a brutal murder called down an evil spirit. "You're an idiot," I chide myself, even as I write Ned's explanations down. It's ridiculous, of course, yet I can't help but wonder. You can call these spirits by committing a great sin, and we had been complicit in one of our country's greatest crimes. Perhaps some sort of spiritual stain lingered, the past itself resurrected as a vengeful fury. Maybe it hovered over us, still.

When I first went to Delal's grandfather's village, the summer we were married, I was toted around to the neighbors' houses where I would dazzle them with a few phrases in Kurdish. They would display effusive delight at my efforts, tickled that a foreigner had taken the time to learn anything in their mother tongue, a language once forbidden by law.

Then one day, on Dede's balcony, we were all chatting over tea. Dede was there, as were Delal and her Aunt Cemile. Dede and I were talking about fathers, and I was trying to tell him about mine, but I was finding it difficult to decide what exactly to say. What would this ninety-year-old Kurdish gentleman, a man who had worked hard all his life, a man revered by everyone in the region for his industry, make of Bob Gibbs, the alcoholic who rarely worked and ended his own life on a train track? At some point, I noticed that no one was listening to me anymore but rather looking at something behind me. I turned to find Aunt Cemile with her hand hovering just over my arm. She was whispering something and compulsively yawning. Over and over again, her mouth heaved open until finally she staggered from the balcony and collapsed on a bench in the kitchen with her head in her hands.

"You all right?" Delal asked, following her aunt inside.

"There's something on him," she said. "A *nazar*, an evil eye, something."

Delal laughed, "Aunt Cemile!"

"I recited some verses from the Quran, but whatever-it-is is powerful. You shouldn't take him around and let him speak Kurdish all the time. People jinx him, and that jinx sticks to him."

"Jinx? But I thought they were happy I spoke Kurdish," I said.

"Some are, but it's painful for others. You're speaking a language they've never been safe to speak."

And so, this historical sin the Turks committed against the Kurds gathered against me, a stranger, as a *nazar*. It made me think of the many black men and women my ancestors had come in contact with, how blithely and in some cases, unconsciously, we may have tormented them. In particular, I thought again of John Henry. Where did the terrible energy of that sin gather? I wondered if Aunt Cemile sensed something besides the local evil eye, something much older I'd brought from home, a hex or a curse or a retribution.

I looked over, and she was still yawning.

ELEVEN

It's a late Istanbul spring, 2019. This afternoon, a Friday, as I and everyone else in the English office are packing up to go home, a 7th grader appears at our office door. It's a boy named Ayhan, a student I have never taught but whom I know well from numerous encounters in the hallway. He is funny, bright, and almost certainly on the autism spectrum. He reminds me of many of my own eccentric friends and relatives, and perhaps he senses a kindred spirit somewhere in my reserved-teacher persona because he's often coming up to me to explain his latest wacky idea, or else, to ask a question about relativity, the role of religion in society, or more often than not, the Cold War. Most recently he stopped me at lunch wanting to know if I thought a peaceful uprising of students against the school administration could be justified if the rebels implemented Marxist principles. The next question followed before I had time to process the first: if I were a "kind of booze," what would I be?

"I'd be Kentucky bourbon," he announces proudly. "Nothing fancy. Just a clean shot of Jim Beam." Why a Turkish twelve-year-old identifies with a bottle of Appalachian whiskey, I'll never know. In any case, that's Ayhan.

So, he appears at our office door looking distraught, nervously pushing up his glasses by wrinkling his nose. Six weary English teachers look up. He's blocking the exit, and it's been a long week.

"What's the problem, Ayhan?" I ask.

"I need to speak to Mr. Rands."

It appears my colleague, his actual English teacher, confiscated his iPad earlier in the day because Ayhan was playing games during a lesson. Normally, we would keep it overnight, which in this case, being Friday, meant the whole weekend.

"See you on Monday," Mr. Rands says.

"But it's crucial for my homework," Ayhan protests. "I have a lot to catch up on."

"Like I said, see you on Monday, Ayhan." Mr. Rands puts in his earbuds and waves Ayhan away.

"Oh sure, I'll survive just fine without my iPad!" Ayhan shouts petulantly, throwing up his hands, then adds as he's storming out the door, "Although the school might want to remember, I still have a noose under my bed."

Six weary teachers perk up.

"What did you say?" asks Ms. Martin, the woman who sits across from me.

Ayhan, always obliging, repeats his statement.

"You're not serious, are you?" She stands.

"All I'm saying is, it's there, waiting. Remember Halloween?"

On Halloween, Ayhan showed up dressed in black with lines drawn up and down both arms in red marker. He had a noose hanging around his neck and carried an empty bottle of pills. When I passed his locker, he whirled around suddenly and pulled up the rope so that it tightened around his neck. "I'm dressed as a depressed adolescent," he announced proudly.

That explains the noose.

"If you're serious," Ms. Martin says, "then I need to call a counselor."

Ayhan squeezes his eyes closed and starts breathing heavily, exaggeratingly puffing out his cheeks. His face is getting red. I know an outburst is coming.

"Of course, I'm not serious!" he shouts. "What's wrong with you people?"

"Look," Ms. Martin says, "you can't threaten suicide and expect me to just let you go."

"Oh my God! It was a joke. Any moron would know that."

"Excuse me?"

"Just let me go! You're making everything worse!"

There's something so familiar about the panicked way he starts to push at the crowd of adults gathering around him, eyes still pressed shut. I know he's joking, but there's a protocol.

I phone the counselor. At the sight of her, he starts to wail. "Oh God, have you all gone nuts!"

"Listen," the counselor says. "Just calm down."

"Why are you all acting like there's something wrong with me?" A wall of grown-ups surrounds him now, closing in. His voice has a note of high-pitched despair. "There's nothing wrong with me! There's nothing wrong with me!"

I have this urge to take Ayhan aside, get him to a private room and say, "Look, someone I love killed themselves. You're making a joke about it, maybe, but even the off chance that you're a little bit serious scares the hell out of me!"

He is whisked away in a flurry of adult panic, still crying, toward the counselor's office. He looks overpowered, outnumbered. I put my hands over my face. I don't know why. It's automatic. I'm not crying or embarrassed. I just have this overwhelming urge to hide, to not see, not know, not witness. I keep my eyes closed on the bus ride home. I want everyone to think I'm asleep. I don't want anything disturbing the flood of memories now pouring out of the blackness. I see for some reason an empty sunlit room with a flat gray carpet. Someone is moving in. Us? There's a kitchen at the far end of a hall and cigarette burns in the orange linoleum floor. A voice says, "This will do; this will do." At first, I don't remember anything more about the place, when or why I was there. Where is this? The answer hangs back in the dark.

***

I cannot speculate on curses that pass from generation to generation without mentioning drinking, and whenever I talk about my dad's alcoholism, there's one period in our lives that springs to mind first, not chronologically, mind you, but rather first in terms of explaining most clearly what our family dynamic was when Dad got drunk.

But let me set the stage.

It was the summer before fourth grade, and my parents had decided to get back together one more time. It had been almost two years since the last attempt in Fairbanks. Dad still maintained that living in Lakeland would drag him back into the past—repeating his mantra that it carried too many painful memories—and so again, my mom and I agreed to move to where he was in north Florida, where a more powerful past lived in the forms of his mother and brother.

I remember a tremendous optimism as the three of us drove around searching for a place to live. We looked in Melrose, Keystone, Earleton, always keeping near the family, near Memaw and Uncle Gene, Aunt Nancy and Karin. We wanted a house on the water—Dad still had his Scorpion—but could we afford it? He had landed a job at a car dealership in Gainesville and talked confidently about commissions and promotions. We were going to be raking in the cash, he assured us, and so I gave an enthusiastic yes to every trailer, house, and shack we looked at as long as it came with a lake, guardedly hopeful we were putting our little family back together.

We decided, finally, on a Quonset hut sitting on a canal off of big Lake Santa Fe, just outside the town of Melrose. The hut was basically a commodious tube of corrugated steel created for the Navy in World War II, a storm pipe with rooms. The owner had procured it wholesale from the naval base in Jacksonville where Dad used to watch air-craft carriers roll out to sea as a boy. Some of the salient features of this "metal garage"—as delineated by its manufacturer, Steel Master USA—were that it could be "shipped anywhere, easily bolted together, and assembled or disassembled without skilled labor."

The Quonset had a few other things going for it as well. Mom liked the cheap rent. Dad, I think, saw a clever joke in the whole experiment. Paying to live in discarded surplus military scrap somehow exemplified his view of America.

"It's like this scene in *Catch-22*," he told me, "where Milo Mindbender, the black market wheeler-dealer, buys all the Egyptian cotton just because it's cheap. And of course, he can't get rid of it. It's wartime, who needs cotton?"

"What's *Catch-22*?" I asked.

"Only the greatest book on earth. Anyway, Milo's a clever scoundrel, and normally, he can sell anything, but this stumps him for a bit. Then, with his ironclad faith in the stupidity of his fellow man, he starts peddling a new delicacy, chocolate-covered cotton. Basically, son, we're going to live in the real-estate equivalent of chocolate-covered cotton."

At age nine, I had not yet read Dad's favorite novel to test the accuracy of this scene, but he talked about it all the time. Heller's vision confirmed his own basic view of American humanity. Dad was a committed cynic. He maintained that everyone in the US fell into one of two groups. The first were those who had managed to get rich—a crass gang of carpetbaggers and snake-oil salesmen. The second were those who hadn't and remained the hapless victims of the first, dupes because of their hopeless vulgarity. The type of people, on the one hand, who could get rich by selling storm drains as homes and the type of person that bought them on the other.

I belonged squarely to this second group. I loved the Quonset hut. It was so utterly bizarre. After the owner gave us the tour, I argued vociferously in its favor before we were out of the driveway, talking enthusiastically over my parents' minor doubts. It was round and had a dock! What more could they want?

The deciding factor for Dad was the waterfront, which meant, of course, he could sail. We called it a canal, but that word denotes an artificial waterway like the one leading off the little lake to Lake Alto. Nobody here had dug a thing. It was a natural marshy finger of Santa Fe that snaked back through a wall of cypress trees to form a blackwater inlet. The only adjustment made by human beings had been the clearing of swamp plants to maintain an easy passage to the big lake. This had to be done periodically, as the dense patchwork of banana lilies and spatterdock ceaselessly crept back to create a quilt of green that was a perfect hiding place for gators. They slid into the middle of the canal around sunset, floating on the black surface like logs.

And so, we settled in.

I started fourth grade at Melrose Elementary, a public school this time, no more private academies trying to weasel out of integration. The buildings were old compared to my tidy, modern red-brick school in Lakeland. The gym dated back to 1882, I was told. It was huge, spacious, and made of wood, the slats outside painted pea green. Basketballs echoed like grenades on the polished maple floor. I could see scratches and scuffs beneath the latest layer of lacquer, relics of a century of kids before me. We'd had no gym in my old school, just a sandy field of crabgrass and asphalt poured sometime in the 60s, so this oldness was all new.

A word about the two towns—Lakeland and Melrose. They were founded at nearly the same time, in the decades right after the Civil War, so whatever past I felt in one should have been evident in the other, but they occupied entirely different slices of time. Subjectively, at least. Perhaps each town was a reflection of my parents. My mother, the transplant from West Virginia, had been a little too wild and scandalous for her small Appalachian town. She'd bounced furiously against its borders until she'd broken through. When Mom flunked out of college for partying too hard and then took up with a boy no one approved of, my Grandma Hodges had decided to whisk her wayward daughter to Florida where she could start fresh. Mom burst into Lakeland, a storm set free, full of excitement, ready to build a new life and a new self among other immigrants intent on the same. My father, on the other hand, was forever retreating into the dark waters of his rural home no matter how many times life cast him onto shore. One embraced the world, the other built defenses against it.

While living in Lakeland, life seemed very bright, focused on the future. We were close enough to Cape Canaveral to go outside as a class during a launch and see rockets blazing up into space through the tropical sky. I'd watched both Voyager 1 and Voyager 2 start their journeys to the outer planets on a ball of fire in first grade. I witnessed the first space shuttle go up in 5th grade. Lakeland was more cosmopolitan, too, closer to the Caribbean culture of south Florida with a population forever in flux from the constant flow of tourists and "snowbirds," Yankees and Canadians who sojourned in Florida for the winter. Before we moved, my mom had been working at the Boy's and Girl's Club of Lakeland, headquartered in the traditionally "black" side of town. I used to go to the club every day after school and join the field trips, make something in the art room or play pool. One of her coworkers was a New York Jew, and all the rest were black. At Crystal Lake, my elementary school, I'd had classmates with parents or grandparents from Turkey, Italy, China, Puerto Rico. Our art teacher was Jamaican. My best friend was my neighbor Kevin, the son of an Irishman from Rhode Island. The students in Melrose, in contrast, were all Southern white, monotone, children of families who had lived in the town since its founding.

I have blips and fragments of memory from this time.

I am sitting bored in math class as my red-headed teacher explains three-digit addition and subtraction, something I mastered two years before. Sunlight pours through the window, filling the room with gold. "Carry the two," the teacher says, and I roll my eyes. I can't remember her name. I remember the name of every teacher I've ever had, all the way back to Mrs. Hawkins in kindergarten, but not this woman's. I think sometimes that Melrose itself is deleting bytes of my own memory, blotting out all evidence of my existence there as if I am an invasive outsider that has to be purged. My aunt and cousins often forget I was ever present. They explain places I already know, tell stories I experienced firsthand, introduce people I've already met. I can't blame them. Dad was always on the outside of the family, and I on the outside of him.

Ms. Mallone. The red-headed teacher's name just popped into my head.

Another scene. I'm in a tiny room drawing images on a blank film strip with a blue wax pencil. I think it's the storage closet for AV equipment. I'm composing a sequel to *The Wizard of Oz*, and this is "gifted class." I get taken out once a day and am the sole kid in the program. Lunch is the only available hour, and so I eat alone with my teacher after whatever activity she's chosen.

Another. I am standing shivering along the side of the highway with a red bell in my hand and a small mallet. It's just before Christmas break. My breath comes out in a cloud of white frost. We're performing Carol of the Bells, and I am waiting to strike my B natural. I'm in chorus, this is our outdoor holiday concert, and my parents are somewhere in the crowd of onlookers, both of them, for the first time in my life. At least, I think they're both there. I have doubts about Dad for some reason. Things are starting to unravel. He's drinking again. I found a half-empty bottle of vodka in the cabinet over the refrigerator the other night. I hadn't told my mother. I'm staring at the bell, listening for my cue.

Last, I am standing on the curb of the school drive watching kid after kid climb in a car with their parents and pull away. Dad is supposed to come get me, but he hasn't shown up yet. He's never been late before. Next to me is a short black woman in a pretty dress. She's the teacher on duty today, and it's her job to make sure we all get home safely.

"Who's coming to get you?" she asks.

As soon as she voices the question, I realize that no one is.

"My dad," I answer.

"What kind of car does he drive?" She peers out toward the gate as if he might be pulling in that very second.

"You know what?" I say. "I forgot. Today is the day I'm supposed to walk home."

"How far do you live?"

I hesitate, my stomach knotting. I know she's not going to let me go unless it's according to the rules. I know her idea of "safe" is not going to fit with what I've got in mind. If she'll just leave me alone, I think I can manage this without causing a bigger scene.

"Oh, it's only a mile."

"Which direction?"

"It's very close."

"But which way?"

I'm too obedient to lie. I tell her I live on the outskirts of town off Highway 26. As soon as it comes out of my mouth, I know how crazy it sounds. My mom dealt with kids all the time in Lakeland, first as a PE teacher and then as manager of the Boys and Girls Club. She used to tell stories about neglectful or abusive parents and how the kids tried to hide it but were so clumsy in their efforts that it was painfully obvious what was really going down. She'd tell me about taking this boy or girl to the counselor to persuade them to spill the tragic story of their dysfunctional families, so they could get the help they needed. We'd shake our heads together in pity and dismay. I have to make it clear to this woman that I am not one of those kids. There's nothing wrong with me. No, ma'am.

"Look, I walk it all the time," I tell her, and then idiotically add, "There's a huge ditch next to the highway. I always make sure to stay on the side away from traffic."

The front of the school is empty now of everyone but us, no straggling teacher, no student or parent. The seconds drag by like hours.

"Where's your mother?"

"At work."

"Why don't we go inside and call her?"

Somehow, what most embarrasses me is not being forgotten by my father, but this teacher having to stay with me past her normal work hours. I want to apologize as she starts guiding me to the principal's office. She'll hate me after this. Her voice is soft, like she's trying to keep me calm. She's being so careful and kind, but I know how kindness works up here from Memaw, who calls you "darling" and "honey" and drowns you in kisses, then seconds later moves just out of sight, into the kitchen or her bedroom, say, to cuss and rage, "You're a goddamn fat, selfish leech, taking everything she owns, etcetera etcetera." Out of sight, but never out of hearing because she wants you to know; that's the whole point of the show.

The teacher is leading me by the hand, asking if I know my mom's work number. I don't. Do I know the name of the place she works? She can look it up in the phone book. "All the way in Gainesville," I say, "at Shands Hospital, near the university." This is at least forty minutes away. This woman will be forced to sit with me that whole time. I can see this awareness settle into her expression. *Look lady, just go home and let me walk. Nobody needs to know*, I think. As we disappear into the principal's office, I steal one last look back at the school entrance, hoping to see Dad's car, but I know what's happened. He's drunk, at home, or maybe at a bar somewhere passed out.

The office is chilly, air-conditioned. There's no need for a phonebook as the number is in my file. The school secretary is helping her—one reads out the digits as the other one dials. They keep glancing up at me, but my eyes roam the room, trying to look bored and inconvenienced, like all this is a colossal waste of time.

***

I don't remember anything after this, but it's a piece of the past which has had a direct and undeniable impact on my behavior. When I get stood up now, it's like a curtain goes up and I relive this entire scene. I stand on that drive with that teacher, the school empty of people, and forty years after the fact, feel a rage at whomever has abandoned me all out of proportion to the crime. No other neurosis has such an obvious, direct origin.

Robert Lenward Sr. abandoned his son many times, vanishing into jails or on drinking binges for months. Only now does it really hit me how strange Dad's choice of Melrose was. He was a man who had avoided naming his newborn son Robert Lenward the Third for fear of tying him to a doomed past. Why, then, just eight years later, would he move that son and wife straight into the very past he was afraid of repeating? Why did he compulsively need to be near the mother who controlled him and the brother he hated, his own childhood family he described with corrosive bitterness? Could the "painful memories" of Lakeland really compare?

This is why I keep coming back to a curse. It was like his foot was caught in a trap. He couldn't wriggle free of whatever misery bound him to Memaw and Uncle Gene, and so we'd had to come to him. I have mentioned my sense of foreboding when I would arrive at Memaw's house on little Lake Santa Fe. I remember our Quonset hut on the canal with the same feeling. No matter the lake, the boat, the fun semicircular house, something needed exorcising there. Fallen angels, old shades of murders past, or just spoiled memories, I don't know, but it was palpable. It had its hands on us every move we made.

***

It turns out that last scene of the teacher calling my mother from school is not quite true.

I didn't know it wasn't when I wrote it. The phone call has always seemed the logical end to all the teacher's questions about where my mother worked, and so I never dwelled on its accuracy. I want to take you through the process of how I found out the real ending just as I did with my first memory because it once again shows how random the reassembly of the past can be, all the interference and avoidance and occasionally, the final epiphany.

I call my mom after writing the section about school in Melrose. She's staying for a few weeks in Birmingham with my nephew, Jeremy, and his girlfriend.

"Your Grandma Hodges is here," she announces, "sitting on the fence."

She's referring to a cardinal. She's outside on the porch, having her morning coffee and "watching for my redbirds," which she claims are the spirits of the dead come back to visit. She saw it on Facebook, apparently. I ask her what she did for work when we lived in Melrose. It's a pesky detail I want clarified.

"I worked at the hospital," she says.

"That much I know. I mean, what did you do there?"

"Well, Shands had a lot of different branches. My job was to call the residents and tell them which one to go to and when they were expected. They didn't like hearing from me, I'll tell you that. They could get downright hateful. I did *not* like that job. I ended up getting fired, though I don't remember why."

"Maybe it was because of that time you had to leave early and pick me up from school," I suggest.

"I don't remember that," she says.

"You don't remember when Dad forgot me?"

"That wasn't a very happy time," she says. "I can't stand all the dogs."

It takes me a second to adjust to the non-sequitur. "What dogs?"

"Jeremy's Great Dane for one. Just a big old horse that thinks he's a lap dog."

"Dozer?"

"And that friend of his from next door, the mutt. They keep coming up on the porch and getting into my coffee. Jeremy doesn't feed him right. You can see his ribs. Ain't that right, Dozer?" There's a pause where I assume she's scratching the dog's head. "You want to talk to Jeff, Dozer? Say hi."

"Mom," I prod. "Did you get fired because of coming to get me?"

"I don't remember coming to get you. What I do remember is the letter of dismissal I got from that old bat that was my boss. 'We would like to inform you we no longer need your services as of such and such date.' Your daddy was fit to be tied. He—and I can still see him doing this, just as clear as day—he put that letter flat on the kitchen table and started scribbling on it with a red pencil, correcting all the commas and periods." She laughs, and a note of pride creeps into her voice, something I never hear when she discusses my father. "He went to town on that letter, boy. He crossed out words he thought were misused and wrote the proper ones. By the time he was finished, it looked like fireworks were flying off the page. 'Big shots,' he grumbled. 'Think they are so high and mighty, yet they can't even compose a sentence in English.' He told me I was to take this 'first draft,' with all his corrections, put it in my boss' hands, and tell her it was from him. Well, I couldn't do it. I was too scared. No, now that's not true. I did do it. But I waited till the end of my two-weeks' notice and ran out of the office."

She sighs.

"But I don't ever remember him forgetting you or having to come get you. Are you sure you aren't making that up for this thing you're writing? To have a little drama?"

"Absolutely."

"He did forget *me* once. In the hospital. I was having an operation, a minor one that I didn't even have to stay overnight for, and he didn't come pick me up. I remember someone else had to take me home, someone who had nothing to do with nothing. I don't remember who, just that I was thinking this person had no business doing this for me, and when I got back, he was passed out on the couch, dead drunk."

And it's after this story that the true ending to the school scene pops into my mind. I'm alone with the teacher. She's asking me if I know my mother's number, and I see Dad pulling in at last. He's in a tan car. He doesn't look at me, just throws open the door and stares straight ahead with that pouty scowl he wears when he's been drinking. It's like he knows what I've assumed happened and is offended by the thought. I get in the car, and he says without prompting, "I was taking a nap and overslept." I sniff at the air, testing it for that sour smell of liquor. Should he even be driving? The teacher closes the car door. I look up at her and smile, to let her know that I'm all right, that she can just go ahead and get lost, wondering if she'll sense it, if she'll stop me from riding home with a drunk. I don't smell anything, and he seems fine. But I know. After a while, you just know.

***

One of my biggest complaints about our home on the inlet was loneliness. There was no one to play with. Before moving to Melrose, we'd lived with my mom's mother, Grandma Hodges, on Hampton Avenue in Lakeland. Grandma's street was teeming with kids. Kevin, who was my age, lived to the right of us with his father Mack, and the girls, Serena and Sonia, lived on the left with their parents, Judy and Jimmy. A rotating cast of kids was in the other Hampton houses—Belinda, Paul, Stacy, Stevie, Nina, Amber, Sam, Claude. Every evening we played kickball, a game called "Spud," or hide-and-seek and its nighttime variant, Bloody Murder. Sometimes we raced our bikes around the neighborhood with gangs of kids from streets parallel to ours. After our move, my only playmate was Cousin Karin whom we visited on the weekends, as she was a half-hour's drive away in Keystone.

Dad liked this isolation. I did not. Not only were there no other kids at the Quonset, there weren't many houses, period. A few trailers sat off by themselves at the back of large empty fields, the properties sealed off by barbed wire and guarded by hunting dogs. I had a bicycle, but the road in front of our house was sand and impossible to ride on. I had to walk my bike to the turn-off for the paved road, which then ran straight about a hundred yards to the highway with no sidewalk or shoulder. I rode those hundred yards back and forth alone, running into the ditch whenever the occasional automobile passed. Sometimes I fished alone, with the same lack of luck I'd had at the little lake. We had a little sheltie named Laddie for a time, but we had to put him down because of arthritis.

Mom felt sorry for me. Neither of us was built to be recluses. She arranged playdates with a boy named Yuri, the son of a doctor at the hospital where she worked and the doctor's Russian husband. Yuri was slightly younger than me, very thin and very blonde. Both his parents were the refined intellectual type. On summer weekends, I'd spend the day at his house on big Lake Santa Fe. In fact, one of my favorite memories of childhood is of an afternoon with this Russian kid catching tadpoles. It was Yuri's idea. We grabbed bait buckets and roamed the shallows around the cypress knees near shore, scooping up the fat black pollywogs. The water was a bright amber color, the soft lake sand a light gold like French vanilla ice cream. If you remember, I was a wreck of a fisherman because I hated touching worms and fish. When Yuri first suggested a full day of catching slimy things that swam in the water, I was sure I was doomed. I would whine and cringe, fail the 'boy' test and be outed as the sissy I knew myself to be. But to my surprise, I absolutely loved grabbing the little proto-frogs. And I was good at it. My bucket was full when Yuri still barely had two or three. He expressed his admiration, even asked for help. Compared to him, I was the rough-and-tumble local kid, the macho redneck.

Something that struck me about the Russian family was their collective display of orderliness and decorum against our chaos. Outside in the yard, in the middle of a brutal and sweaty Florida summer of mosquitoes, yellow flies, and lake mud, Yuri's mother wore button-down blouses, slacks, and sandals. My mom, even at more formal family events, kicked back barefoot in a T-shirt and shorts. Lunch was a formal affair out on the lawn with a picnic table, tablecloth, and place settings. We were served sandwiches and cucumber slices precisely at noon, with apple quarters for dessert. At our house, we would have grabbed ourselves a Coke and a bag of chips, then shoved the whole mess in our mouths as we waded in the shallows.

I found all the protocol at Yuri's house both baffling and suffocating. Our way was much more fun, and yet I sensed that their order was somehow connected to their stability, that it was a part of the reason they owned a house on a lake with a motorboat and water skis.

Other than Yuri, our only other social outlet was our crazy neighbor, Harry, a Vietnam vet, and his two springer spaniels. He owned a Quonset hut next to ours.

Mom doesn't remember him until I describe the dogs.

"That's right! He's the one with all the prisms. He had about twenty of them hanging in the living room window, and in the afternoon, they cast rainbows everywhere."

An image pops into my head of a shadowed room filled with a dozen glittering crystals.

"He was a bit of a hippy, wasn't he?" I say. "I remember Dad always going off about Harry having a screw loose."

"Well, he didn't work, I remember that. Some injury from Vietnam. I think he was on disability. There was something just...off about him all around, but he was nice enough."

Harry was husky, with a big belly and a thick black beard. He used to sit in the yard under the horse chestnut tree with Dad. They'd have a beer together, and Harry would talk about his boat or auras or the war. His dogs were always at the shoreline, poking their wet noses around in the lake grass. The cinnamon-colored female was called Mariah, but I don't remember the name of the black-spotted male. He disappeared one evening. I remember Harry standing out in the yard whistling for him, his eyes scanning the patch of banana lily near the swamp where the dog loved to swim.

"A gator got him," Harry said. "I just know it."

Harry was a big fan of backgammon and taught all of us to play. In fact, it was thanks to him that I could hold my own when I came to Turkey, where backgammon is almost the national game. We, for our part, taught him Wahoo and all the variations. The four of us would sit up late into the night on weekends, moving marbles and rolling dice. Harry would bring a sixpack of Dad's favorite beer, Milwaukee Lite, for the adults. I'd have sweet tea. One fall night, the four of us were playing Wahoo in the living room when something large struck the screen door. We all jumped. An animal snorted outside, one clearly very large. I saw a gigantic black eye press against the screen, gleaming.

"Bob! Do something!" Mom hissed. Dad was starting to stand just as a cow suddenly pushed open the door and poked her head into the living room. A tentative hoof stepped in.

"Well, shit," Dad said, and at the sound of his voice, the cow lumbered back out of our house and let out a plaintive moo. It became perhaps the sole good memory of that whole Quonset hut experiment.

***

Perhaps it was our great isolation in Melrose that made the visit of my sister and Grandma Hodges so important. They came up for Thanksgiving, and I was so excited I helped my mom clean the whole house the day before their arrival.

I had missed them both intensely. Michele had been my constant companion back in Lakeland. She took me to her softball games, horseback riding at the rodeo stadium, to her cousin's pool. Grandma, for her part, was the grand matron of the family and the epitome of respectability. She had worked all her life, first supporting her mother, her siblings and their kids, then later her daughter and me, and she expected the same industry of everyone, so Dad was a little intimidated by her.

Maybe that's what drove him over the edge. He'd just lost another job and now his hyper-responsible, no-nonsense mountain woman mother-in-law was coming for a visit. She'd never approved of his hobo tendencies, those fateful characteristics passed down from his father.

Here's the scene. My sister, mother, Grandma, and I are in the living room watching television. It's dark, the only light the flashing blue from the TV screen. I look up and catch sight of my dad bumbling down the hall in his boxer shorts. I can tell from the way he lists back and forth and from the telltale pout that he's drunk. He stops in front of the TV, gives us a strange look, then pulls down his pants and squats over the carpet. His eyes flutter, and he turns up his nose slightly, as if realizing he's in the presence of disagreeable riffraff. I look first at the spot under his white ass, wondering if he's really going to do it, shit right there on the floor, and then I look up at the open bathroom door. Just a few more feet and he would have been in the actual toilet. There's another bathroom just down the hall from which he'd come. Why hadn't he gone there? This display is as deliberate as the loud fits of rage his mother indulged in once she left the room you were in. Michele is glaring at him, her eyebrows arched. She's scrunched up in the chair as if she might press herself straight through the back of it. I look at Grandma Hodges, who keeps her eyes on the TV as if she notices nothing, and I take my cue from her. I won't see. I won't be a witness. Her presence fills me with an intense, eviscerating shame. I want to disappear. Eventually, Dad stands, pulls up his pants, and walks back the way he came. The floor is clean, no human shit marring the flat gray carpet.

The flat gray carpet!

This was the memory resurrected in Istanbul by the incident with Ayhan.

Not long after Grandma left, she sent up her neighbor, Mack, to bring us back. Mack brought his son, Kevin, with him. After spending more than half a year in those friendless woods, I was thrilled to see both of them. I showed Kevin the canal, the dock where I fished, Dad's boat.

But we were in a hurry.

Mom packed our suitcases and a few boxes. Dad sat on the front porch in a lawn chair, looking stone-faced at Mack's blue camper parked in his yard, the one that would take his wife and son away. It was sunset. I vividly remember the deep orange sky. Mack sat next to Dad, leaning in and talking a mile a minute about drinking, about getting control of his life, about responsibility. Part of me was relieved to see someone from outside our family bubble breaking in and taking charge. But Mack was an alcoholic, too, and could be very unpleasant. Back in Lakeland, I'd found Kevin outside at night several times, seeking refuge from his father's rages. Once, he'd been lying flat under our car, another time he tapped on my window and asked me to let him in to hide. Mack used to cuss both Kevin and me out sometimes—I'd never heard the words "fuck" and "cunt" before meeting him, and he routinely called us "little faggots" whenever we did something he didn't approve of. My father said Mack was so crude because he was a Yankee. It must have broken Dad to be lectured by such a man and to have that man be in the right. Mack may have drunk himself into oblivion on the weekends, but he kept a job; he kept his family together.

I don't remember hugging Dad when I left. I don't remember saying goodbye or I love you. All I remember is walking into the yard toward the truck when an iron came flying out the window, shattering the glass. It landed with a thump in the yard. Had he thrown it *at* us? There was no other movement or sound, no scream of rage or frustration, no plea for us to come back.

"Just keep walking," Mack said.

I got into the back of the truck, and we drove away, leaving Dad alone in that haunted house with his demons and his whiskey.

***

An unpleasant feeling comes over me as I finish this section. It's like I shouldn't write about these things, not because they are private and embarrassing, but because they are so tawdry. What the hell was I thinking to try to make them into some kind of pretentious literature? There is nothing noble, nothing worth others knowing. I think of that combination of animal pity and contempt people often feel for homeless madmen raving in the streets or lying on the sidewalk wrapped in blankets that reek of piss. I feel that for Dad and for what I was then.

I need to get away; I need refuge. I leave our apartment and start walking. I jump on the metro and venture out into Üsküdar, one of the oldest neighborhoods in Istanbul. I stroll along the blue Bosporus, weaving in and out of simit sellers and kids with kites. It is intensely crowded. More people are here, wandering on this promenade than live in the three towns of Earleton, Melrose, and Keystone combined. I climb the stairs to a seaside cafe. I speak Turkish, order a rose-mint hookah pipe. I read an article on the upcoming election, study a little Kurdish. The cafe sits among a cluster of mosques, and when the ezan sounds, I watch startled swallows take flight and weave among their domes. One of them, the mosque of Mihrimah Sultan, was built in the 1500s, a century before the first Gibbses even set foot on American shores. I am immersed in Turkey, in other, and only then does the feeling mercifully wash off of me, that stench of the backwater Florida, of cheap whiskey and the South.

TWELVE

It's the year 2000, four years after Dad died, and I am a graduate student in Tucson. I work nights and weekends for a company that provides mental health care services at clients' homes. The company is owned and managed by the families of the people it serves: people living with a variety of disabilities and challenges ranging from Down's and schizophrenia to addictions and severe cognitive disabilities. Sometimes it's a combination of several things.

I chose this job specifically because of my father. I've lived with an alcoholic suicide, after all. My dad was a man who might have used this company's services. I figure it's only natural that I now try to help others like him. I have inherited his affinity for the downcast and forgotten, assumed his duty to the world's castoffs. Many of the other people I meet working there fit a similar profile—we have all had loved ones who might benefit from what we do.

I have a dizzying variety of difficult clients my first year, and the take-charge decisiveness required to handle them is not something that comes naturally to me. I'm always letting things slip, not being forceful enough, confident enough, bold enough. One woman is bipolar and struggling with an intellectual disability. She's also a compulsive firebug. One day she swipes a book of matches from the counter of her favorite restaurant, a Love's Truck Stop on Interstate 10, then sneaks out of the house after I put her to bed. I have to track her down, then follow her through neighbors' yards to make sure she doesn't set fire to another dumpster, car, or fence as she apparently did last year. Another client charges out of his house in a rage and breaks a cinder block over his head. We have to rush him to the hospital as blood pours down his face. Still another is in the final stages of Alzheimer's and greets me one afternoon with a butter knife and a death threat.

"I'm going to kill you," he says in both English and Spanish and starts to shuffle slowly forward with the blade extended.

It's a stressful job, and one day I simply stop sleeping. For nearly a week, I don't get a second of rest, and by the end, I honestly fear it might be time to check into a mental hospital and become a client myself. The university counselor suggests the insomnia might be the result of having to be alert all the time at work, ready for anything, and so my supervisor changes my assignment to a fairly-easy house in the Santa Rita foothills, south of the city. My two new clients are men a little younger than me, both working full-time at a landscape company and struggling with mild cognitive disabilities and the behavior issues that go along with them.

I will call them Mitchell and José.

I have the evening shift. My job is to help the manager of the house, a man named Richard, pick up the guys from work, make dinner, and administer the night meds. My first day, I pull into the driveway only to find Mitchell and José already home. Richard greets me at the door and shakes my hand vigorously. "I picked the guys up early today," he explains. Richard is about twenty years older than me with skin weathered and brown from the relentless Arizona sun. He wears a green Michelob trucker hat, a checkered shirt, and sports a scraggly beard. Something about him reminds me of Dad, and then I realize it's the sweet smell of tobacco clinging to his clothes.

Richard introduces me to the guys. José's in the kitchen cleaning out his lunch box, carefully washing each item in the sink—thermos, cup, Tupperware box. He wears a white uniform with the landscape company's logo embroidered in red over the breast. Mitchell has already gone to his room to play video games and has to be coaxed out, then chastised for leaving his work things scattered over the kitchen counter. Mitchell is taller than me, broad-shouldered with a hefty belly and thick, wavy brown hair. He fidgets a lot, scratching his head or rubbing his palms together suddenly while letting out a high-pitched cackle. They both shake my hand warily, refrain from making eye contact. My questions are answered with evasive, clipped yeses and nos.

"The guys have been through a lot of caretakers," Richard says by way of explanation. "They're burned out. That's why they trust me. They know I'll stick around."

It's my first night, so I try to follow Richard's lead. I don't know the guys, after all, and he's been head counselor at the house for over a year. I can tell from the way José and Mitchell joke with Richard that they've established a close bond.

"Mitchell has a bit of an anger problem," Richard tells me while the man in question is boiling water in the kitchen for pasta. It's his turn to prepare dinner. "Ain't that right, Mitchell?"

"Yeah," Mitchell says with a grin as he stares into the pot. He gives his head a violent scratch and steam drifts around his large face.

"We gotta get you a girlfriend," Richard says. "Someone to give you a kiss when you get worked up."

Mitchell lets go of the spoon and claps his hands loudly together. "That'd be sweet."

"José over here," Richard says with a jerk of his thumb toward the other client, "is already a lady killer. He don't need help from an old man like me."

"Richard!" José says, blushing.

"He's even got a girlfriend."

"You do?" I ask.

"I met her at work," he answers shyly, then slips from the room.

After dinner, we go out on the back patio. José likes Kool-Aid, so as a treat, we make a batch of strawberry. We have to sweeten it with Splenda because Mitchell is diabetic. Then we fill four Big Gulp cups to the rim and kick back in our lawn chairs as we gaze down over the desert valley glittering with lights. I crunch on the ice.

"This house is nicer than any I've worked in," I say. "It must have cost a fortune."

"I think someone donated it," Richard says. "But yeah, we like it. Don't we, guys?"

Mitchell and José nod enthusiastically.

"Sometimes quail come up in the yard," José says.

"It's a cakewalk here," Richard says. "The guys have their routine, and they like to stick to it. They're both pretty independent, though, and like I said earlier, Mitchell has trouble managing his anger sometimes. He punched clean through a wall on one occasion, but we've made a lot of progress on that, haven't we, Mitchie?"

"Damn right," says Mitchell.

"I've worked in a lot of houses," Richard continues, "but this is the first one where I actually have friends." He raises his cup. "I love these guys. They're my brothers."

"Yeah, brothers," echoes José, and the three of them touch their plastic cups together.

"The hardest thing about this place," Richard says, taking a sip, "is keeping up with all the meds. They both take about a thousand pills each, and you gotta get it just right, or it can send somebody into a seizure real fast."

"Of course," I say.

Richard has pushed his chair against a corner of the house, and as we talk, I see him reach down, remove a brick from the wall, and take out a bottle of whiskey. There's been another smell hovering about this whole time that I've ignored, one every bit as familiar as tobacco.

"Sometimes it does get stressful here," Richard says, as he pours a draught into his Kool-Aid, then fixes his eyes straight on me. "If you want to call the manager and tattle, go ahead. You'll just lose me the job that lets me support my kid and deprive the guys here of the only stable friend they've ever had. Fuck, I can't even take José to visit his dad because the bastard beats him. Came back covered in bruises last time."

Richard takes a drink, and I look at Mitchell and José, trying to read their faces. They don't seem fazed at all, both still gazing out over the valley. *Maybe it's just a one-time thing,* I think. *Maybe he spikes his drink a little at the beginning of the night to take the edge off.* Even as these thoughts run through my head, I find myself scanning the patio for anywhere else he might hide a bottle, instantly alert; it's an instinctual reaction, and then I am startled out of my inspection by the sight of him reaching over and pouring a swig of whiskey into each of the guys' cups.

"You boys deserve a break," he says. "You worked your asses off today." Then he holds the bottle out to me, gives it a little shake.

"Want some, cowboy?"

"No, thanks," I say.

"You're going to get me fired, aren't you?" he says. "You probably should just go ahead and make the call. What do you think, guys?"

He turns toward José and Mitchell.

"No," they both say in unison.

Richard picks up the cordless phone off the patio table next to his chair. Each house comes with one of these massive battery-powered contraptions.

"Go on. Take it, Miss Priss."

I grab the phone but don't call anyone. "Come on, man," I whisper. "You just said they're on a lot of meds. You don't know how that could interact with alcohol."

"Drink up, guys," he says, sitting back with a laugh. "This guy's not calling anybody."

I should do exactly what he's taunting me to do; I know. But there's a feeling building in my gut, one that I haven't felt in a long time. I can almost hear it, like an old machine being dragged out of the closet and plugged in, the rev and hum of the motor. Lights flicker on, and I am again the little boy sitting in the chair as his dad squats in front of his grandmother to take a shit, the kid waiting to be picked up from school and lying to the teacher charged with taking care of him, the boy who finds the bottle in the woods after months of his father's supposed abstinence and puts it right back in its place. Pretend nothing is happening. Cover your eyes. Wait for the storm to pass and try to manage the worst of the damage yourself. And so, within an hour, all three of them are drunk, and we are racing down Golf Links Road in the company jeep, Richard at the wheel with Mitchell in the passenger seat while José and I sit in the back, me eyeing the speedometer's needle as it whips past eighty. We've stopped by a liquor store to pick up a case of beer, and now, according to Richard, we are headed to a strip joint to get everyone laid. Mitchell is cheering out the front passenger-side window, belting out celebratory hoots and hammering the side of the door with the flat of his hand, but José, who is with me in the back, starts to cry.

"I don't wanna go to a strip joint," he says. "I have a girlfriend."

"Don't cockblock your roommate," Richard says and takes a swig of beer. "We gotta get Mitchell a girl before his balls explode!" He swerves into the right lane and sends a car there bouncing onto the shoulder.

"You shouldn't be driving!" José protests.

"Relax. Have I ever let you guys down?"

"Yeah," echoes Mitchell. "Has he ever let us down?"

We zip through a red light. It's at this point that José looks at me, his eyes begging me to act, and something finally clicks. I take the phone I have never let go of and make the call I should have made hours before. Richard glares at me from the rearview mirror as I explain what's happening to the supervisor.

"Where are you?" the supervisor asks, instantly alarmed.

"I don't know exactly," I answer. "Heading into the south side."

"How much has Richard had?"

"I'm not sure. But the guys have been drinking, too."

"What! Why the hell didn't you call earlier? Don't you know how dangerous that is with their meds? What the fuck were you thinking?"

"I'm sorry."

"Tell Richard to stop the car, then you drive them home. If you can't get him to do it, call me back and I'll tell him myself. Otherwise, I'll meet you at the house."

I hang up.

"Stop the car," I tell Richard. To my incredulous relief, he obeys and climbs compliantly into the seat where I was just seconds before. I expect him to try and turn the guys against me, to run off perhaps, but once things are in motion, his will seems to collapse. It's like he's gotten exactly what he's been after the whole time. He stares straight ahead, a haughty scowl on his face like the world is against him and he's just proven it again. I've seen the same expression so many times on my father.

"Thought I'd finally caught a break," he tells me as we pull into the driveway. "And here you went and fucked it all up."

Let me be clear. I do not feel guilty in the least for getting Richard fired. I do feel guilty for letting him put Mitchell and José in danger, for letting myself fall into old patterns, for still acting like a passive victim. He so precisely mimicked Dad's worst behavior that I switched into a kind of autopilot. The past isn't past. The programming is very much intact, and I am helpless against it. The company is staffed by people like me, however, and my supervisor is more than understanding.

"I want to apologize for yelling at you when you called," he says after Richard has been hauled off by the police and the guys are in bed. "It was your first night in a house you didn't know, and you had a lot of shit to deal with. You were the outsider and the one in control was a fuck-up."

"I just feel so bad."

"Richard's been in jail before. He'll weather it fine."

"I was talking about the guys."

And then he says something that catches me totally by surprise.

"You should know both José and Mitchell were impressed with you. Both of them said you handled things exactly as you should have."

"I don't see how."

"You have a quality that I think, in the long term, works out well in a job like this where you have to walk into a stranger's home and take over. You don't immediately judge and impose your own will. You get a feel for how things already are and try to jibe with that. It's something that works well with the guys. You respect them. They see that, and they trust you."

I blush. I can't quite understand the compliment. Something that I long believed was a debilitating and irredeemable character flaw might actually be useful? A wild hope that my experiences with my father might serve a purpose led me to work at the company in the first place. Maybe I hadn't been so naive. Maybe I was right.

The next night, I go to a local shrine in downtown Tucson called "El Tiradito," the little castoff. It sits in what was once the Old Barrio in a pocket of sacred space near the convention center, hidden among the small-city clutter of restaurants, billboards, and bus stops. I walk down a sidewalk underneath the glare of sodium lamps and then turn left to see a patch of quiet darkness gathered over the burnt ruins of an old Spanish mission. The rubble is illuminated with candlelight. Sometimes there are hundreds of candles, sometimes just a dozen. Most are votives, in tall glass containers adorned with pictures of Jesus, his heart bared and radiating red light, or else Mary in brightly-colored robes surrounded by flowers. The air is filled with the scents of wax and roses. The candles have tiny pictures sitting among them. Other photos are pushed into cracks in the adobe, face after face of loved ones lost to suicide, jail, addiction, accident. Some have just disappeared. My father was, of course, all those things at one point or another.

The shrine is named after a sinner, a young man who, in the 1870s, had an affair with his mother-in-law and was murdered on this very spot, chopped into pieces by his father-in-law with an ax. The church refused to bury him on sacred ground, and so his lover placed him where he fell. He became the unofficial martyr to all those abandoned by the official powers-that-be, to all the strays and outsiders, and the shrine itself a symbol, in a way, of how much we can love the damaged and the lost. It reminds me of my father's burial place; of the sneaky backdoor way I had done it. Of the fuck-the-world defiance I felt.

I buy a candle from a convenience store on the way to the shrine. I climb the back wall and set it at the highest point before lighting it, then scramble back down, igniting older candles that have gone out. There's a legend that only those whose candles burn all night get their prayers answered, and I want to help out my fellow children of castoffs. El Tiradito is also known as a wishing shrine. If you come with a forgiving heart, it says on the Tucson Museum's website, you will pass through the ruins unscathed by the spirits here and may even have your wish fulfilled. If not, then you may invoke the sins that bring you and begin an endless cycle of history repeating itself. Standing before the dozens of candle flames, I whisper a prayer for Dad, asking that he be at peace, that whatever spirits there are in the world show mercy on him. Then I add a prayer for Richard. I say I forgive him and ask to be free of whatever weakness might lurk inside my own soul.

***

The past replays on large and small scales, over generations or over the course of a year, in a society, or in the life of one individual who just can't break a habit. That's partly what history is, really, addictive behavior, compulsion. It's why we repeat it as countries and as individuals, so stupidly and open-eyed. It turns us into automatons, like the Jeff Gibbs riding helplessly in the back of the drunk's jeep, though he was a full-grown man and had the power to stop the whole nightmare. Dad had conditioned Mom and me to keep living the same catastrophe with the same dumbstruck helplessness, over and over again, first the gasp of wonder, as at the launch of some experimental rocket, followed by an explosion and the rain of radioactive debris into the ocean and all the crushing disappointment. And yet we gathered for every attempt, watched the sky anxiously and felt surprised every time we saw the ball of flame.

How to explain those explosions? Where was the black box?

Back on that first day I met Uncle Clark and Cousin Lisa, the day I was so hopeful to gain some brief insight into my father's life from a man close to him before I was even born, alcoholism was one of the first things mentioned.

"Bob certainly liked to drink," Clark said with the same exaggerated scowl of distaste I had often seen on Memaw's face, the "Hamner snarl." I pressed him a little. Had Dad always drunk too much? When had it started?

"I don't know," Clark says.

"Well, do you remember him getting drunk a lot when you two were hanging out?"

He shakes his head. "My memory is so shot I barely remember why I'm sitting here. He just drank! That's all."

The drinking is as inexplicable as the suicide—without cause or logic. That's the impression I get.

Later, as we're touring the countryside, Clark will point out a trailer and tell me that it belonged to his Uncle Sleepy.

"Uncle Sleepy?" I ask.

"That was your memaw's brother, Carlton. He liked himself a nip or two. People found him passed out in all sorts of places, so he got the nickname Sleepy Hamner. Sometimes when he went on one of his benders, his wife would call up Uncle Russel, the youngest brother and a cop, and she'd have him keep Sleepy down at the jail till he dried out."

"Aunt Nancy said that Memaw's mom, Miss Linnie, used to keep a little whiskey flask under her mattress that she referred to as her 'medicine,'" I say.

"And I remember Grandmama saying her Grandaddy Bridges was rather wild, too," Lisa adds from the driver's seat. "Someone told him once, and I can't forget this, 'I'll blast your teeth out the back of your skull.' And apparently, that's just how he died."

I asked Dad myself once, in a letter I wrote from Japan, how his alcoholism had started. I made sure to preface it with lots of reassuring words about how I loved him either way, everyone had their faults, I didn't think it was a big deal and didn't feel at all damaged by it, etcetera etcetera. He wrote back what I thought was a disappointing and superficial answer: "In my late twenties," he said, "I went to lots of parties and was getting drunk every weekend, basically. Then it turned to two nights a week, and then three. It just snuck up on me in the end and became a habit."

I think of Mac, Grandma's next-door neighbor, the man who brought us back from Melrose because of Dad's "habit." Mac got drunk every weekend and downed a couple whiskeys nightly. He always smelled of booze, but I wouldn't have called him an alcoholic. Or maybe Mac was the alcoholic, and Dad was another thing. There was something qualitatively different about my father's drinking. When Mac drank, it was like the liquor spawned another persona, created his Mr. Hyde. It brought out the flights of emotion, the extreme anger, the blistering crudity. With Dad, it was the opposite. The other persona, the shadow, spawned the drinking; the extremes of emotion demanded the alcohol. Mac was the man with a habit he couldn't break, but Dad's drinking was a symptom of a deeper disease of the soul. When he lived with Memaw, Dad could go for months or even years at a time without touching a drop, but even without his "medicine," the shadow never lifted. I always felt its presence, and I think that even if he had quit drinking altogether and found a steady job, or if he had never drunk at all, he would still have been sitting on the railroad track in Starke that morning in April of 1996.

***

As I write, I decide to Skype Mom again to see if I can trick her into recalling something unpleasant. She's once again at my nephew's house in Alabama, out on the front porch.

"When do you first remember thinking 'this man drinks too much?'"

"He drank from the get-go."

"Yeah, but y'all dated and partied a lot, right? You both probably drank quite a bit. When did you realize something was different about his drinking?"

She knits her brow, looks off to the right. I'm expecting her to change the subject, but instead, she shakes her head and says, "That's a good question."

"Was it because he drank alone?" I suggest. "When no one else was?"

"Yes," she says immediately. "That's exactly it. And I think I always knew. My stepfather was an alcoholic, too, so I recognized it. With Bob, I just used the excuse that he never went to bars when he drank; he stayed home. As a teenager, I used to have to go pick Jim up."

"Jim?"

"My stepdad. In fact, that's how he died in the end. They found him shut up in his truck in the Elks Lodge parking lot, asphyxiated."

"Jesus, Mom. I didn't know."

"The real problem with your dad was his work."

"What do you mean?"

"When he worked at the chemical company, he would sell a couple of big drums and get a huge bonus. That's when he would get drunk, not when things were going badly, but when everyone was proud of him. It wasn't just because he had money to spend on booze—there was always money enough for that. I think it was success. Whenever he did something good, he drank. If he sold a car and got a commission, the only way he could handle that feeling was to get drunk. He just didn't know how to deal with things going well. Does that make any sense?"

"When you think about his family," I say, "I mean, Memaw and the rest, maybe it does."

"I've told you this, I think, but we used to be real good friends with the pastor of your grandma's Methodist Church, Stan. He was the one who baptized you. I remember you didn't like anyone touching you, and everyone knew it, so when I started to hand you to Stan that Sunday, his eyes went wide and he said, 'What am I supposed to do?' And I said, 'Just take him!' He just knew you were going to throw a fit!"

"What does that have to do with Dad's drinking?"

"Nothing! But one time Stan was running this 'Trust Seminar' for couples, and we had to do trust falls and such as that. In one of these games, they blindfolded all the wives and had the husbands lead them around the room. There was lots of nervousness on the women's part, they'd squeak and squeal, 'Where are you leading me?' And the men were no better, running the women into pretty much everything. There were lots of stubbed toes! But your daddy guided me perfectly around that room. I never had one little grain of doubt he would let me get hurt in any way." She pauses. "At least not physically."

We sit together on that last sentence for a second in silence.

"Anyway, Stan had us perform as an example to the others. And then we all went to our house, and your dad was feeling so good, he offered Stan a beer. Stan laughed and said, 'I could sure use one!' or something like that, and your Grandma Hodges' jaw dropped through the floor. She just could not believe her preacher was drinking! That did not happen in West Virginia."

"See? That's what I mean," I say. "There's a perfectly good example of you guys drinking socially, normally, and no one seemed bothered by Dad having the beer."

"Do you remember when he was house-sitting on that lake in the middle of nowhere?"

"Lake Elizabeth," I half-whisper. This is the first time Mom has initiated a question about Dad.

"That was not a happy time either," she says.

"You only came up with me to Lake Elizabeth once," I say to Mom. "Or maybe twice. How many memories can you possibly have of that place?"

"Enough."

"It can't have been all bad," I tease. "I remember getting up in the middle of the night to get a drink of water, and as I was coming back to my room, Dad popped out of y'all's room stark naked. There was this kind of startled rush, and I got so flustered that in trying to avoid him, I ended up bumping slap into him. Neither of us said a word. We both just kind of slunk off, pretending we were too sleepy to know what had happened."

Mom turns red, and I laugh.

"Well, thanks for sharing!" she says, flustered. "You know," she adds mischievously, "you think you're so smart, but you're not telling me anything all that special. Your dad always slept in the buff!"

And this time, we both laugh.

***

Lake Elizabeth was Dad's next attempt to rise after our lives in Melrose so spectacularly blew apart. At first, after losing the Quonset hut, he'd gone back to Memaw's house on Lake Santa Fe but then soon found a job on nearby Elizabeth, a tiny, swampy lake connected to Santa Fe through a system of wetland and bayou. A construction company from Gainesville was planning the next big waterfront housing development and had built a network of roads through the marsh, even clearing a few lots of land. One model home had been hastily thrown up, and they needed someone to live there and handle any potential buyers who came by to look at a property.

It was Dad's ideal job, all alone a million miles from nowhere on a lake in the wilderness. Maybe one potential customer visited a week, the boss almost never. Dad could spend his days contemplating the folly and greed of Florida's development craze while sailing his Scorpion. The isolation also meant he could get drunk with impunity.

***

The first time I visit Dad at Lake Elizabeth, I'm around eleven. It's just me alone, up for summer vacation. He takes me outside right after we wake up.

"Come on, we gotta feed Charlotte," he says.

"Charlotte" is Dad's pet out here in the woods, a banana spider as big as my hand who has built her web across the front sidewalk between the corner of the house and a pine tree. She's bright yellow like her namesake, with long legs striped black. Dad plucks a lethargic moth from the porch lightbulb, which is still burning, and tosses it into the sticky strands. Charlotte scampers over and begins wrapping the flailing insect in silk.

"She's a member of one of the most ancient spider species in the world," he says quietly, with obvious respect. "Over 165 million years old. Not important, but nice to know. This isn't the first Charlotte, either. There was another one when I moved in. I watched her build her egg sacks, waited for them to hatch. She died about a month after the babies emerged. This little bit of real estate stood empty for a few weeks, then Charlotte the Second showed up."

Dad's relationship with the banana spider, I think, speaks volumes. First, there's his methodical, scientific interest. He notes which insects she prefers as food, when she'll attack something caught in her web and when she won't. He observes her entire life cycle with the appropriate detachment (several Charlottes come and go during his sojourn at the lake, each passing without mourning), yet he coos at her whenever he goes outside as if he were talking to a pampered kitten. She's a companion out here in the woods, just the sort he would choose, too. His favorite animals, like his favorite people, are shunned by most—street dogs and lost cats—or else they are grotesque, appreciated only by him, like this prehistoric arachnid. When my mother, who's got a pathological fear of spiders, tells him that she won't stay in that house until he tears the web down, he just grins. He's not laughing at her but confirming something about himself through her reaction. *I'm the only one who gets it.*

He doesn't tear the web down, of course.

In fact, he is respectful of Charlotte's territory. We never use the front door, for example, because that would mean destroying her nest as it hangs over the spot where the sidewalk meets the driveway. It's the same with the sugar ants who have a mound along the sand path to the lake (we feed them cookie crumbs), with the bull gator that slides out from the banana lilies to the right of the dock and with the gopher turtle digging up the northern edge of the yard.

Their homes are protected, their habits observed and catalogued. The ones that are solitary get proper names. The gator is Buzz; the tortoise is Gomer.

***

Many of my memories from the Lake Elizabeth period were of the sort Mom referred to as "nice things."

One morning, Dad taught me his method for making breakfast. It was one of those times Mom was up visiting with me.

"Cook your bacon first," he said and instructed me to fill the skillet until the marbled strips of pork were climbing the sides. I started to remove one or two to make room. "Just leave it alone," he ordered. "That's going to shrink down." We started the grits while the meat was heating up, bringing the water to a boil and then setting it on simmer. "You'll want to stir them a few times," he said, "but basically you can let them wait till everything else is done. Always make sure you add your salt before they cook, otherwise, the flavor won't soak in." When the bacon was done and draining on a napkin, I started to pour out the drippings. "Stop!" he said. "You want that to fry your eggs in." As a family, we preferred our eggs over-easy, and it was taking me a long time to learn to flip them without busting the yolks. His secret was to toss hot bacon grease over the top of them with a spoon as they cooked.

"This is all about timing and economy," he explained. "It should all be ready and hot at the same time. You have to think of what takes longest to cook and what you can use from one thing to make another. Capeesh?"

He ran me through the whole process several mornings in a row until I performed it flawlessly, at which point he put me in charge. And I was proud somehow. I had reached a milestone. Until now, every time we had cooked together, he finished whatever I was doing as if he didn't quite trust me. It was always one last stir of the spoon, whether it was batter for apple cake or filling for pecan and chess pies or tomato sauce for his famous steak and spaghetti. Now, at last, he completely left me alone.

Another "nice" memory.

I'm twelve years old. Dad has suggested, to my terror and delight, that the back roads through the future housing development will be the perfect place to learn to drive. The car is a blue El Camino with a manual transmission, the company jalopy. He takes it out to the entrance and parks it next to the weathered sign that spells "Lake Elizabeth Estates." There are no houses anywhere, nothing important to crash into, only grassy fields of white sand and oaks.

We switch places. I slide across the front seat, and he climbs out. I watch him lope coolly around the front of the car. *The man never loses his reserve*, I think, *is never anxious or worried*. My stomach is doing backflips. He climbs in the passenger side, pushes the seat all the way back until his long legs are no longer crammed up to his chin, then plucks a Pall Mall from the front pocket of his red-checked shirt and lights up. There's the sweet tobacco smell, then smoke.

I adjust the Camino's mirrors and try to find the lever that pulls up the driver's seat—I can't reach the pedals even with my toes stretched out. He waits patiently, blowing smoke rings out the window. Once I'm situated, he explains the clutch, the gas, and first gear.

"It's a balance between the two," he says. "Letting go of one while feeding the other."

I nod.

"Then give it a go."

The engine revs, screams. I ease up on the clutch and with a violent jolt, the car switches off.

"Too fast," Dad says. "You gotta ease into it."

It's only after an hour of failures that I'm finally able to consistently hit the right balance and keep us in motion. At first, I poke along at about five miles an hour in first gear, making the engine whine painfully, until Dad says, "Get the molasses out of your ass, son." I shift into second and press the gas pedal. "Faster," he insists.

I go to third, then fourth.

Pretty soon, I'm zipping down the newly paved road that runs along the back of the property, a straight shot between oak scrub on the right side and dense pine forest on the left. I'm feeling pretty cocky. The windows are down, the radio is blasting Kenny Rogers' "The Gambler," and Dad's tapping out the rhythm on the outside of the door, his arm draped outside the window. Then a raccoon darts out in front of us. I swerve, bounce off the pavement, and now we are crashing through palmettos and ferns toward a clutch of pine trees. Dad calmly tells me to hit the brakes, but in my panic, I slam down on the accelerator, and we lunge forward. Limbs thud against the roof, vines skip across the windshield. We're done for. I release the wheel and he clamps my hands back down on it. "You need to hit the brakes," he says softly. By some miracle, my foot obeys. We lurch to a halt a fraction of an inch before the trunk of a gigantic live oak.

"That was close," he says. We breathe in silence for a good long while, contemplating mortality and the green moss on the bark, and then I say, "I didn't want to hit the raccoon."

"Jeffrey," he answers, his voice still restrained and steady. "You are never, ever to put our lives in danger for an animal. Capeesh?"

"Sorry."

"No, you did good. Just as I was trying to figure out how to swing my leg over the gear shift and slam on the brakes myself, you took control of the situation."

My heart is ricocheting between my chest and my throat, my hands shaking. Instead of letting me relinquish the wheel, he orders me to back us out the way we came, and we continue the lesson.

***

One night that same year when I'm up for Christmas break, he takes me camping. We drive out to the end of the road where I'd nearly killed us and park the Camino in a cul-de-sac of broken asphalt already sinking back into the black peat of the marsh it'd been spilled on. We cut a trail through hammock and wetland till we find a relatively dry point at the eastern edge of the lake. It's not ideal, but at least it's not muddy. He spends half an hour with a machete hacking us a space in the palmetto big enough for our campsite. He teaches me to pitch a tent and build a fire. I learn all the basics, not to use green or wet wood, avoid moss and rotten branches, break off a piece of the turpentine-filled lighter knot at the heart of a pine branch to get the flames started. It's knowledge whose origin I'll remember the rest of my life. For dinner, we have a packet of Saltines with potted meat and Vienna sausages. He's bought them special just for tonight.

"You have to know the right meal to have with the right situation," he instructs as he smears a bit of the ham mash on a cracker with the blade of his pocketknife. "Me and the boys used to eat this stuff in the Army Reserves. We had to spend nights in the woods sometimes outside of Jacksonville, and this was all we had. Though I wouldn't have touched it with a ten-foot pole back in civilization, it sure was good somehow in the boonies, accompanied by some baked beans, of course, heated over the coals and partaken right out of the can." He hands me a spoon and says "Bon Appétite." The hot beans steam in the firelight. After dinner, we let the fire die down and watch for meteors over the lake.

What I remember most is the next morning. He's brought along all the fixings for breakfast. I'm in charge again. I have this image of pushing around the eggs in the black iron skillet with a spatula as they fry in the bacon fat. It's chilly. There's a dusting of crisp frost on the palmetto fronds and on the pine straw. A white mist drifts over the lake surface, and we hear the croak of a nearby gator off on a morning hunt, and somehow the food tastes a hundred times better out here, like this. It's the right meal for the right situation. I love him intensely that morning. I am groggy but resolutely myself, a boy with his father, his shoulder tight against mine for warmth. Everything's in place. The sun appears and pierces the tree trunks in a blast of yellow flame. Higher and higher the light rises.

***

On one of the visits when Mom comes up with me, he gets drunk. I don't know when or how. Most likely he's been swiping sips from a hidden stash all day, a bottle in the top of the closet or in the garage or in the sailboat or all of the above. But then, I've searched all those places, several times, always on the lookout.

I don't know why he's drunk, either, but I sense it's a show of defiance. How dare we think everything might proceed without incident. Who do we think we are? He's wearing nothing but his boxers and plops down in the armchair in front of the TV. Mom and he are arguing again, and I get the same guilty feeling I got a long time ago when they were fighting about why I didn't call him Dad. Both their eyes are fixed on me, hers worried, his bitter and trying to focus.

"Come here," he says and pats the arm of the chair. "I want to give you a hug."

I stay by the kitchen counter and look at Mom.

"Don't look at her," he says. "Look at me. I want you to come over and sit here."

He's got that sullen expression on his face again. *I'm too old for this*, I think, almost a teenager. Besides, I've never sat in his lap or snuggled with him in a chair, not even as a small child. That's just not our thing. When I refuse to move, he struggles to his feet, scowls at us both, and staggers toward his bedroom.

"Well, fuck you, then." I have never heard him say the f-word.

Or maybe before this, I *do* slink over and perch on the arm of the chair. I seem to have some recollection of that, sitting uncomfortably for a few minutes before the blaring television neither of us are watching. I don't know. The only image I clearly retain is that moment of him trying to stand and falling to the side. His hairless chest is pale, his cheap cotton boxers long and white. Mom, I know without needing to ask, has made the decision to leave the next day.

***

When visits to Lake Elizabeth go really south and Mom is not with me, I end up staying at Memaw's. She'll pick me up and spirit me to "safety" at her house on Santa Fe. At night, in front of the TV, she will regard me from her own armchair and shake her head in pity.

"My poor doll baby," she'll say. "I pray you don't ever start drinking. I pray every night."

***

I have thought long over the issue of genetics. When I'm home in Florida and my sister finds out, for example, that I've been to St. Augustine with Delal and tried a guava daiquiri, she will lower her voice and say gently, "You do remember your father and grandfather were both alcoholics, don't you?" Or when my niece's husband brings over a bottle of wine for a family dinner, I'll enthusiastically have a glass, and though Michele will hold her tongue, she'll make sure to catch my eye, at which point she'll glumly shake her head to let me know the sight of me with wine confirms my surrender to heredity.

And I get it. Michele spent a few years living with my dad as his stepdaughter. Maybe she witnessed her share of humiliating behavior. Maybe she felt a similar disappointment. She'll tell me stories sometimes, of the fun Bob Gibbs, of being his "first mate" on his sailboat when he raced. They liked each other to some extent, and that's an essential precursor to feeling let down. I wonder sometimes if her own anxiety has more in common with mine than I realize. Could it have the same origin? Maybe she, too, qualifies as a child of an alcoholic. When I picture my brother attacking my father with a baseball bat that night when I was three, I see it as a story of a boy defending his mother from an outsider, the stepfather, an unwanted interloper whose banishment will make the family whole again. Had they ever accepted him? Michele wasn't even living with us, after all, but had gone back to her own father, her *real* father. When Dad finally left Lakeland, I had always assumed that for my brother and sister, it

187

meant a return to normal, while for me it was the moment normal broke apart. My brother Mike never talks about my dad. I've never asked him if he remembers the incident with the bat. I don't think he'd tell me much, and it'd just make him grumpy. "Why do you dwell on such unhappy memories?" he'd want to know.

I don't trust Michele's memory either. She tells me I shouldn't blame my father too much. Mom was an alcoholic, too, she'll say, shaking her head in mournful disapproval. "She liked to party. She was out all the time."

I know my mom likes to party. Even now, at eighty-two, when we go out to eat some place with a happy hour, she'll order herself a daiquiri and then insist they go ahead and bring the free one so she can sip from both. One of the mother-son activities we enjoy when I'm visiting is knocking back margaritas on the screened-in porch. She'll buy a cheap canned drink mix from the grocery store, and I'll spruce it up with fresh lime juice and salt.

"Partying" is not what Dad did.

Michele has a Southern view of drinking, a Baptist view, a Wiregrass view. It's the Devil's brew, the evil refuge of the sinner, a family scandal, something that the Lost do in secret, sipping from bottles hidden under the bed like Miss Linnie or else, like Pepaw, stumbling out of the woods after binge drinking for a week only to raise hell and get arrested. It's an unforgiving way of seeing the world, one that Memaw held far more fanatically than my sister. I think the petulant pout that Dad sported when he drank may have been a reaction to that, a rebellious "Don't you dare judge me!" but also a sign that he had completely internalized the voice that did the judging, and not just of drinking. Of everything.

***

When Dad lost his job at Lake Elizabeth, he moved back in with Memaw. By that time, she had sold the Santa Fe house, unable to bear the property taxes after Grandpa Zillman's death. She bought a smaller place closer to Uncle Gene in Keystone Heights. This would be the house in which Dad would live out the rest of his life, a newly-built brick home in a newly-cleared housing development called Geneva Lake Estates. Despite the name, there was no waterfront property—it was a subdivision surrounded by pastureland—so Dad had to give up his sailboat for good. Somehow, he never thought to store it at his brother's house on the actual Lake Geneva, which was now just a ten-minute walk down an orange clay road. And what a beautiful walk it was, too, the road framed by giant live oaks heavy with Spanish moss. The branches formed a cathedral-like arch, letting through pillars of sunlight. To the left and right were fields of racehorses. We walked that tunnel of trees hundreds of times, me and Karin or me and Dad. One night, he took me down a side road that cut into the woods, and we found ourselves in the middle of a cloud of green fireflies. I'd never seen anything like it, nor have I since, a lazy galaxy of hundreds of blinking stars swirling upward out of the mud.

"Let's be still here a while, son," he said.

There would be no further attempts to get back together with Mom. No real attempts to break out ever again.

But my memory is wrong, as I have discovered over and over in writing this narrative.

This past winter break, while in Florida on vacation, I am digging through a box of old photos when one turns up of my father at a family gathering in Lakeland. I must have been in 6th or 7th grade. We are at my sister's doublewide trailer, a crowd gathered in the kitchen. Everyone is there who usually wasn't when my dad was around: my brother, Mike, with his first wife and stepson; my sister, Michele, with her first husband "Little Mike" and her mother-in-law, a woman preacher who performed exorcisms; and Mom's best friend, Aunt Sue. My mom is there, too, of course, as is my sister's other half-brother from her father's side. Dad is standing in the back, towering over all the shorter people. He wears a blank expression, stares off to the side.

"When the hell is this?" I ask Mom.

"You don't remember?" she says.

"This is Lakeland. He was never in Lakeland."

"That's the Thanksgiving I had to beg the hospital for special permission to let him out."

"Out of where?"

"I'd had him committed."

"Are you talking about the time he got thrown in the drunk tank?"

"No, that was earlier. When you were little."

"So, when you say 'committed,' you mean to a mental hospital?"

"Yes. Your memaw helped me do it. She signed the papers or something."

"Why? What happened?"

"Oh, I don't remember."

I close my eyes and think back to this trailer, this group of people. Not an image, not a story, not even an impression of my dad surfaces.

"I think it was that time he came down to live with us," she says.

And then a couple of fragments click into place, and a scene fires up. I see him on the back patio at Grandma Hodges' house on Hampton Avenue where we moved after she died. He's come to live with us there, to give it yet another go. He's out on the patio because he has to get away from all "those people" inside the house. My mom's cousin Butch is down visiting from West Virginia with his new wife and two kids. Dad is sitting on a cement block, his long legs jutting out awkwardly. He's in a white T-shirt, smoking nervously. Behind him is the tall wooden fence that separates our yard from Mack's.

"I don't know if I can stay here, Jeffrey," he says.

This sort of thing is no longer a surprise. "Why not?"

"I can't take all these *people*. I came here to be with my family, but it's never just the three of us."

"Uncle Butch is only visiting," I protest, thinking how much I like it that they are here and realizing there is something different about my father that I will never understand. He actually wants that isolation of Melrose and Lake Elizabeth. This is the first time I think that maybe he can't leave that little cluster of woods in north Florida. He's like some enchanted character from a fairy tale, bound by a witch's spell to a border her magic has determined.

He continues, "When it's not them, it's someone else. The neighbors or your mama's friends, or Michele and her family, Mike and his family, or all their cousins and second cousins and their friends. Even that boy is here every weekend, what's-his-name, the son of her first husband and his second wife."

"He's Mike and Michele's half-brother, too," I remind him. "Just like me."

"It's weird, Jeffrey. Who keeps hanging out with all the old in-laws after they're married to someone else?"

***

Another memory. It's just after he's first arrived, and I've taken him to see *E.T.* It's my third or fourth viewing. At twelve years of age, I see it as essential watching for anyone pretending to be cultured, and given all our stargazing on Lake Elizabeth, all our long talks on Lake Santa Fe about astronomy and the possibility of life elsewhere in the universe, I am sure he will be caught up in the magic, too. After all, the story is what we always fantasize about.

The movie's over. We are walking back to the car, the sky is overcast, and I ask him what he thought. He lights up a cigarette and says, "What I think is that the kids in that movie were spoiled smart-asses."

"I thought they were totally normal," I say, baffled. *E.T.* featured clever children living with an overworked single mom trying to make up for an absent father. How much more normal could it get?

"If that's a 'normal' family these days, then the whole world's going to hell. Where I come from, you respect your elders when you talk to them. You sit down to a home-cooked meal and ask to be excused when you leave the table." He lets out a quick breath of smoke. "That bunch in the movie lived in constant chaos. The kids controlled the house. Everything was noise and mess twenty-four hours a day."

And I know he's talking about us. But I liked the noise and chaos and messiness of our lives, and I knew it would never square with the order Dad thought he wanted.

***

He works for Lakeland Chevrolet. One night after he sells a car and makes a hefty commission, he announces that he's taking us out to dinner at the Sampan, our local Chinese restaurant, a place he considers a bit on the expensive side and therefore a suitable destination for a family wanting to celebrate something with a little extravagance. The three of us dress up in our best clothes. We are honoring not only his successful sale, after all, but his return and our reunion as a family. We order appetizers and then before the waitress can gather up the menus, Dad says he'd like a pair of cocktails, one for him and one for Mom. It's happy hour.

Funny how as I write, more details come into focus. I see the round red moon gate that leads back to the kitchen, the sweat on the water glasses, the crimson paper lanterns. We sit at a table in the center of the room. The drinks are gin tonics with a slice of lime. When they arrive, I freeze and stare stonily at the tabletop as Dad tries to act casual, asking us about our days. I must be putting on quite a show because eventually Mom turns to me and wants to know what's wrong. I hem, I haw, but to my credit, I get it out. "I don't want Dad drinking." It feels like the words are covered in thorns coming up my throat. Dad rolls his eyes, lets out a frustrated sigh, and beckons the waitress over.

"Happy now?" he asks sarcastically as she takes the drink away. I nod, but from that moment on, he is sullen. He has the old expression, that defiant pout, and it sours the whole evening. But I feel quietly triumphant. Maybe I've prevented the crash I've been waiting for.

Was it shortly after this Mom had to have him committed? Did success undo him again?

Or was it me?

If I had just left it alone. If I had let Dad feel normal that night, have his drink, celebrate. If I had not been the little Dixie prude. Maybe what made him sick was the South itself, all its dour Old Testament judgment for which I and so many others served as unwitting conduits. Was the whole problem one of geography? How would things have been different if Dad had been born somewhere else, in one of the places I have lived for example? What would he have become without all those nagging, belittling Southern-accented inner voices?

Here, in Turkey for instance, just like in the South, conservative religious people frown on alcohol, so drinking has become a political symbol of the non-religious. It marks you as urbane, enlightened, democratic. Atatürk, the man who founded the secular republic from the ashes of the medieval Ottoman caliphate, was a heavy drinker who looked toward France as an example of advanced civilization, and so to ostentatiously enjoy alcohol is to ally yourself with this national hero and his dream of European sophistication. A beer at dinner means you reject the narrow-minded zealots longing for a return to the old Islamic empire. And while this is a bit of an oversimplification on my part, and although this perception often does not match reality, Delal and I do sometimes use booze as a rough key to suss out people we've just met. Someone cracks open a cold beer in the middle of Ramadan? She's cool. She is, to some extent, willing to buck the system. Here, Dad's boozing might have told us that he was an ally.

I think of him one spring break, for example, when we go to the village of Datça on the Aegean, and the owner of our hotel invites us to a grilled fish and raki dinner. Raki is the local spirit, distilled from grapes and flavored with aniseed. It is drunk in a kind of ritual with seafood, melon, feta cheese, and a dozen local appetizers called meze. The invitation indicates immediately what kind of person the owner is—generous, cosmopolitan, cultured—and that he has deemed us the same. It's early in the season; there are no other guests, so he invites all his neighbors, a group of Istanbul emigres living out their retirement on the sea.

"At this table, we are forward-looking people," our host announces and holds up a bottle as proof. "We are not like those backward fanatics in the government."

What follows are hours of conversation over politics, local history (there were Greek ruins everywhere), and a life well-lived, just the sort of conversation my father loved and could never find in the Wiregrass woods. I pull back and imagine him sitting at the head of the table, next to the host. What would Robert Lenward Gibbs have been like if this had been his drinking culture? An alternative vibrant community of like-minded people, defiant and loud right in the middle of all that medieval religious condemnation?

Could we have saved him?

THIRTEEN

I dreamed last night I was home in Florida. It was one of those rare dreams that seem to come from outside of me, one whose presence lingers in the air after I wake, like a draft from a window left open somewhere in the house.

I was flying over a river that ran through the swamps and wound in curves like a moccasin. The water was filled with people in white baptismal robes. No preachers or prophets stood at their backs; they were on their own. As I passed over, each one fell back into the river as if it were my presence pushing them under, and I watched the water close over their faces, turning them first amber, then brown, then black as they sank. They smiled, blissful, and their robes billowed out like spilled sand. The trees were tall and electric green, draped with Spanish moss. At the end, I came to rest on a tall cliff of red rock. I had a key in my hand made of the same stone. I placed it in a notch in the rock at the top of the cliffs and turned back toward the river below.

Then I woke.

***

I've tried to be honest during this whole process, and I've tried to be accurate, though I've had to arrange things in a certain way so the story flows, so it makes narrative sense. That means choosing details to include and details to cut, sometimes best-guessing the words of a conversation back into existence or filling in lacunae with information from other people or even from the internet, like the name of the Japanese department store I will mention shortly. And it means leaving out large chunks of time while I'm revising, rethinking, rewriting.

It's now two years after the initial journey to see Lisa and Clark. I've just returned from a trip home where I rummaged through the boxes I packed away when I first moved to Turkey and discovered, to my utter shock, all the things connected to my father's suicide that I had thought lost when I wrote the first chapters. There they were in a plastic carton—the belongings found in his room by the hotel manager, the homicide report given to me by the Starke police department, the death certificates, the old pictures, the autopsy report documenting the locations of the worst abrasions and contusions on his corpse, the letters of mine he kept, old pay stubs, a gold tie pin with a Gothic G that once belonged to Pepaw, my old journals. All of it.

I haven't had access to this material in a long time. I take each item in hand, turn it over and back. Sometimes I close my eyes and sit with an object, let the emotions rush past me, like when you swim against large waves in the ocean and have to sink down to let them by; you wait on the bottom because at the surface the force of the wave will toss and roll you uncontrollably.

I've discussed the archaeology of memory before, how you can collect a few artifacts from an unexpected corner and tease out a world. With these new fragments, this debris from my father's wrecked life and shabby death, I make a lot of rediscoveries that correct details I've scribbled down in earlier sections or fill in others I had forgotten. Sometimes something sets off whole stretches of continuous memory. Only once do I outwardly cry, when I read through the witness statement of the train engineer. It's a few convulsions that quickly settle. I have given you the beginning of this story before, about how Dad looked up into the engine light and then away, but the rest I have blocked for two decades. Or forgotten. The gloom that falls over me once I pack all the artifacts to take home to Turkey doesn't fade for weeks. I don't suppose it ever had, even when I sank it below the surface, which is the point of this whole endeavor.

One of the items I find in the box of old things from home is a rent receipt for the Magnolia Hotel in Starke, Florida. It's signed by Dad and covers a full month in room 24 starting from March 19th, the day after his birthday. The sight of that date is like a seed around which crystals grow, one after the other spreading outward to fill the empty substrate, building and building, and I remember: There was going to be a birthday party. Everyone had been on their way to Memaw's house for some sort of begrudging celebration—Memaw, Gene, and Karin in my uncle's brown truck—and Dad was cooking, steak and spaghetti, but he hadn't wanted this party in the first place and had gotten drunk.

Just a few weeks ago, I was debating with my friend Julie over the phone about the details of the incident with the Ouija board, about when he'd disappeared. I insisted our amateur seance had taken place at least three months before Dad's death in the winter. I was absolutely certain. She kept saying she thought it had only been a few days prior.

"It spelled 'Eating grass, ha ha,' and then you got the news the next day, two days later at most," she said.

I dug in. I couldn't give so much credit to that goddamned Ouija board. But she'd been right. Why couldn't I remember something so important correctly?

And why his birthday? Why had it all fallen apart then? Was it the mix-up with the birth certificate and passport?

***

I go out for breakfast with my mom to a rinky-dink diner on the east side of Lakeland. It's owned by a Greek family, the manager a fresh immigrant from Rhodes, and the walls are covered with American nostalgia—pictures of Elvis and Marilyn and old cowboy movie posters. Over sausage gravy and biscuits, I finally tell my mother what I've been writing for the past two years, and I can see from her eyes she doesn't approve.

"I feel like this still bothers you a lot," she says.

"No," I answer reflexively. Denial is always my first instinct, but then I become aware of what I'm doing and say, "Yes, it bothers me. It *should* bother me. It should bother all of us. And it's not wrong to talk about it." I decide to provoke, to say something I said to my sister just the night before and which I said to you at the beginning of this book.

"When it happened, I wasn't surprised at all."

Her eyes jump up. "What do you mean?"

"Think about it," I say. "For years, he'd been living with his mother, whom he hated, losing job after job. I imagine he started looking toward the day she died and wondering what he'd do with himself then and thinking about what he hadn't been able to do for fifty-nine years. Honestly, I can't understand why I was the only one *not* surprised."

"You can't do that," my mom snaps.

"Do what?"

"You can't assume you know things like that, what goes on inside people's heads!"

"Mom, it was staring us all in the face for a long, long time."

***

I've avoided talking about my father's "funeral." I know. But I needed to get you to a place where you might see what it meant. I had to make you live through a few things. And I have also been afraid of fucking the whole thing up. Or just afraid. Plus, there were so many pieces I couldn't remember.

But then I found that box.

For almost a quarter of a century I've sat on this story. When I look in my journal from the time, I see barely ten lines devoted to the topic, though I was scribbling pages and pages about any little thing that happened in Japan.

May 5, 1996.

I am unexpectedly returning home for a few weeks today. You see, my dad is dead, and I have to go back and bury him. It seems like something out of a movie. The ticket I'm using now should have been his. This trip should have been him coming to see me, not me going there. He killed himself, or more accurately, let himself be killed. What should I feel about this? He and I were never in a clear-cut Better Homes and Garden father-son relationship. Dai, just thirteen years old, told me I was his best friend when I left. They all saw me off at the airport; he, Kuniko, and Eiichiro, the only people in this whole country who even know my dad existed. It's difficult to part with them today. They're family, and I love them. I hope I am strong enough for whatever comes next.

That paragraph is the only thing I wrote about his suicide for the next twenty-five years. And I have written absolutely nothing about those days in Japan after finding out, or about that trip home. Until now.

***

The morning after I went to my knees in the shower, I called in sick to work, bought a plane ticket home for the earliest possible date (two days later) then traveled into Tokyo for a long walk. I wanted to wander until my legs collapsed. I have a few memories from that trek across one of the world's largest cities, that first day of loss, vivid film clips I can put on without struggling for the details or asking anyone for help.

The lights go out. The images burst alive in the darkness.

I'm in an Indian restaurant in the Ginza district, Tokyo's poshest neighborhood, and have just ordered a meal of garlic naan and butter chicken. This is not an indulgence but a sacrament, for my relationship with Dad was built around the enjoyment of good food. Remembering him must include a meal.

The walls are hung with colorful tapestries, pashas in green and orange on horseback with tall turbans, blue Krishnas, Ganesh in a nimbus of pink light. The waiter is a young Indian, movie-star handsome—I can still see his perfectly-coiffed hair and stiff white collar. When he brings my meal, he pauses before setting my plate down and asks, "Are you all right?" I haven't cried yet. I've shown no signs of grief. I've behaved well, smiled, said please and thank you.

"Yes," I say.

"No," he answers gently. "I don't think you are."

The plate hangs in the air. He tilts his head and knots his brow in concern. How does he know? Why does he care?

***

Later, I'm on the sidewalk. I still haven't cried. I'm starting to have doubts about myself. Maybe I didn't love Dad at all. (I stumble over the past tense; it's brand new.) Maybe I don't even feel sad. Maybe my reasoning for the extravagant meal was just an excuse, and I am using his suicide as a justification for calling into work. I despise my job.

I'm passing Mitsukoshi department store with these thoughts dragging at my heart. In the display window is a mannequin dressed in a luxurious purple kimono with gold embroidery. Cranes with orange feathers fly across misty hills. Each window holds a kimono of a different color—red, yellow, blue. On the sidewalk outside, a young woman stands in front of a table bearing stacks of advertisements. She wears a pale green suit, a green pillbox hat, and hands out flyers. On her left, a banner flutters in the wind advertising a Spring sale. From a loudspeaker inside the store comes the low somber entry of a cello into Pachabel's "Canon in D," followed by the high plaintive notes of the first violin in echo of the bass, then the second. The sun is bright, the sky a strangely clean blue for the city, and when the final violin breaks into the melody, it seems to burn a hole into my chest. I take in a breath and start to sob right there, among the clicking shoes of the pedestrians. I can't stop. I don't want to. *This is real*, I think. Finally, after all these years, I know what I feel for him. Finally.

The night before I leave, I go to my Japanese drum class. This is where I first met Kuniko and her family three years before, where I'd taken Mom on her visit and fantasized about taking Dad. Beating the surface of the *taiko*, disappearing in that collective thunder is cathartic. When we are packing our stuff to leave, one of the drum teachers hands me an envelope. Inside is one thousand dollars in Japanese yen.

"We've taken up a collection for you," she says. "To help you on your trip home."

I look at the money, then up at the faces of my classmates, thirty people ranging in age from twelve to sixty.

"I can't," I say.

Kuniko is behind me. She closes my fingers over the envelope. "It's okay," she says.

I bow deeply so that I don't start sobbing. If I meet their eyes, I'll fall apart.

***

On the plane, I think, *Things will be different now.* This is too big for everything to just proceed as it always has. A death changes people. Suicide changes everything. Uncle Gene will finally show love for my father. I'll see him cry. He'll share memories of good times they had together. He'll start sentences with the words, "My brother." Memaw will show regret, guilt. Her well-put-together facade will melt, and I'll finally see a real person. It will be for them like it was for me on that sidewalk in Ginza. The impact of that train will break the family open and reveal what they really feel. We'll weep together and rebuild something new from the ruins.

***

I understand how stupid I've been when I get to my mother's house in Lakeland and phone Aunt Nancy. She tells the story as she has every story I've ever heard her tell. No tears, no breaks in her voice. She might be talking about Janine's motorcycle-riding boyfriend or cremating Uncle Gene in the burn barrel or Memaw's attack with the soap bottle.

"Yeah! Your memaw got a call from the police up in Starke, and they wanted her to come down and identify the body, so she phoned your Uncle Gene and demanded he go with her. He said he would but grumbled when he hung up the phone. Didn't want to go, not if it took him away from his precious TV. Bitched all the way to the truck, goddamn this and goddamn that. He's a son of a bitch and always has been a son of a bitch. He's just like his mommy, Rosemary and her baby, I always say. Yeah! Two peas in a pod."

The rest of this spiel I know by heart. When I hang up, I ask my mom if Nancy cried when she first told her the news.

"I don't remember," she says. "I think so."

"Did you?"

"Of course." She hesitates, "But mostly, I was thinking about how you would feel."

"I'm fine," I tell her. "I'm not the one who killed myself."

When Mom isn't around, my sister Michele tells me the pastor at her church is willing to talk to me about what happened. "It would be good to get it out," she says.

"We'll see," I say.

"Your memaw didn't want anyone to know," she says. "She was mad your Aunt Nancy called us at all. She said it was her private business."

Nothing has changed. A man could kill himself and his brother would complain about having to identify the body, his sister-in-law would incorporate the story as a new piece in her repertoire of family gossip, and his mother would stake a claim on his corpse. That's when I made my decision about the funeral. I would do it alone. The rest of them could go fuck themselves.

I buy the tree and order the gravestone. It needs to be of good quality but simple. It's what Dad would have wanted, I think. I pick a rectangular marble slab and have nothing carved on it save his name, birthday, and date of death. No Bible verses, no flowers or vines or praying hands. Memaw had wanted no stone at all, just his ashes to scatter anonymously into Santa Fe. When I write the check to pay for it, I sense a transfer of power. Memaw has handled all of his business until this moment. Now I am taking over.

***

Zack, an old friend from college, agrees to drive me up to Melrose. The previous year his own father committed suicide, and now he's promised to help me through my ordeal. He's doting, attentive. He writes me a long letter and gives me something from his late father's belongings, a pouch from an antique shop in New Orleans with a gold necklace inside.

"Dad sent all of his personal stuff to me," he writes. "And this was one thing. You have it because I grieve for you."

The night before the trip to Melrose, he invites me to a party in Orlando to get my mind off things. He says it will be right up my alley, a gathering of smart young Americans who have lived overseas. The host is the daughter of an ambassador, and very pretty, he assures me. We'll have a lot in common.

When he and I get to the party, we realize we are comically underdressed. The women are all wearing formal dresses, the men slacks, coats, and button-up dress shirts. I am in my Florida shorts and t-shirt combo, Zack in khakis. The house is full of artifacts rather than decorations, a tall African mask, a large Chinese vase. There aren't any pictures of living people anywhere. Our host, who is indeed very beautiful, with long brown hair and bright green eyes, is able to give short lectures on each piece, gesturing with a wine glass in her hand as she speaks.

"Both my parents have been all over the world," she says. "So our house ends up like a museum exhibit. It totally sucked as a kid. You had to be careful of *everything*."

"I know what you mean," another guest says. She's a thin blonde woman with short curly hair. "My dad is a chemistry professor, and the living room is full of expensive books and models of molecules or whatever. We were never allowed to play there."

"My dad was in the State Senate for a while," a young man says. "So, for like, years, we had to be really put together in public and even at home. Important people were always visiting, so the house sometimes felt more like a showroom than a place to live."

"Sometimes you just want to make a mess, right?" our host says. "Or break something without it destroying thousands of years of irreplaceable history."

They all laugh, and she turns to us.

"What do your parents do?"

"My dad shot himself in his trailer last year," Zack says. He lets that sentence sink in before adding, "And Jeff's killed himself just last month. He sat on the railroad track and let a train hit him. That's why Jeff's home. Where did it happen again, Gainesville?" He looks at me, raising his wine glass quizzically.

"Starke," I clarify, clinking my glass against his. "But he was homeless at the time."

At the sudden, stunned silence, both of us burst into laughter.

***

There's a point in the drive up the next day when I look out the car window and notice fields blanketed in color. Pink and red and white and purple. I audibly gasp.

"What?" Zack asks.

"My God, look at the flowers," I say. "They're everywhere."

It's May in north central Florida, and phlox flood the open spaces. They make the trip up different than it's ever been. The sense of being haunted is gone. Instead, everywhere I look between the Green Swamp and Melrose are blankets of bright pastel. The cow pastures after Tarrytown are cotton-candy pink, the medians of Highway 301 white and red, the horses on the farms north of Ocala graze in rolling fields of lavender and lilac. We are passing through a series of Impressionist paintings. The flowers spring out of the drainage ditches, from the grass around the parking lot at the Bevilles Corner bar, in the spaces beneath the crumbling billboards advertising the defunct Silver Springs, the Orange Shop, and the I Risqué. I have never seen this many phlox in bloom before.

"This is for you, Dad," I whisper. Wiregrass country is saying goodbye.

***

Zack is sitting with me in Aunt Nancy's kitchen. I've made the introductions. She pours us glasses of tea, opens a bag of chips, and immediately launches into one of her monologues.

"Yeah," she says. "Don't expect to find a grieving mommy. Your memaw hasn't changed a bit. She drove him to it, if you ask me. She'll send us all down to the tracks before it's over. Your sister Michele told her as much on the phone, or at least that's what your mama said, and Nell threatened to go down there with her rifle and fill Michele full of buckshot. Yeah. Lee put me on watch. I had to stake out your memaw's house to make sure she didn't go shoot up your sister and give you two bodies to bury. You never know with that one. I remember that time she got after your daddy with the .22. What was that for again? It was around the time she hooked up the garden hose to her tailpipe and left the car on. Your daddy found the Pontiac running in the garage with the door closed, like she was planning to kill herself, see? She was supposedly taking the wrong drugs and it drove her crazy, at least that's what Gene said, and the doctor had to fix the prescription later, but I think she did it for attention. She was trying to get Gene to feel sorry for her. Poor Mommy. Too bad she gave up on her own little suicide project. Might have saved us all a lot of trouble later on, and your daddy might still be here."

Zack taps me on the shoulder.

"She knows I'm here, right?"

I laugh, despite everything. Aunt Nancy hands me the obituary from the Starke paper.

"I don't know if anyone would have found out if not for the paper," she says. "Nell wanted everything to be her little secret. She ordered Gene not to tell a soul, then it comes out in the *Bradford County Telegraph* for the whole world to see."

Melrose man killed sitting on train tracks
By Kevin Miller, Telegraph Staff Writer
A 59-year-old Melrose man was killed early morning (sic) on April 23rd in Starke when he was struck and thrown about 40 feet in the air by a CSX freight train.

Robert L. Gibbs was apparently sitting on the railroad track in downtown Starke near Teal Tile and Carpet early Tuesday morning at approximately 5:15 when a CSX train headed north struck him and threw him about 40 feet from the site of the impact, according to Police Chief Jimmie Epps. Epps said the collision was so forceful, Gibbs probably died on impact. He added the preliminary investigation indicates suicide, noting that family members said Gibbs had a long history of problems with alcohol. The medical examiner's office will conduct an autopsy to determine the blood-alcohol content at the time Gibbs was killed.

An empty bottle of liquor was found near the site of the collision, but it hasn't been determined if it belonged to Gibbs or not, according to Epps.
After the accident, traffic was tied up in Starke for more than an hour since the train was blocking all of the crossings in town south of SR-16. Epps said that extra officers were called in to direct traffic to SR-16 in order to cross the tracks.
Gibbs had moved to Starke about five weeks ago and had been staying at the Magnolia Hotel, just two blocks from the railroad tracks. Before coming to Starke, his last known address was in Melrose where his parents and a brother live.

"Your memaw loves that bit about the empty bottle," Aunt Nancy says, tapping the article with her finger. "But I don't think it was his. He wasn't drunk. I'm sure of it."

***

When my mom's mother died back when I was twelve, we flew up to West Virginia and were met at the Clarksburg airport by her cousin's husband. Though we'd never met, I remember flinging myself into his arms right there on the runway and sobbing helplessly. He cried, too. Everyone we met did—all of

Grandma's sisters and brothers, her nieces and nephews. We spent a week hugging and weeping from house to house to house, the whole extended family of second cousins and third cousins once removed and great aunts and uncles-in-law. At the funeral, my sister and I had sat in the front row, holding hands and blubbering.

I am waiting for something similar now, but Uncle Gene still sits in his chair in the living room with his jar of tea and newspaper. I go in to say hello, and he reminds me that my father was a drinker, but it's a tragedy anyway, and how is everything over there in "that country?" When my cousin Ray comes over, we have an awkward moment standing several feet apart in the yard where he says he's sorry to hear about Bob. His wife Donna gives me a hug, tells me to let her know if I need anything. They're here to pick up their sons, whom Aunt Nancy babysits. Donna lingers in the kitchen, chats with Nancy about work. Ray joins his father in front of the TV, and the kids keep playing outside.

I ask Zack to stay until Karin gets home from work. I walk him down the hill to the lake where we sit on the dock talking until she arrives.

***

When Karin drives me to Starke, it's getting dark. Our first stop is the police station where I pick up a copy of the official report.

"It's not an easy read," the officer warns. "Are you sure you want this?"

"I need to know," I tell him.

"I think I ought to tell you that the engineer is really upset about the whole thing. He feels like it was his fault."

I can't take my eyes off the report. The words "Traffic Homicide Investigation" are in all caps below a City of Starke police badge and the Florida state seal.

"It was a suicide," I say bluntly. "Tell him I don't blame him in any way."

"Maybe you could tell him yourself. It might mean more. His address is in there." He taps the report with his finger.

"I will," I say. I never did.

The engineer's statement is handwritten, sandwiched between pages three and four.

I am Kerry Alan Coats, age 39, of Callahan, Florida. I am employed as an Engineer with CSX Transportation. On April 23rd, 1996, I was working as Engineer on train Q250 on a run from Wildwood to Baldwin. The train had two locomotives with #5890 in the lead hauling 74 cars. At around 5:15 AM with weather clear and conditions dark, we were northbound on the west track traveling at 45 mph. The train's headlight, ditch lights, horn and bell were all operating, and the lights were working at the crossing when I saw an object sitting on the west rail. This individual looked in my direction, and I blew the horn thinking he would move off the tracks. He did not, and I applied the train brakes. The man was struck, and the train then stopped north of the man.

What happened when "the man was struck" is meticulously documented by the investigating officer on page six.

P-1 was sitting on the west rail of the west track approximately 100 feet north of the Call St. (SR 230) intersection. Vehicle was northbound on the west track and struck P-1. After being struck, P-1 became airborne approximately 107 feet, then struck the west rock bed, causing a 13-foot gouge. P-1 then became airborne again for another 30 feet, causing another gouge mark in the west ditch. P-1 became airborne again for another 15 feet before coming to rest on the upward slope of the western ditch approximately 60 feet from the Jackson Street crossing.

The train's lead engine had no damage. The only signs of impact was the impression of blue jean material on the lower left cow catcher and three finger marks 30 inches above the material impression. Also found was a small amount of flesh and blood on the large brake line.

Finger marks. He'd reached up as if to stop the train. I see his huge hand on the black metal of the "cowcatcher" right before it hits. I see his long body skipping 107 feet across railroad slag like a ragdoll, bending at odd angles before becoming airborne again. I see the gore in the brake line, the pieces of him torn away.

They were talking about my daddy.

I see Uncle Gene in his armchair at the house in Lake Geneva, Memaw in hers a few miles away.

"I walked south down the railroad tracks from Jackson Street," writes the chief investigating officer.

Approximately 75 yards away, I observed a white male lying face down in the ditch. The subject's upper body was pointing in a northwesterly direction and his feet in a southeasterly direction. The subject was wearing jeans, a red and white striped shirt, a brown leather belt, and white socks. There were no shoes.

I then received a brown single-fold wallet from CPL. JOHNSON. Upon opening the wallet, I observed a State of Florida driver's identification card displaying the name Robert. L. Gibbs, D.O.B March 18, 1937. There was also one Putnam County/Melrose Branch library card, one Clay County/Keystone Branch library card, one Bradford County library card, and one State of Georgia birth certificate issued in Tift County on 11-19-52. I then assisted CPL. JOHNSON by taking photographs, including the deceased, his surroundings, and two shoes found on the scene.

I ask Karin to pull into the municipal parking lot at the end of Jefferson Street. I hop the chain-link fence and follow the tracks until I'm behind the carpet store. Kudzu vines are starting to crawl up the cinder-block wall. I estimate the distances and find the patch of crabgrass where he finally came to rest. I pick up chunks of granite from the railbed and squeeze them in my fist. I sit on the west track and look south, then close my fingers over the rails. I'm trying to feel something, summon something.

"You're facing everything," I tell myself. "You're looking it all directly in the eye."

There should be a ghost, a presence in the orangish glare of the sodium lights.

There's a whiskey bottle in the ditch lying sideways in a patch of weeds. It's cracked and covered in some kind of white scum. It looks like it's been there for months or even years. Is this the one the newspaper mentioned? The autopsy report is attached to the end of the homicide report. It clears up any doubts about his sobriety at the time of death. Every test for intoxicants comes up negative. In the middle of the report is a crude diagram of the body, marking places on the head and belly where there are scrapes and cuts, then on the shin and forearms where bits of flesh were torn away. I scan over the clinical descriptions of his remains, lacerations of face and right frontal scalp region, multiple cuts through the brain and upper cervical spinal cord, a multiplicity of rib fractures.

"I knew he wasn't drunk," I tell Karin. "But even if he had been, what the fuck difference would it have made?"

This is the first time I've cursed in front of a family member.

We go by the Magnolia Hotel and meet Wyatt, the white middle-aged night manager from California. He shows me to room 24.

"After I heard about the accident," Wyatt explains on the way up the stairs, "I went to Mr. Gibbs' room to see how much stuff I'd have to put into storage, you know, until the family came to get it. It was locked, but I found the key in the door. I didn't touch a thing. I figured the police would want to have a look around. Everything is just as he left it."

Inside, I find a couple of small notebooks on the end table by the bed and a brown satchel full of pictures, mostly of me, though there are a few of Jennie, including a copy of her first driver's license.

"I can't believe Memaw didn't come get this stuff," I say. "Was there no note?"

"Not that I found. Mr. Gibbs mostly kept to himself. He did say he was having domestic problems, and he had either to come to this hotel or go to jail, but he wouldn't go into detail. He said his cousin paid the rent for that first month, but there'd be no one to pay it after that."

Also in the satchel, sealed in a large Zip-Lock bag, are a stack of letters and postcards, again, mostly from me. A beat-up blue suitcase is half-packed with clothes and his old checkered shirts hang in the closet smelling of tobacco. An empty vodka bottle lies in a small chest next to the door. I open the Zip-Lock and start sifting through the papers inside. He's annotated one of my letters, the very first one I sent from Tokyo, making proud-parent exegesis in the margins like "shows ambition," "makes own destiny," and "others have no vision."

A New Year's card decorated with origami cranes reads:

Dear Pa, Sorry you couldn't make it here for the Holidays, but like I said, look toward April. The cranes on this card are called "tsuru" in Japanese. They represent happiness and longevity. I thought they were pretty cool. Anyway, hope to see you soon. Love, Jeff.

Happiness and longevity. There are also remnants of a care package I'd sent him, a huge box full of different Japanese snacks and sauces for him to try along with a letter explaining the use of each one.

The noodle-looking things are called soba. The ketchup-shaped orange bottle has special sauce for dipping them in. You can heat it up and add a dash of finely chopped green onions and/or shredded radish. And I mean finely chopped!

I turn to Karin, the letters held out like an offering.
"I didn't completely neglect him."

***

In the car, we cross the tracks with a thunk and start heading back toward Keystone on Route 100.

"That weird religious commune he used to stay at is around here somewhere," I say.

"I forgot all about that," she answers.

"Will you go with me to get his ashes from Memaw tomorrow?" I ask.

"Of course."

"Did you cry when he died?"

"Yes," she says quietly.

"Did anybody else?" I can't stop barraging her with questions.

"My mom did. She was really shocked."

"Is it true that Memaw tried to keep it all a secret?"

"She went ahead and had him cremated before we even knew something had happened. She wanted to go toss them in Lake Santa Fe immediately, but Dad convinced her to wait for you. I don't think she's doing too well. She seems a little crazy."

"She's always been crazy." I hesitate, and then something cracks inside, and the thing I've been trying to summon since the railroad tracks arrives.

"Why did they all hate each other so much?" I ask.

Karin grabs my hand and looks at me. It's dark in the cab of her truck. The lights of the dashboard cast a pale glow over her face. When I meet her eyes, my body starts to shake.

"How can you hate your own brother like that? Or your mother? Or your son?"

I start to sob, and Karin pulls over on the shoulder of the road and wraps her arms around me. It's the first time in our lives, I think, that we've ever hugged. It seems to mark some irrevocable transition. We're not kids anymore. The responsibility for this family is ours now. The older people cannot be trusted. They were never trustworthy.

"It should have been her!" I say. "She should be dead, not him."

"I know," she says. "I know."

"I wish they were all dead! All of them!"

I know I am saying a terrible thing, but I can't stop myself. I am so angry, so beyond angry. I'm thinking this is what I have felt all my life, and my father's suicide now gives me the courage and clarity to voice it. I straighten up, wipe the tears out of my eyes and apologize. Karin puts the car in drive and says it's okay, she gets it. The road is so dark. It's late, midnight in the woods.

"Do you think she'll give me the ashes tomorrow?"

"I don't know."

"You told her we're coming?"

"Yes."

"Because I don't want to talk to her. I don't want her involved in this at all. I want to get him out of her hands as soon as possible. What if she's already done something with them, taken them out and tossed them in the woods?"

"I don't think she would do that."

"She's insane," I say. "She might do anything."

***

The next morning, Karin drives me over to Memaw's. I'm dreading facing her. I haven't even called her since he died. Memaw's house has a circular driveway of white sand covered in pine straw and mulch. When we pull in, a cloud of fine dust envelops the car. All I can think is, *She has dumped my father in the yard.* Karin and I both look at each other, eyes wide.

"She wouldn't," I say.

My stomach in knots, I knock on the front door. *I have to save him from her,* I think. I have to get him out of her control at long last. It's my duty now. She opens. I let her hug me. She doesn't cry but gives a choked little sob and says something about how she misses him. I don't remember what. She smells of powders and make-up, her hair wispy and thin.

The next moment we are standing in the living room. I remember the blue carpet, the fireplace, and the decorative dish propped up on the mantle. I am cold, detached. I try to watch myself from the outside as if I'm a character from a movie. I don't want to go any deeper into the house. I don't want a glass of tea or a bite to eat. I don't want to chat. She brings the box of ashes from her bedroom. It's white, cardboard, like a carton for Chinese take-out.

"I'm sure he was drunk," she says, handing it to me. I am surprised it's so easy. "What are you going to do with them?"

"I'm going to Omega to bury him next to his father," I say. "I think it was the only place he was ever truly happy."

She nods, and I'm angry that I've told her where I'm taking him and that I'm not telling her what I told Karin last night, that I hate her, that it's her fault.

It should have been you.

But she seems so frail, and she was his mother after all, despite everything. When we get back in the car, I look in the box. The ashes are in a thick plastic bag. It seems full.

"Maybe she didn't," I say, and we drive back to Karin's house.

***

I sit in the kitchen with the box in my lap. "Well," Aunt Nancy says. "It looks like they're all there, but you never know. When my daddy died, I went up to my brother's and snuck a bit of Daddy's ashes out of the urn when nobody was looking. No one missed a thing. Half of him's right up there in the sugar canister now, on top of the fridge. I just hope I got the top half. Gotta make sure people don't put him in their coffee."

Dad's ashes are surprisingly fine, almost like baby powder. *If someone were to put them in coffee*, I think, *they would float to the top.*

***

My mother drives up with my brother-in-law that afternoon. They're going to take me to Omega to do the job, and then we'll all go home to Lakeland. They've got the tree and the headstone in the back of the car. This is my sister's second husband James. At first, I wanted just my mom, but she insisted a man come with her, and to my surprise, I'm glad he's along. James is more stable than my last brother-in-law. He's got steady work, a house. He's reliable in a way no man in my family has ever been. And he's willing to open up and talk. On the way to Georgia, he asks me questions, and I find myself telling stories about my father, then James tells some of his, and it's good to have the voice of an older male on that long and lonely drive north to bury Dad. I'm glad he's there to help plant the tree, too, but he goes back to the car when it's time to place the headstone. The sun is setting, the sky is a deep orange. I lay the stone at the trunk of the little oak and step back, taking my mother's hand.

"I miss him," I say.

"Me too," she says. And we stand there for a long moment in the fading light, hand in hand, a family of three for the last time ever.

FOURTEEN

Dear Dad,

I've been avoiding talking to you directly for hundreds of pages. I've started a dozen times, writing you letters from home or from cafes here in the city to try and share with you something about Istanbul and Delal and who I am now. It never felt real, somehow, never more than a gimmick. It still doesn't. I think you're dead. I think no trace of you is left in any dimension. You've been utterly obliterated, just as I will be one day. Eating grass, only I fixed it so the grass was eating you. Capeesh? Not in any fairy-tale metaphorical way, but literally, scientifically; the atoms in your ashes dissolved into the soil and were drawn up into the roots of the grass in Omega's cemetery.

I think that description from the engineer has gotten to me. I see it so clearly, as if it were my own memory. The train's light catches you. At first, you're staring firmly to the left, but when the train whistle sounds, you turn toward me as if you have one last thing to say.

The thing is, after burying you, I waited for a long time beside your grave. I have visited the tracks where you died, and I've slept in your room, each time expecting a ghost, a sign, a word. I woke last night thinking I heard movement upstairs. When I went to check, I wondered if you'd returned, summoned back by my writing this book about you, but of course, it was only a pigeon warming itself on the metal pipe of our radiator vent.

You would have chided me for this. You, the consummate nonbeliever, denying everything, God, love, redemption.

"There's nothing after death, son."

Then this is me talking to myself.

***

Dear Dad,

After you died, I went to grad school in Arizona. You would have been proud of that, I think, the first of us not only to graduate college but to get his master's as well.

One spring, my friend Zack came out to visit. He was the one who drove me up to bury you back in '96. From Tucson, we traveled up through the Superstition Mountains to the Grand Canyon. For a long time, I'd wanted to hike down to the bottom and camp along the Colorado River, and Zack was game. He was always game for adventures like that. In fact, when I couldn't get you to Japan that Christmas, I sprung the last-minute ticket on him, and he'd immediately hopped on the plane. All the places I'd arranged for you and me, I took him.

Now, Zack was an unusual friend, Dad. He had convinced me he could conjure spirits. Well, not spirits exactly, but when he was a teenager, he'd been locked up in a mental hospital for schizophrenia. He used to hear voices, talk to demons, travel to other dimensions. The way he'd finally learned to deal with it, he told me, was, at the suggestion of his psychiatrist, to imagine the schizophrenic state as another world with an entrance deep inside his belly. Then, he had to picture building a door to cover that entrance. When he closed and locked that door, the world beyond could no longer affect him. It was important, however, that Zack had control, that the door was his to open whenever he wanted.

"So, I still have access to that place," he used to tell me, "if I need it."

"Why in the world would you need it?" I asked.

"It's so much more colorful there," he said. "Everything charged with meaning. It's here that life feels empty. It's hard to keep the door closed."

I wouldn't have put much stock into this story, thought of "the door" as anything more than a therapy method, except Zack seemed to have powers of perception that to me, bordered on the supernatural. He could read people, total strangers even, like a psychic. When we first met, we went out for lunch at a diner. Over burgers and fries, he asked about my family, where I was from. I mentioned Lakeland, Mom's job at the Boy's and Girl's Club. I claimed you were a car salesman, which I guess you had been from time to time. At that point, he clamped his hand down on my wrist and said, "Your dad's an alcoholic, isn't he?"

I was stunned. "How did you know?"

"The hesitation before you told me about him," he answered. "And the way your hand was fiddling nervously with the napkin."

"But all that might have told you was that I had issues with my father."

"Yeah, but I *saw* it."

"What does that mean?"

"I saw it. That's all."

Anyway, that night at the bottom of the Grand Canyon, we set up our tent, and I built the fire as you had taught me years before on Lake Elizabeth, the way I had built fires dozens of times, following your rituals. Maybe that was what put you in my thoughts, but I had a dream of you that night. I don't remember the details, just that it was one of the recurring dreams I have about once a year. You're alive somewhere. You have been all along, and you've been waiting for me to visit, annoyed that I've been telling people you killed yourself.

The next morning, as Zack and I trudged our way back up to the rim, he sensed something was askew.

"You okay?" he asked.

"Yeah," I said. "Just this walk up is a lot harder than the walk down."

"That's not it."

I had learned over the years not to pretend with Zack. Plus, he was the son of a suicide, too, after all, so I told him about the dream, told him about how often I'd had it, about how it nagged.

"I wonder why he keeps coming back to you," he said.

"Isn't it normal to dream about the dead?"

"Yes, of course, but there's something else to this dream of yours."

I don't remember all the questions he asked me now, but sometimes with Zack, it wasn't necessarily what he asked, but the timber of his voice, a kind of hypnosis, like while you were distracted with his words, something else was coming out of him and probing around in your mind, or in your belly, opening your own door. While we talked, we came to a point on the trail where we had to pass into a tunnel, and I froze.

"What's wrong?" he asked.

"I'm scared to go in there."

"Why?"

"It's stupid."

"Just say it."

"Dad is in there."

I stared into that deep shadow in the red rock, and I thought I sensed you filling the space.

"Would it be so terrible?" Zack asked. "Wouldn't it be great to see him again?"

"No," I said instantly, and surprised myself.

"Why not?"

"Because he wants me to die, too."

213

"Why would he want that? He's your dad."

"He needs me. Because in life, I was his only friend. I was the only one he could talk to. How many times did he tell me that? He wants me to follow him."

"There! That's the real meaning of the dream," Zack said.

And I was crying again like I did when I first lost you, but the darkness had cleared. I was no longer afraid. And this is the point of this story, Dad. Standing in front of that tunnel was the only time I ever felt any kind of supernatural presence from you, and it turned out to be just some deep-seated fear and resentment of my own manifesting itself subconsciously. I never felt anything like it again. And I still have those dreams.

***

Dear Dad,

Okay, you would laugh at this, too, but I have to admit I put a lot of stock in dreams, especially since that day in the Grand Canyon. Most are nonsensical mishmashes of the day's events and random thoughts popping through the brain, yes, but some come from deeper down, like the ones I have of you, and a few seem to come from the outside bearing messages.

I had one of those dreams a few years ago, before Delal's grandfather died.

I was in a forest, and there was a tower of mud in front of me, just my height and vaguely pyramidal. It was lopsided and lumpy, like something a kid might have built on the beach, and I started punching it, knocking out large chunks until it lay in goopy ruins at my feet. My field of vision zoomed out then, and I saw that I was surrounded by dozens of red-robed Buddhist monks, each tending one of these mud towers, revolving around them like planets. I realized the towers looked so primitive because they were incredibly ancient, the first pagodas ever built by human beings. These monks and their predecessors had been protecting them for millennia. Horrified and ashamed, I slinked away into the jungle to hide.

This dream felt charged, electric. I couldn't stop thinking about it all day—even the humidity of the forest lingered. When I told Delal about it, she suggested I ask her grandfather.

"Dede believes in the power of dreams," she said. "And he's pretty good at interpreting them."

So, I went over to Dede's house and presented the dream just as I told you.

"Aha!" he said, slapping his knee. "It means you lack faith."

"Religious faith?"

"There is another world out there," he said, "whether you see it or not. You said you only noticed the monks when you zoomed out. You denied the sacred until it was spelled out for you. But that's not how sacred things work."

I often wonder what you would have made of Dede, Dad. I sometimes saw him as a replacement for you, the older man in my life who provided guidance, someone whose wisdom I'd like to pass on, as a son should.

***

Dear Dad,

I think you may have visited me.

In the middle of writing one of the middle chapters several months ago, I was overcome with despair. Nothing was going well. Why tell this story? What purpose did it serve? As Mom always said, why pick at these scabs? This effort to find some meaning in your life and death, and especially to tie it to a grander history, seemed beyond my capability at best, and selfish at worst. Who would care? Who even should? The past was dead.

I turned off the computer and decided to take a bath. Delal and I had just moved to our new apartment, and one of the perks was a bathtub, a rare commodity in Turkey. I planned to soak in scalding hot water and read. I wanted something dry and intellectual, something to take me totally out of the world my writing was preoccupied with, out of America and the South, and so I grabbed a book off the shelf, a six-hundred-page tome on the history of Armenians from Eastern Turkey I hadn't touched in years. As I was carrying it to the bathroom, an envelope dropped out onto the floor. I looked down to see my name scrawled on the front, with an old Lakeland address of Mom's. There was no stamp or postmark. Whatever this was had never been mailed. I picked it up and opened it. To my utter surprise, I found the receipt for your tombstone inside, dated May 5th, 1996. How it ever got in that book, I have no idea. The box of stuff connected with your death was still packed away back in the States. I hadn't seen it in a decade.

I sat down on the side of the tub, thinking about Dede's words.

"You lack faith."

Was it you?

***

Dear Dad,

I surround my desk with pictures of you to bolster my shaky faith. Many of these photos are from a time before I even existed. There's one of you on the beach. You look so young, barely thirty. Your old sailing buddy, Dave, is standing in the shallow green water, right at the prow, wearing a blue cap and sunglasses with his fist on his hip. You are peeking out from behind the sail, just behind the stern, wearing the same sunglasses and hat as your partner, your big ears the only thing that distinguishes you from him. This has to be the Gulf of Mexico. Behind you is a long strand of white sand and palm trees. You both wear grins that cut your faces in half, part goofy, part young-man cocky.

In another picture you're sitting on a couch with a drink, wearing a black turtleneck sweater and shorts. You're smiling here, too, the kind that distorts your entire face. You look a little buzzed, frankly, but I have that same smile. I see the shape of my cheekbones and forehead, the curve of my lips. These pictures are both from '69, the year you and Mom got married.

You wear a different kind of smile in the first picture taken after I was born. I'm on your lap, just over four months old. You're wearing a white undershirt and you've grown the mustache I'll never see you without. We're leaning together against the side of a house. It looks like Uncle Gene's Lake Geneva place. I recognize the wood shingles and the tree shadows that dapple us in patches of light. The back of the photo bears Memaw's handwriting, *Jeffrey and Bob, January 1972*. Half of your face is caught in the sun, and you are looking off to the side, away from me, but your smile is content. You look utterly at peace with life.

I never saw any of these smiles.

***

Dear Dad,

I'll talk to the picture of you with the sailboat.

I've had so many imaginary conversations with you while living in Turkey. They're usually about food, history or politics, sometimes about all three. It's a constant internal dialogue. Just last night, Delal and I went to a tapas bar on the European side of Istanbul, and I fantasized about you sitting in the third chair as we dug into a plate of Spanish pinchos. We talked about the salmon, the roasted eggplant, and evaluated the quality of the toasted bread. You said,

"Jeffrey, this is the fanciest meal I've eaten in a long time." We discussed the war in Syria, and I kept track of how many glasses of sangria you downed.

Years ago, one hot August day, Delal and I and the rest of the family went to a festival in Dersim, a mountainous region near Delal's village. It was maybe my second time visiting Conag, and everything was still new to me. In my mind, I kept telling you about all I was seeing and feeling, writing you mental letters.

The festival took place at a restaurant located in a small canyon on the edge of the Peri River, a tributary of the Euphrates. Underground volcanic springs poured scalding mineral water from the cliff walls all along the shore, and some enterprising young locals had built a hot spring resort from one of them. At the entrance to the resort was a ruined fortress dating back thousands of years. Tablets written in cuneiform had been found in the ruins. Cuneiform, Dad. The first writing ever!

Anyway, we were splitting our time between the hot water pools at the river's edge and the table laden with food at the picnic pavilions. You would have been in heaven. There were long tables of kebabs and wings and salads drizzled in pomegranate sauce, grilled onions with sumac, and a special dish called *goştê selê*—roasted chunks of lamb cooked in a wide metal pan and then drizzled in a sauce made of butter, yogurt, and garlic. What made me really think of you was the tea. Everyone was guzzling tea, glass after glass, just like you used to do back home.

Here's something not important, but nice to know. This festival was a bit on the illegal side. It was during Ramadan when the rest of the country was on a fast during the day. Restaurants were closed. Most people slept through the afternoons. But this was Dersim, and these people were not Muslims but Alevis, a different religion in many ways, a mishmash of animism and Zoroastrianism overlaid with a flimsy patina of Shi'a Islam. They did not observe the fast and in fact, enjoyed flaunting their disobedience in this way at a festival.

A young man, curious about what the hell an American was doing so far from home, struck up a conversation with me over lunch. Where was I from? Why had I come? I asked him the same questions in return.

"I'm from Istanbul," he said. "But I just learned recently my family has roots here."

"Why just recently?" I asked.

"The state killed a lot of Alevis back in '38," he said. "It wasn't always safe to admit you were from Dersim. It still isn't, really. But for my family, it was even worse. We weren't even truly Alevi, but Armenian. My great-grandparents fled the Genocide of 1915 and came to these mountains where the Alevi Kurds hid them from the Turkish soldiers. See that river? Most of us were marched to a bridge just north of here, to a place called Kuresan. The 'special forces' in charge of gathering up the Armenians tied all the men and boys from our village together, then shot the one at the head of the line. They didn't want to waste bullets, see? When the first person went over, he dragged along the rest, and they all drowned together. My great-grandmother escaped somehow and took refuge in Dersim where she pretended to be an Alevi Kurd in order to survive. They came for the Alevis just twenty years later."

He points across the Peri River, brilliant green against the red cliffs.

"See that castle over there? It was ours once. The Turks used it during the Genocide. They locked Armenians up in the rooms and set them on fire. Then they threw their remains over the side into the water."

It's such a heavy history, Dad.

Talking about it used to be a crime. When I wrote about this story for my blog, I was called a liar, a dupe, an agent. I even got a death threat. Why did I insist on dishonoring the Turkish race? Commenters asked. How could I so viciously insult the country that hosted me? I was just another outsider stirring up trouble. I would never understand what the Turks went through with the Armenians and the Kurds.

These arguments sounded so familiar. How many Southerners say the same things when faced with parts of our own history we want to deny?

I wanted to tell you about it all. I make sense of things, sometimes, by going back to Keystone, sitting on that back porch and explaining what I've learned to you.

***

Dear Dad,

It doesn't take much for me to start talking to you. I don't need anything profound. Last night, Delal made a simple salad for supper, tomatoes and peppers with feta cheese and walnuts, dressed in olive oil and a hint of pomegranate syrup. I thought, *Dad, you would have loved this.* I think of you when we crack walnuts, a staple in Turkey. It reminds me of shelling those pecans we used to gather in the groves on Lake Santa Fe. I think of you when I'm heading toward the ferry at night, and I see three vagrants in dusty sports coats gathered around a makeshift fire they've built against the metal grate of a fishing goods store closed for the night. Cigarettes dangle from their mustachioed lips. They toss trash in the flames.

***

Dear Dad,

I get closer with each repetition of that salutation.

***

Dear Dad,

I wish you had lived long enough to meet the woman I married. You would have liked Delal, I think. She's incredibly beautiful, brilliant, and strong. And before you say anything, she's strong in a way that strengthens those around her, not tears them down, not like the strength of your mother. Delal's laughter, her wit, her compassion radiate an energy that charges the air. We all drink from it.

Her strength is also communal, drawn from her connection to a people and a history, to the Kurds in Turkey and the century-long political struggle that has forged their character. Through them and their movement, she has access to a collective dignity that is humbling and completely baffling sometimes.

I've been dying to talk to you about this for a long time. My preoccupation with politics came from you, after all, and it's one of the elements that sustains my marriage. Whenever Delal comes to the States, she is surprised by how little people care about the subject, and I'll tell her about you, how you were different. We always talked politics.

I wish the three of us—you, Delal and I—could sit out on the Santa Fe dock or on Memaw's back porch and discuss political systems and philosophies like we used to, though to be honest, she would dance circles around you.

"Well," you'd have said. "Americans follow a capitalist system because we know human beings are essentially selfish, always on the lookout for number one, and the system uses our mutual greed as a check. It's the ideal solution for a species like us."

I picture you taking a drag of your cigarette at this point, blowing the smoke toward the ceiling. We'd all sip our sweet tea.

"Capitalism has reached its limit," Delal might have said as she put her glass down. "Our system—and I don't mean the state system, which is shit, but rather the cultural system of the Kurds and the Middle East in general—is based on mutual aid and empathy. We're a vast network of relationships where you put your own needs last."

And you would have laughed. What would you know of a vast network of empathetic relationships, isolated your entire life in that hell of a nuclear family? But I have lived what she describes for the past twelve years. I have seen it in action. Earlier in this book, I wondered when I saw your picture on the bookshelf hovering over one of our family parties, the house bursting with people, how your life would have been different in this culture, where everyone in that room, all thirty of them, would have felt responsible for you. When news came that a Kurdish cousin living in the UK was struggling with alcohol, the entire clan mobilized. We formulated a plan of action and divvied up the tasks. Who would we dispatch to England? Who would buy the ticket? When he came home, who would find him a job, and how would we monitor his movements to make sure he stayed afloat?

"Where do you think the power of your collective identity comes from?" I ask Delal one night.

"What do you mean?"

"You always talk about how being Kurdish gives you an identity others don't have. If you had to explain that to someone who wasn't Kurdish, what would you say?"

"Oppression," she answers without hesitation. "People instinctively know how others under the same oppression feel."

If she sees something on the news about a police raid on a family's house in the Kurdish city of Urfa, she says, or the army bombing a village in Van, she knows what they are going through because either she or someone she loves has lived through the same thing. Any Kurd feels this instinctively. If one of them suffers, they all suffer, because they have all experienced the same heartache.

"The state tries to erase you as a people," she says. "So, you respond as a people. Our language was outlawed, then when it started to die, the state said it was proof there was no Kurdish language. Record companies stole our songs, fitted them with Turkish lyrics, and played them on the radio, then said we didn't have a culture. Our parents and grandparents were arrested, our villages bombed and evacuated. Every Kurd elected to office in the East is thrown in prison and replaced. These things don't happen to me, Delal, but to all of us as a whole, and we respond as a whole.

"But I think maybe it's their hatred that unites us most. We face it together, just because of who we are, but we can't understand it. You can assimilate totally and forget you're Kurdish, and it doesn't matter in the end. You can't change what you are in their eyes. Why do they hate us so much? It's such a natural part of their lives they don't even notice it. A twelve-year-old Kurdish shepherd girl is killed 'accidentally' by a Howitzer rocket, her body parts scattered all over the field and people back in Istanbul celebrate. 'One less terrorist,' they say. In Cizre, a soldier shoots an eleven-year-old girl in the street, and the family has to store her body in their freezer because there's a curfew and the army will fire on them if they go outside. Turks ask what business she had on the street in the first place. Our children's deaths are reasons to rejoice. Where can such hatred come from?"

She's crying now, angry tears. It's the reason I try to be careful asking about this. The list of atrocities she rattled off is more than news stories. They're experiences. She has her own stories, and that's true for most Kurds. If Karin and I share an invisible bond because of what we witnessed in our family, then think of the bond among millions of people who have witnessed far greater traumas.

Delal is a community leader in Kurdish politics. Whenever she goes to rallies and demonstrations, I worry because for the last five years in Turkey, public gatherings of any kind have been attacked by police armed with tear gas and tanks, the leaders arrested and sometimes disappeared. But she has an instinct. "I didn't like the look of things tonight," she'll say of a gathering on Women's Day, "So we dispersed early." Or at a rally announcing the local candidates for Parliament, "The police are here, but you can tell they're not going to attack." She reads the signs like you used to read the winds and water when out on the Scorpion.

I imagine sharing all this with you, and I imagine you understanding, but honestly, I'm not sure. You and I always got snagged on the subject of race and politics. Maybe that's why I can't stop explaining it to you.

***

Dear Dad,

You would love summers at Dede's house in the village. So much would strike you as familiar. We spend evenings sipping endless tea and chatting on the balcony. We sometimes munch on vegetables from the garden or fruit from the trees by the fence, plums and apricots and mulberries. At night, we follow the calls of the little Scops owls whistling from the darkness, and sometimes we go to the railing to try and pinpoint their location just as you and I used to go to the screen windows on Memaw's porch to triangulate the positions of the barn owls hooting from the wall of trees. On the table was our tea, a plate of tomatoes and onions from your garden or a bit of apple cake.

I said earlier that Dede was like a replacement for you. He was also another me because he grew up without a dad. When Dede was an infant, his father abandoned him, and his mother went to America. We think he traveled with a group of Armenians from the surrounding villages who were fleeing the pogroms to find work in the New World. He returned thirty-five years later, with no explanation of where he'd been or what he'd been doing there. There was a picture of two blonde children he carried around in his pocket and another of himself sitting at the end of a long bar, staring forlornly into the camera with a fedora pushed back on his head, but all he would reveal was that the children were not his, and the bar was in a town called Lodi in California. So, Dede and I had mysterious fathers in common.

***

Dear Dad,

A picture of Memaw's back porch makes talking to you feel more natural. The house is flooded in sunlight, and a shadow falls over your chair, so I can imagine you there, contained within that shade. Another picture of you strengthens the spell, one taken closer to the last time I saw you—aging, thinning black hair streaked with gray. You're putting an empty pan in the oven. I remember when it was taken because I have a copy of my own that you sent to Japan for me to "show the natives." It was a response to my care package of food, a contribution, you said, to the "anthropological research on primitive Occidental folkways." On the back, you'd written, "Exhibit A: Male places baking implement into heat chamber."

I still depend on your sense of irony. It was always a source of oxygen in our sometimes suffocating Southern world of zealots, those unflinching, unquestioning Christians and patriots.

"Politics and religion are the domains of scoundrels," you'd say. You'd thrust your chin toward the living room, then, where Memaw would often be sitting in her chair flipping through the Bible. "Scoundrel number one right there. There isn't a book holy enough to save her."

I have needed you, Dad.

I needed you most when Delal's father was arrested. It was just a few months after our wedding in October of 2011. He was a language teacher at the local academy of the Kurdish political party and was charged with "training terrorists." It was actually part of a political purge that swept nearly ten thousand Kurdish men and women into prison—city counselors, teachers, lawyers, campaign workers—in short, anyone remotely capable of leading.

Delal waited to tell me till I got off work. We had tickets to a concert near Galata Tower and were going to meet at the ferry dock to ride over together, but she called to say that before the concert, we had to stop by the neighborhood of Aksaray. She wouldn't explain why over the phone.

"I can't," she insisted.

I couldn't figure it out—there was nothing worth seeing in Aksaray—just a mall and the Istanbul police station where I had to go occasionally to renew my residence permit. It was very much out of the way. When I met her at the wharf, I could tell immediately something was wrong. Her face was drawn and anxious, and she couldn't look me in the eye.

"They've taken my dad away," she said.

I'll never forget that ferry ride. I felt so angry and helpless. Delal held her father's diabetes medicine in her hands, cradling it in her lap. She thought they might let her see him if she had some sort of medical excuse. I got her a tea from the boat's concession stand, I held her hand, I hugged her as hard as I could. I tried to be any kind of comfort I could be.

The police station was a drab fortress of slab concrete. As we passed through security, I stared at the ten-story Turkish flag hanging from the A-wing just outside. Next to it was an equally gigantic picture of Atatürk, the founder of the Turkish Republic who had written the constitution defining anyone within the country's borders as a Turk. No more Armenians or Greeks or Kurds. Saying otherwise was a crime, a "terrorist" attempt to divide the nation.

We were let into Ward C, the anti-terrorism department. They took the diabetes medicine but wouldn't promise to give it to him without a doctor's note, which we didn't have. A doddering old guard with bushy white hair manned the information desk. "Don't be scared," he told us. "If anything happens, they'll run him immediately to the hospital. We have heaters in all the rooms. And pillows! No one gets tortured anymore!"

On a news program that night, one of the pundits said, "We should have completely assimilated the Kurds when we had the chance. Left no trace of them."

Over the next three years, I spent weekends at my father-in-law's trials. They tried the detainees from Istanbul en masse, ninety-five people at once. You and

I could have sneered together at the absurdity. At one point, the guest list for my and Delal's wedding was given as evidence, all the foreign names indicating my father-in-law was in league with foreign provocateurs. That's right. Mom was apparently an operative of the American deep state. (Yes, that makes me giggle, too). At night in bed, I used to recount all of this in long conversations to you before I went to sleep.

Once, during a recess, we went to have lunch in the prison canteen. Or maybe it belonged to the courtroom. It's hard to tell because one was right next to the other. (You'd have had a comment about that!) A friend of the family was talking with us—her mother was also one of the defendants—and she asked me if I regretted coming to Turkey.

"Stuff like this doesn't happen in America, I bet."

"I'm not so sure," I answered.

"Oh?" she said. "Has your father ever been in prison?"

I thought of the time you went to jail because you shared Pepaw's name, of the nights you spent in the drunk tank, and of that final time after Memaw kicked you out. I didn't want to reveal any of them.

"He passed away a long time ago," I said instead.

Once, I tried to explain what was happening to another foreigner at school, an older British math teacher who was married to a Turkish woman. We sat across from each other in the cafeteria, eating school spaghetti. I went through the whole story of the arrest and the trials. He nodded sagely, poked his fork in my face, and said:

"You have to be careful, mate. Your father-in-law may have been involved in things you didn't know about."

"I've known him for three years at this point," I said. "And I went to the place he taught several times, the so-called 'terrorist training center.' I think I know my own family pretty well."

"These people can hide things," he warned. "You never know."

These people. And so, I stopped talking to him altogether, to anyone outside the inner circle of our own immediate family.

I needed you. I needed you to ridicule them all, the smug idiot at lunch and the patriotic pundit and the judge and the old guard of Ward C. I needed you to crack sardonic jokes that made the faithful squirm. I needed you to be on my side, to stand with me against the world.

I needed Bob Gibbs. I needed my dad.

***

Dear Dad,

To be frank, I finally started writing you directly because of the gore, because of the sentence in your homicide report that described pieces of your body caught in the brake lines. It made me think of Wayne's story, of how his grandfather had been struck in the face by a piece of meat that flew from the body of the man he and the lynch mob were shooting. It made me think of the thumb in Aunt Nancy's father's jar and of all the pieces of flesh I've read about being torn or cut or hacked from John Henry Williams and all the other lynching victims around the South, then taken home as souvenirs.

The thought of those pieces of you in the metal grate of the cowcatcher—even the name of that part of the train was demeaning—broke me down again, left me sobbing and pawing at pictures of you. I felt small and unclean. What did all the relatives of these black men and women feel, then, as pieces of their fathers and mothers and sons were passed around as gifts?

As Delal said, it's hard to understand that hatred.

***

Dear Dad,

That picture of the back porch gathers energy.

We used to read together there during the day, then discuss what we had read that night. You had your history books on the Old South, the Civil War, and World War II. Or your spy novels. In a notepad I found at the Magnolia, you had scribbled three authors' names on the last page as "must reads:" Leonard Scott, J.C. Pollock, and Mark Berent, all three Vietnam veterans who penned political thrillers about the war. Maybe one of them wrote the last book you ever read.

I remember the books I would bring, Maya Angelou's *I Know Why the Caged Bird Sings* in 7th grade, a history of Jim Crow in 8th grade, and when you took me to the Clay County library in 9th and insisted I pick out a book by your favorite James Michener, I chose *The Covenant*, his stab at explaining South African Apartheid.

Something was nagging me about race and your attitude toward it. I had no idea what it was, but I couldn't let it go. You hated the overt bigotry of Memaw and Uncle Gene but would insist I was wrong, too, in believing everyone was the same. I was young, you'd say. I saw things in absolutes, right or wrong, but there were nuances I couldn't get till I was older.

So, now I'm older. Let's talk about it again, through books like we used to.

***

Dear Dad,

So, my book is called *At the Hands of Persons Unknown: The Lynching of Black America* by a man named Philip Dray, and yes, he's a Yankee, born in Chicago and currently living in Brooklyn, an outsider stirring up trouble like me with my blog in Turkey. It's one of the books I picked up to help me understand the lynching of John Henry, and it makes me want to ask you about a few things.

I find myself thinking of rivers, of the Peri that runs near Delal's village, of the Munzur in Dersim, and of our rivers back in Georgia. All have swallowed victims of mass murder and spit them back up in pieces. Your father was born in Ty Ty, in a pinewood farmhouse on the Little River where his great-grandfather had established a homestead. Four generations of Gibbs lived on that little tributary of the Withlacoochee. Not ten years after Pepaw's birth, about an hour south and on this same waterway, a mob of white Georgia patriots first tortured, then murdered a woman named Mary Turner and her child.

This story is harrowing, Dad, so much so that I feel we should stop and warn any readers who've stuck with us this far, for I know it's them I am really talking to, isn't it? Though I try so hard to talk to you.

In May of 1918, a black man named Sidney Johnson shot and killed his employer, Hampton Smith. Smith owned a plantation in Brooks County, just south of Tifton. People said Smith was a brutal boss; he took advantage of Georgia's convict leasing system to work his land with cheap labor and treated them like expendable slaves. He'd bought Sidney Johnson, for example, by paying the thirty-dollar fine Johnson owed for gambling, then beat him several times, once for refusing to work when sick.

Dray's book says Smith's murder was most likely an act of retaliation, but the lynch mob that formed to avenge the white farmer's death didn't stop to ask why it had happened or even who did it. In a two-week rampage, they murdered thirteen black men throughout the county. Chime Riley in Barney, Georgia, for example, had no connection to Smith's death. It was just chance that put him in the mob's path when they were on the hunt. They hung Chime, then threw him into the Little River, tying clay turpentine cups to his hands to weigh down his corpse. Three more dead bodies turned up in the Little soon after, all black men, their remains too mutilated to be identified.

In Valdosta, where Janine lived for a few years after abandoning you, a black man named Hayes Turner was arrested for being Johnson's accomplice and locked up in the county jail. Threats of lynching grew too intense to ignore, and so police tried to transfer him to Moultrie, but a group of whites intercepted them on the road and hung Turner from a tree on the Okapilco Creek, the same creek that ran through Autreyville, the same creek on which Memaw and your grandparents were living at the time.

Hayes' wife, Mary, publicly protested her husband's murder, and the whites turned their fury on her. Atlanta's newspaper reported that she had "made unwise remarks," that "the people were angered by her attitude." A newspaper article like this in Turkey, Dad, would be recognized as a covert call to mobilize the mob. It was a similar sentence that preceded the assassination of the Armenian Hrant Dink I mentioned way back in the third chapter.

Valdosta's sheriff arrested Mary, then surrendered her to a group of white men who drove her north toward Tifton, stopping at a place in the woods along the Little River called Folsom's Bridge. There, before an audience including wives and children of the mob, she was stripped, hung upside down by the ankles and soaked in gasoline. She was eight-months pregnant at the time, and as she burned, a man took the kind of knife used for butchering hogs and cut the baby from her belly. The infant fell to the ground at which point a group of men trampled it to death. The mob buried the child beneath the tree where its mother had hung. One of them marked the site with an empty whiskey bottle and a cigar jammed in its neck. Far from being ashamed of what they'd done, one of the murderers took NAACP investigator Walter White to the site and bragged, "Mister, you ought to have heard that n—— wench howl!"

I think of all the accounts I've read of the Armenian Genocide here in Turkey, of Turkish soldiers cutting open pregnant women with their bayonets and skewering the infants. I thought them too medieval to be true, the kind of exaggeration you spread about your enemy in order to make them appear even more demonic in the eyes of the world, yet here in our own backyard, Dad, at the same time as the Genocide, our people performed the same barbaric acts and felt pride. Whole families came to watch as if it were a high school band performance.

And I can't comfort myself by saying this was an aberration. This torture, this terrorism was one of the traditions of our South.

In 1893, in Memphis, a black man named Lee Walker was arrested for "aggressively approaching" two white women as they drove along in their buggy. A mob busted him out of jail, hoisted him up a telegraph pole, and hacked off his penis. The crowd then played a game in which they excitedly swung the body back and forth around the pole like a tetherball. When they grew bored, they cut Lee down and threw him into a fire. Women were escorted to the front to get an unobstructed view of the burning flesh. When the fire died down, people reached into the warm ash and took teeth, nails, and bits of burned flesh as keepsakes.

In 1922, in Kirvin, Texas, a seventeen-year-old white girl named Eula Ausley was murdered in much the same manner as Loreena Wilkes, her throat cut from ear to ear and her body dumped in a clearing. Her grandfather, John King, one of the wealthiest ranchers in the area, urged the sheriff not to allow any lynchings of black people because he suspected his neighbors, the Powells; the King and Powell families were feuding at the time. The warning didn't matter, of course. Three black ranch hands—McKinley Curry, Mose Jones, and John Cornish—were seized by a mob, tied to a cultivator, and dragged through the streets to an empty lot between two churches. The crowd cut off fingers, ears, and testicles. "No organ of the negroes was allowed to remain protruding," a local newspaper bragged. The men were doused in oil and set on fire, a blaze kept burning for six hours by enthusiastic stoking from the crowd, including small boys younger than ten. As always, when the ashes were cool, everyone in the audience reached in to snap off a souvenir.

In 1904, in Mississippi, a farmer named James Eastland was killed in a shootout with a black farmhand. The alleged murderer, Luther Holbert, and his wife were captured by a posse, taken to the woods, and tied to a tree. Before an audience that, again, included women and children, the mob cut off their ears and fingers, distributing the pieces among the crowd as gifts. Then, before setting them on fire, they tortured them with corkscrews, boring straight into their bodies to twist out chunks of flesh.

In 1946, in Minden, Louisiana, World War II veteran John C. Jones was charged with loitering in a white woman's yard. A mob took him to a bayou three miles outside of town, chopped off his hands with a meat cleaver, then burned the flesh from his face and chest with a blow torch.

And beheadings, Dad, the hallmark of ISIS, the apocalyptic terrorists that rampaged for so many years on the border of the country I call home. ISIS madmen posted gruesome videos on the net as they decapitated James Foley, David Haines, and Haruna Yukawa. Such barbarism rightly sickened us. What, then, do we say of Cairo, Louisiana, where a mob lynched William James in 1909, then chopped off his head and mounted it on a fence post before tearing out his heart and other organs to sell as souvenirs?

There was one argument you and I had repeatedly, Dad. We had it when I was reading *I Know Why the Caged Bird Sings* and *The Covenant* and pretty much every time I brought up the subject of race. It haunted me then and still does now, because though you would admit using the n-word was wrong, that slavery and Jim Crow and lynchings were all crimes, you insisted there was a fundamental difference between the races that I refused to see.

"It's something you have to accept, Jeffrey," you'd say. "It doesn't mean you can treat them badly, but you can't expect blacks and whites to hang out together as equals."

I wonder if anyone could have distinguished the pieces of your body on that cowcatcher from those of Lee Walker, Mose Jones, William James, the Holberts, Mary Turner, or, of course, John Henry Williams?

Here's something that's not important, but nice to know.

Do you remember showing me those cuts in the pine trees while walking in the woods around Santa Fe? You told me all about the convict labor system, how prisoners were used as free laborers to extract the resin. Well, I've found out quite a bit about that in another book I'm reading, *Slavery by Any Other Name* by Douglas A. Blackmon.

As you once told me, there's a clause in the 13th Amendment which says that slavery is forever abolished "except as a punishment for crime." The South decided to take advantage of this loophole and expand the definition of crime. The state you died in, Florida, passed "vagrancy laws" to increase the convict population and thus the pool of cheap workers the former Confederates needed for the various development projects they were planning. Under these laws, police arrested:

> *common drunkards...persons who neglect their calling or employment and misspend what they earn...idle persons, including those who neglect lawful business...persons who are able to work but who are habitually idle or live upon the earning of their wives or children, and all able-bodied male persons over eighteen years of age without means of support.*

In other words, Dad, you. You would have been leased out and worked to death alongside all the black men these laws were designed to snare. What differences between the races would there have been as you mined pine resin, laid asphalt for the state's highways, or built Florida's railroad?

The gore, Dad, is why I'm talking to you again. Pieces of a loved one's body.

I visited the Agricultural Museum in Tifton. Your great-grandfather's cabin is there, memorialized as one of the first homesteads in the region. There was also an exhibit dedicated to Joel Chandler Harris, Georgia's famous author of the Uncle Remus fables. You used to read "Br'er Rabbit and the Tarbaby" to me when we lived on Tradewinds. I came across a story in Dray's book connected to Harris and Wiregrass Country.

"The great civil rights activist, W.E.B Dubois," Dray writes, "smartly dressed and with walking cane in hand stepped out of his Atlanta home and began strolling down Mitchell Street. In his pocket was a letter of introduction to Harris who was an editor at the *Atlanta Constitution* at the time. Sam Hose had just been brutally lynched in Newnan for the murder of his boss, and thousands of people from all over the state had boarded trains to Newnan in order to take part. Dubois wanted to enlist the paper's help to stop such lynchings for good. 'It occurred to me,' he said later, 'That I might go down to the *Atlanta Constitution* and talk with Joel Chandler Harris and try to put before the South what happened in cases of this sort and see if I couldn't start some sort of movement.'"

But within a few minutes of leaving his house, a passerby told Dubois that Sam Hose's barbecued knuckles were for sale in a grocer's window on the next block. At the news, Dubois froze, then turned around. He walked home "in a distracted manner," slowly coming to the realization that telling the truth was no answer. People already knew the truth, and they didn't care. You could sell parts of a human being's body in a grocery store with no consequence.

"I had overworked a theory," Dubois said, "That the cause of the problem was ignorance. The cure wasn't simply telling people the truth, it was inducing them to act on it."

***

Dear Dad,

I hear your objections, the same objections you used to raise to those other books I read as a teenager. The author, this Dray guy, is a smug Northerner who cannot understand the South. He exaggerates, but I've double-checked the sources, local newspapers from the time and eye-witness accounts. They don't differ in what happened, only in how we should feel about it. We burn human beings, yes, we cut off parts of their body for keepsakes, but it's justice. We're outraged and defiant and proud.

Pride, Dad. People felt pride in these scenes from some medieval painting of hell they acted out on their neighbors. They commemorated it, took pictures even, and traded them like baseball cards. In 1891, a postcard from Clanton, Alabama was printed showing a group of nine-year-old boys posing beneath the corpse of a lynched black man. Such postcards were mailed legally until they were banned in 1908, and then they kept circulating illegally.

In 1935, in Fort Lauderdale, a man named Reuben Stacy was arrested for threatening a white woman with a knife. Locals hung Stacy from a pine tree with a wire clothesline, and a group of little girls posed for a picture beneath the swinging corpse. One is four, one is seven, one looks about nine. Most of the girls look uncomfortably at the camera, but the nine-year-old smirks, her eyes focused on the corpse. She appears immensely pleased, but her hands clutch at her skirts, wadding the cloth in her fingers, betraying another emotion perhaps? I think of Memaw at the same age when John Henry was tortured and burned. A clipping from the NAACP's paper, *The Crisis*, published the photo with this caption, "Rubin Stacy suffered physical torture for a few short hours, but what psychological havoc is being wrought on the minds of the white children? Into what kinds of citizens are they being transformed?"

You protest.

"Jeffrey, these were awful crimes, but as I've told you before, there are good whites and bad whites, just as there are good blacks and bad blacks. These things were done by bad whites."

But it was everyone, Dad.

In Memphis, when Ell Persons was set on fire, the whole town came out. Two white men stepped into the flames and cut off his ears, then his lower lip. Members of the crowd grew so anxious to get a piece of their own for a keepsake, they had to be restrained with a rope. The local papers had announced the lynching as if it were a concert or a county fair, and many parents sent notes to school, asking that their children be excused to attend. Vendors sold sandwiches and chewing gum to the crowd.

It was everyone.

In Greenville, Mississippi, in 1903, a black man was hanged from a telegraph pole downtown. A reporter wrote, "Girls looked on and applauded.

Everything was orderly, there was not a shot, but much laughing and hilarious excitement. It was quite a gala occasion, and as soon as the corpse was cut down, all the crowd took themselves to the park for a game of baseball."

In Bartow, Florida, when sixteen-year-old Fred Rochelle was lynched, the town gathered at a bridge over the Peace River. They set him on fire, of course, and as he burned, served drinks and snacks to the crowd. Afterward, everybody cut off a piece of the body and took it home. The whole town, Dad! And this was just ten miles from our house in Lakeland. These grisly killings were not exceptions, but as part of the pattern as Cracker Jacks and baseball.

The whole thing stinks of genocide, Dad. I have spent too long in Turkey not to notice the similarities. Sometimes whites took out whole towns.

In 1934, in Mariana, Florida, a group gathered at the courthouse to watch the lynching of Claude Neal, but Neal had already been killed in the woods by a different mob who'd castrated him and forced him to eat his genitals before shooting him. Disappointed, the people at the courthouse turned on every black man, woman, or child they saw, driving them out of the stores, beating women and children in the streets. Black people fled the town in droves, their property seized and never given back. They did the same to the black citizens of Forsyth County, Georgia and Pierce City, Missouri and Harrison, Arkansas and both Rosewood and Ocilla in Florida.

But Jeffrey, that was just how things were then, you say, things have changed. This is your final objection.

Undoubtedly, things are different now, just as I am not the same raving hobo alcoholic my grandfather was. Our demons evolve as history does. So, I am an anxiety-ridden, co-dependent who needs a weekly therapist to avoid a nervous breakdown. I attend meetings of Al-Anon here in Istanbul and see so much of my behavior reflected in ten strangers there. It's all the classic pattern of the child of an alcoholic, apparently. Your drinking turned me into that, however unwittingly, and your suicide turned me into something else. Let's not forget Jennie, either, and the effect your abandonment had on her life or that your behavior, in turn, was caused by whatever the hell Memaw and Pepaw did to you, and undoubtedly their own issues were seeded by something in their mutual pasts, by its violence both physical and spiritual, individual and collective.

Consequences of our histories are passed down like genes, and we in turn affect those who love us, our spouses and friends and children. How can the fucked-up childhood of your parents still carry on through me and Jennie, and yet, the hatred that motivated these lynchings and ethnic cleansings of thousands upon thousands of people not still be rippling out?

It was long ago, Dad, but it matters. That's the whole point. Just like things long ago still mattered when you went to the railroad tracks three days before your mother's birthday. The savage murder of John Henry Williams was not an isolated storm of outrage against a single target, but a wave of depravity stretching from century to century. Those waters don't recede overnight.

Dubois said the cure wasn't telling people the truth but inducing them to act on it. He was speaking of a whole country, but it could apply to a single person as well. I felt the same about one man in the spring of 1996, after all. Everyone around you knew exactly what you were heading toward but did not act. So, I took your ashes away from the Gibbses in Florida, the people that watched you die and did not raise a finger, and I buried you illegally in Miss Hattie's plot, partly to put you near your father and beloved grandmother, yes, but also to stir the others up, all those Georgia relatives who should have known but chose not to reach out, not to be responsible, not to act.

I was no better than the rest of them, Dad, in regard to you, but in regard to the other part of that past, I've decided to know and to act.

I've harangued you enough with the books I've been reading. I want to hear your voice. Haunt me if you want. Tell me about your last book. Those three authors' names were the only written words you left behind when you abandoned that room to die. I search the internet for them as if finding the title might yield a trace of you. Maybe your final read was *The Iron Men* by Leonard B. Scott. It's a thriller. The summary reads: "Two German World War II vets and one American Vietnam vet meet in Berlin just before the Fall of the Wall to confront the legacy of the past...and defeat it."

FIFTEEN

I need to circle back to the beginning, to the first page, to Cousin Clark and Lisa, and to the blog I found that set all this in motion, the daily chronicle of lynchings in America, *Strange Fruit and Spanish Moss*.

At the time, I was not sure if my fuzzy memory of the story Memaw had told me connected in any way to the lynching of John Henry Williams of Autreyville. As I have mentioned before, all I knew was that Memaw had been born in Sparks, nearly forty miles away and too far for people escaping from a mob to flee on foot and hide in my great-grandmother's cane field. My ignorance of the Hamner side of the family and their movements was total. I thought any relative who might know anything was dead, so instead I wrote the author of the blog, explained who I was and what I wanted, and asked her if she knew anything more about Williams' murder. She didn't, but she did say that shortly before my email, she had received a message from a woman living in Florida who also had relatives involved in the lynching.

That's how I met Polly Yates.

I wrote Polly an introductory email explaining everything I thought I knew. She sent a reply almost immediately:

Dear Mr. Gibbs,

Thank you for this information. I will share with you all that I know.

I have been interested in John Henry Williams' horrific circumstances since my mother first recounted her understandings when I was a youngster. She has long since passed, and I have been doing my own research off and on for years.

My mother was only three at the time, and so heard many stories of John Henry Williams as she was growing up. She lived very near where the twelve-year-old girl was found. My grandfather was deputized, as were many of the property owners at the time, and was involved in the circumstances. I have been attempting to decipher bits from articles in the "white" newspapers as well as some in the "black" newspapers. I have woven together information from my mother and from the stories that she heard.

My mother reported that the KKK was very active in the community at the time and that her father was a (somewhat reluctant) member. I find this understanding of a grandfather that I never knew alarming, and I have searched for reasons to lessen the implications. I have mostly discouraging information about my grandfather's participation in this horrific act. I have more reason to believe that Mr. Williams was framed and was part of a widespread tactic, especially in rural areas to persecute, scare, and drive out people of color.

I do have some information that indicates my grandfather used his influence to protect Mr. Williams' wife and helped her move to Atlanta after or during the events that took place. As my mother was so little at the time, all the stories she heard would have most likely been favorable in terms of her father's intentions or turned favorable over the years. I have come to realize that there was a great deal of energy that surrounded this horrific event and that not all that energy was KKK sponsored, though much of it was. I suspect we will never know the specifics in the way I would like to. I do believe my grandfather and grandmother must have felt that John Henry Williams was not guilty, as the stories have come down to me with that slant. But it may just mean that my grandfather was one of the ones that it didn't matter to. I have come to understand that those times and people (like now) carried energy and intentions that ranged in intensity and understanding of each other and of their God, when they had any understanding at all of either.

Ultimately, I would like to find a descendant of Mr. Williams and share openly the painful pieces that I have left. I know this is unrealistic and perhaps very selfish of me. I have some idea that the energy shared between who I am now and my understanding of this event and the energy left here on this earth from John Henry Williams through his descendants could actually add to a very hopeful tipping point of reconciliation. I do not think this idea is too grandiose. After all, God as I know Him/Her is the ALL that IS.

Thank you again for your sharing.

Sincerely,
Polly Yates

I read over Polly's email several times, pausing on the line about her grandfather being in the Klan. I wondered if that meant my own great-grandfather and great-uncles had also been members? It was something I had never considered, but it was certainly possible. The group had been newly resurrected right there in Georgia after all, in 1915, by a preacher named William Joseph Simmons. Klan membership in the late teens and early twenties was a way of life for many and would not necessarily have been something to hide. The group portrayed itself as a mere Christian fraternal order along the lines of the Masons—pious, loyal, patriotic. In 1921, when Williams was murdered, a circular listed the ABCs of the Klan as "America First, Benevolence, and Clannishness." Under this creed, they sponsored picnics and baby beauty pageants, lynched black people, lashed young women found riding in cars with men, officiated at weddings, bullied Jews, and punished men who abused their wives. They marched openly in Washington DC in 1925 and even ran candidates for public office. Clifford Walker, for example, governor of Georgia in the mid-twenties, was in the Klan. If my great-grandfather had been a member, it would not have been that remarkable.

Polly and I resolved to meet. I would go to Georgia and see what I could find out about the Hamner store where I imagined the scene with Miss Linnie and the sharecroppers had taken place, and Polly would drive up from her home in north Florida to show me Autreyville, her family's old property and the area where John Henry Williams had been tortured and murdered. This was the other reason I wanted to meet Cousin Clark, to see if I could discover a physical connection between my family and that century-old crime. I just hadn't realized how tangled up Dad's suicide was with my intentions.

It was from the beginning, of course. When I first related this story, I said Memaw had told me about the lynching of John Henry on a visit after my college graduation, just before I went to Japan. I was wrong. In the boxes of my father's things I rediscovered in Lakeland were several of my old journals where a quick perusal through the pages written after Dad's death revealed notes about John Henry and Miss Linnie I'd taken in January of 1999. As had happened so many times before, the nudge of one piece of evidence brought all the facts and dates and memories I'd been struggling to access tumbling out.

I'd stopped by Memaw's house in 1999 on the way out to Tucson and graduate school. It would be the last time I saw her alive and also the first time I'd spoken to her or seen that house since taking the box of ashes out of her hands. I went, in part, because I wanted to confront my father's ghost, but there were other reasons. One was to face down the woman I blamed for his suicide, but I think a second was because a part of me cared for her, despite the hatred I confessed to Karin that night in her car. She had been sending me letters again recently, begging me to visit.

"My Darling Jeff," began one written that Christmas. "I haven't heard from you in a while. Why? Have tried to call your mother several times, but she is no longer at the number I have. Write or call. Please don't forget that I love you."

No doubt she had her own demons to face.

So, I forgave her. I stayed the night with her and let her spend time with me, the last remnant of her youngest son. I could see that was important somehow, that when she looked at me, she pretended she was looking at him again. I let her tell me about her first memory and had dinner with her. She made her famous blueberry crisp because she knew how much I liked it, and I made myself eat a second helping because it seemed to give her some kind of comfort. She was my father's mother in the end, and I could not just cut her out of my life, however justified that might have been. Maybe this was part of my white Southern heritage as well, that mix of love and hatred, that duty that ensures loyalty even to those who damage us. I was not the only one who felt it. Despite her own considerable animosity toward our grandmother, my cousin Karin took care of Memaw until her death, attending her in the nursing home where she lived out the last years of her life. In the end, Memaw came down with Alzheimer's and could no longer take care of herself. In fact, her disease was so fierce it wiped her memories clean.

"She became almost kind after that," Karin said. "I liked going to see her. Just think, once she forgot who she was, she was genuinely pleasant to be around."

***

Delal and I are heading south toward State Road 319. I have arranged to meet Polly in the parking lot of the Autreyville Baptist Church. We have just said goodbye to Lisa and Clark at the Cracker Barrel. At first, I didn't tell either of them about John Henry Williams or my intent to research his murder. I'm not sure why. It may have been out of that same sense of duty that took me to Memaw's that day because somehow, I was feeling guilty, as if I were betraying them and the family in seeking these answers. At the last moment, as we hugged in the parking lot, I decided to tell Lisa where we were heading.

"How interesting," she said. "Grandmama never told me about a lynching!"

"I don't think Aunt Dorothy would have been born yet," I told her. "Hell, I'm not even sure it's true. I don't think they ever lived near where it happened."

"Like I told you before, I just remember Grandmama talking about Tallokas Road. But more than that, I don't know."

***

We are supposed to meet Polly at two o'clock and are running early. Delal being Delal, she wants to pick up a gift before we meet, so we stop by a farm south of Tifton and buy a bag of candied pecans and fresh peaches. We kill time with scoops of peach ice cream on the farm store's front porch, fending off gnats as we sit in rocking chairs that overlook the orchard and a line of square fishponds.

"I'm a little nervous," I say.

"Why?" Delal asks.

I shrug my shoulders. I don't have an answer.

We drive through Moultrie and stop at the courthouse, taking pictures of the east entrance where the papers said John Henry had been escorted out by dozens of police and then seized by the mob. It's a grand building, neoclassical, with white Corinthian columns rising three stories to support the entablature and a hexagonal clock tower crowning the whole edifice. On the courthouse lawn, a red-brick patio circles a fountain, and a row of magnolias shades the sidewalk that leads to the street. A rhythmic buzz of cicadas throbs from the trees. The air is unbelievably hot. Delal won't even get out of the car. The ubiquitous gnats dart over my face as I walk the lawn, trying to get a feel for what this place might have been like a century before, with hundreds of men from all over south Georgia swarming the grass, bent on murder. Maybe my great-grandfather and Uncle Fred were among them. Where would they have stood?

We head south through the outskirts of Moultrie until we cross a highway, at which point there is only open land, cow pastures, and ponds with the occasional farmhouse or trailer set off far from the highway. I scan the scenery, unsure what exactly I am looking for or how I'll know if I find it. I keep thinking how far this is from either Memaw's birthplace in Sparks or the site of the store Clark showed me near Omega. And we are only getting farther away. How can her story possibly be true?

The church is the first building we see on the right, red brick with a tall, white steeple and a parking lot sprawling to the north bordered by a patch of woods. A single silver hatchback sits under the shade of an ash tree. Someone waves from the driver's seat as we pull in, and I assume that it's Polly. A woman with a gray ponytail steps out of the car. She looks to be in her late fifties and is wearing a bright turquoise, tie-dyed blouse over shorts and white sandals.

"It's hot!" she exclaims and vigorously shakes my hand. Delal gives her a hug and hands over the pecans and peaches.

"You shouldn't have!" she exclaims. "Oh, I didn't get anything for you!"

"Let's just call it Kurdish hospitality," Delal says.

"Well, we've got our Southern hospitality, too, and I didn't bring a thing!"

In a way, it feels like we are meeting an old friend. We hop in Polly's air-conditioned car and pull out on the highway.

"I thought there would be more to the town than this," I say. "Aren't there any stores or a gas station, at least?"

"I'm afraid this is all there is," Polly says. "The nearest gas station is ten miles back the way you came. Where do y'all want to start?"

"I'm not sure," I say. "You said you know where the lynching happened?"

"I just know the road. It's right past that old market up ahead, the one painted red."

On the left stands an abandoned clapboard building with a collapsing front porch and tin roof. It's colored a deep maroon.

"That's the very store Loreena Wilkes was returning home from when she was attacked," Polly says.

The mood changes instantly.

"Her momma supposedly sent her for some kerosene and other things," Polly continues. "And when Loreena didn't come back, she and her other daughter went out looking for her. One of the papers says they noticed a place by the road where there looked like there'd been a scuffle, so they walked into the woods and found the pond. It was the sister that spied the hand sticking out of the water. Someone had weighted the body down with logs and cut the girl's throat from ear to ear."

We turn right after the red store onto Pryor Road, named for one of the families who still own property here. It's unpaved, with a sandy clay surface and a wall of ash, oak and pine on either side casting us in flickering summer shadows.

"So, this is the road Loreena walked that day," I say.

"It's beautiful," Delal says.

She's right. With its dangling curtains of Spanish moss, it's a postcard-perfect picture of a bucolic, Southern country lane. I imagine the pool of blood described in the papers, the pale dead hand in the black water.

"Just think," I say. "If John Henry Williams was innocent, then someone got away with something monstrous."

"My momma told me that her family used to talk all the time about the lynching when she was growing up," Polly says. "She was only three at the time, but her mother, my grandmother, claimed that some men had wanted her to go to the trial in Moultrie and testify that John Henry had come by the house to ask for work and that she had noticed his clothes were wet. That was supposedly one of the key pieces of evidence. They found wet clothes in a barrel at his house, and the mud on them matched the mud in the pond. In the end, though, there was never any need for her to go to court, and grandma was relieved for some reason. That's what makes me think she didn't believe he did it. My grandmother was not a meek person. If she thought that man had killed Loreena Wilkes and she could help prove it, she would have done so gladly. My feeling was that she was being asked to lie and didn't want to do it."

A creek passes through a storm pipe that runs beneath the road.

"I wonder if this is where they found her," I say.

We stop the car, and all three of us get out. The water is tannic like Lake Santa Fe, a pale honey brown. The trees are wrapped in muscadine and kudzu vines; the green is thick and buzzing so loudly with cicadas that it's difficult to hear one another.

"I thought you said it was a pond," Delal says.

"Yeah," I answer. "But there might be one back in the briar."

"I wonder if any Wilkes still live out here?" Polly asks.

"I've been looking around in newspaper archives online," I say. "I found the obituary for Willie Wilkes, Loreena's father. He died in 1920, not even a year before the murder, leaving behind a forty-seven-year-old widow and five daughters."

"I saw that, too. I imagine a houseful of girls all alone on a farm out here would have been a target to a lot of people."

"My grandmother told me the mother died in a 'crazy house.'"

"Let's keep looking," Polly suggests. "The papers said she lived about a mile from the store."

We drive farther than a mile. On either side of the road are cotton fields watered with gigantic industrial sprinklers, more trailers and the occasional modern homes with ruined houses in the backyard rotting into tangles of vine and briar. We study the mailbox plaques for familiar names from the newspaper articles and census archives and scan the landscape for ponds. There are several on my cell's satellite map but none visible from the road. We reach the end of the pavement, having found absolutely nothing, and stop at the entrance to a two-lane highway.

"That's it, I guess," Delal says.

"Let's go back and have another look," I suggest, though I have the feeling this has been a wild goose chase. Why did I expect to find any clues to something that happened a century ago, millions of miles from nowhere? If Memaw had ever lived out here, I would never know.

It's as we are turning around that I notice the sign: Tallokas Road.

"Stop!" I say.

"What is it?" Both Delal and Polly look at me.

"Tallokas," I say. "This is the road where Lisa said Aunt Dorothy was born. This is where my grandmother lived!"

***

When Memaw went into the nursing home, Karin mailed me a box of our grandmother's memorabilia—old pictures, letters, and other items she couldn't take with her. One of the pictures was of her mother, Linnie, holding three fat puppies with Memaw's two youngest sisters at either side. Aunt Dorothy, nothing more than a toddler, stares at the chubby dogs in her mother's lap, and Aunt Carolyn, who died before I was born, kneels at Linnie's side, smirking mischievously up at the camera. Miss Linnie looks young, with thick brown hair pinned back and smooth pale skin. Her gaze is turned toward the animals squirming on her knees, so I can't see her eyes. Behind them is a clapboard house painted white and kept off the ground by squat brick columns. Judging from Aunt Dorothy's age, the picture was most likely taken in the mid-20s. Only the bottom third of the house is visible, and I study the details wondering if it could be one of those ruins we passed on Pryor Road.

Nell Hamner and her family appear in the 1920 census living on farm number 30 in Autreyville, Colquitt County. Nell is just six years old, soon to turn seven in April. ("Enumerated on the 3rd of January" is written in a flourish of cursive at the top.) The Hamners are renters, and her father Claude is listed as "overseer on a general farm." Their neighbors on farms number 25, 26, 27, 28, and 29 are all black, renters like themselves. I have mentioned some of their names before—the Browns, McCrays, and Mathises; the Stubs, Petersons, and Johnsons.

I want to pause on these six families for a moment because they were most likely the ones who asked to hide in Miss Linnie's cane fields that fateful night in June of 1921. I'd like to consider what exactly they were fleeing from.

Loreena Wilkes was found on Monday morning, June 13th, 1921. According to the *Moultrie Observer*, "Suspicion immediately fell on John Henry Williams, a negro, because he had been seen in the area at the time of the murder, chipping wood." By whom he'd been seen, it does not say. The accuser remains anonymous. The truth was, as in hundreds of other cases across the South, Williams' color had already marked him as guilty. He made a handy target, after all, having only been released from a prison chain gang a few months before.

Racial tension was already high in June 1921. Loreena's murder occurred just two weeks after the most violent race massacre in American history, a ruthless ethnic cleansing in Oklahoma that had also been ignited by a black man's supposed harassment of a white woman. In Tulsa, the *Moultrie Observer* reported on June 2nd that whites had killed "one hundred negroes" and burned the black district of Greenwood to the ground. Thousands of homeless black families were camping at the county fairgrounds while still thousands more remained in hiding. White mobs had attacked Greenwood from the ground and from the air, using private planes to raze thirty-five blocks of homes, churches, and businesses.

The terror of this catastrophe was certainly fresh on the minds of Autreyville's black residents as they watched suspicion crystallize rapidly around their community. Within just a few hours of finding the girl's body, Williams had already been arrested and was being held on the property of Polly's grandfather, Van Crosby. A mob converged immediately on Crosby's house, in such numbers and so quickly, Polly suggests to me later, that it might have been organized beforehand. She has a point. The *Thomasville Times* reports that on a workday, in the space of an hour or two, in a rural district with few phones and poor roads, "Men came by horse, by car, and on foot to the site of the arrest in order to assist in unraveling the mystery."

People must have wondered if they were about to have another Tulsa right there in south Georgia. The whites massing on Crosby's land were bent on a lynching, and so the Colquitt County sheriff, a young man named Thomas Valentine Beard, decided that if he wanted his prisoner to have a fair shot, he had to get him out of Autreyville without delay. He borrowed the small but sporty Jordan car of a man named Mayo Kendall and raced south out of town toward the community of Thomasville near the Florida border. According to the *Bainbridge Post Searchlight*, the hundred or so cars that chased after Sheriff Beard made up "the greatest mob ever assembled in south Georgia." More cars from

Moultrie and two other Colquitt County towns, Doerun and Pavo, joined the pursuit, meeting up with still more in Thomasville where the sheriff finally managed to elude them, transferring his prisoner to the sheriff of Thomas County after ducking down an alley behind the Baptist church. The caravan continued to follow Beard, while the Thomas County sheriff spirited Williams out of town.

When the mob found out they'd been duped, they were enraged. Rumors flew. Some said Williams went south to Tallahassee, Florida, others north to Cairo. Men immediately split off, heading for both. Before they left, however, "infuriated and determined," some broke into local hardware stores and stole ammunition, rifles, and pistols.

That night in Autreyville, according to the *Moultrie Observer*, "members of a crowd" burned down a "negro" church, and two black women were severely beaten as whites "went to every negro house to find Williams' wife." One of the women was tortured, barely clinging to life. The *Bainbridge Post* adds that windows and doors were smashed during the search and that black people found outside were lashed with whips. Baltimore's *Washington Eagle* reports that whites "tore down colored farmer's fences and chased wealthy colored farmers from their homes" then severely beat a woman and her son. According to the *Associated Press*, several houses were also burned, as well as a black Masonic lodge.

The violence continued on Tuesday night. The *Moultrie Observer* says that another crowd gathered in Autreyville that evening when they heard a rumor that Williams had been caught in nearby Bainbridge and was being brought back to town. "While waiting, some members burned down two negro houses, one of them the house in which Williams lived." Another church was torched at the junction of the Autreyville and Thomasville roads.

> One negro, Everett Hill, was wounded during the night and came to Moultrie to have his injuries treated. When a party came to his home to ask for information, the negro was belligerent and tried to use his gun. He was fired on, and some bird shot struck him in the face.

Everett Hill's wife and children fled into the darkness at which point the mob "fired many rounds into the house." Perhaps the Hills were the ones who came to Linnie's farm, to that little white house with the puppies? In *100 Years of Lynching*, Ralph Ginzburg writes that, "A sick woman and her child, who had nothing to do with the matter, were beaten into insensibility and left to die." Was this someone who failed to find Miss Linnie's field in time, or what happened after they left?

In the space of two nights, an entire community was driven out by their neighbors, its houses and churches burned, its women hunted, tortured, and beaten. And this purge continued for another week until "not a negro was left in the district" according to the *Thomasville Times*. It's not until the following Monday, June 20th, after the lynching is over, that the *Moultrie Observer* speculates, "Perhaps the negroes who fled their homes during the lawlessness last week and the missing people will return as they were notified it would be safe."

The implication of this is profound. A whole week of arson, floggings, and shootings by the largest mob in south Georgia's history armed with stolen rifles and pistols. Who were the "missing" people? Were they just hiding, or had something worse happened to them? Who was charged with "notifying" them that it was safe to go back? Had Linnie sheltered people in the cane field for a week, or were they caught? What did her husband and oldest son say when they got back from whatever they were doing during the terror and found the mobs' targets lying in their fields, for Memaw clearly told me that her father and oldest brother had joined "the posse?"

I will probably never know. But thanks to the online archives, I can find out if their black neighbors did indeed return, those six families on farms 25 through 29. In the 1930 census, the Mathises are still around but the Petersons have moved to downtown Moultrie, where two of the daughters work as servants for wealthy white women. Everett Hill has taken his wife and children to Los Angeles. No trace remains of the others. I can't say there was an ethnic cleansing because there are dozens of black families still living in Autreyville in 1930, but almost no one was left of Miss Linnie's terrified neighbors. My own family, the Hamners, moved as well. In 1930, they are renting another farm between Omega and Ty Ty where Memaw will soon meet my alcoholic, dashing grandfather at a house party and steal him from his girlfriend.

***

Polly, Delal, and I retrace our drive down Pryor Road. We watch the speedometer to estimate a mile from the red store and pull over next to a barbed-wire fence marked with a "No Trespassing" sign.

"It happened somewhere around here, I guess," Polly says.

Some sort of mill lies beyond the fence, the buildings and machinery are half-rusted and overgrown with weeds. We walk the edge of the road on either side searching for signs of a pond, though I'm thinking that even if we find one, how could we ever possibly know it's the one we are looking for? We spot nothing very enlightening and climb back in the car.

"I'll take you over to Crosby Road where my cousins still have land," Polly announces, and then we notice a pick-up truck pull out of a driveway up ahead. In the bed are two shirtless little boys, both standing; one holds onto the side of the truck, the other to the top of the cab. A hound dog trots behind barking frantically. At the wheel is an old man in a trucker hat, and I feel like I'm in a scene from a Hollywood movie about the Civil-Rights Era South. What's coming toward us is a stereotype sprung to life. My whole body tenses up, ready for a confrontation.

The truck stops alongside our car, and Polly rolls down the window.

"Hi there," the man says.

"Hi," Polly says back. Delal and I lean over and wave. The two boys in the back of the truck peer curiously through our windshield.

"Can I ask what y'all are doing out here?" the man asks.

"Well, my momma was born out here," Polly says. "And she told me about a lynching that happened when she was a girl. We're out here just kind of investigating, seeing what we can find."

I close my eyes thinking, *Jesus, Polly, don't tell this man what we're up to! He could be a descendant of one of the lynchers and see us as "outside agitators" come to dishonor their family.*

"Well," the man says, "I don't mean to be rude, but we were robbed recently, and you have to forgive me, but I get a little suspicious these days whenever I see a car I don't know."

"That's certainly understandable," Polly says.

"You say you're researching a lynching?" he asks.

"Yeah. A man named John Henry Williams was killed in 1921 for raping a white girl, and they burned him to death somewhere out here."

"Well," the man says, "that happened on my property. Right back there."

I lean forward, dumbfounded that he says it so freely.

"Really?" Polly asks.

"The pond dried up a while back. The stump he was tied to was still there till a couple of years ago, but we had to pull it out with a tractor. You say your mother saw it happen?"

"She was just three, so I doubt it, but my grandfather did. His name was Van Crosby." She gestures to where I'm sitting in the passenger seat. "His great-granddaddy was there, too."

"So was my father," the man says. "Look, if you're so interested in this thing, you should go talk to the schoolteacher. She did a bunch of research last year and could tell you a lot more than I could. Went around conducting interviews and the whole shebang."

He gives us the teacher's address and continues toward the highway in a cloud of dust. The hound dog lopes back the way it came.

"Well, that went better than I thought it would," I say.

***

"Grandmama always said you can't escape your genes," Lisa tells me one day in an email.

I think of the black neighbors and the little white family they met that night on the porch of the Hamner farmhouse while their other white neighbors burned houses, attacked farmers, and beat women. Did the mothers gather their children to them, those kids Memaw had played with as a small girl, Franklin and Mary Peterson, Lacy and Dan Mathis, Ellina and Lilly McCray? Did the women huddle together in terror, listening to the gunshots and the screams and the snap of the whips echo through the wilderness? Why did they make the decision to hide in the Hamner fields as opposed to fleeing into the woods?

"They knew Mama would help them," Memaw had said. "She had a reputation."

Did they wait concealed in the trees, then, until the men of the house had left, watch Memaw's father and older brother ride off before rushing into the yard and calling out?

"Miss Linnie! Miss Linnie!"

They would have found my great-grandmother with her younger children assembled around her; Evelyn, the dispenser of two-dollar checks, had just turned fourteen; Carlton, the future Uncle Sleepy, was about to turn eleven; Nell, my kidnapper and Dad's tormentor, was eight; Russel, the war hero, was four; and sister Carolyn had just turned two. Dorothy had not been born yet.

"We were scared," Memaw had told me. "The bunch of us. I hid behind Mother and peered around the edge of her nightdress like a little ol' frightened kitten."

What do I know of this white family and the woman who decided to help

246

the people terrorized by her own community that night? Or of their men who rode out into the violence?

***

In the box of Memaw's things that Karin sent me are a few letters to Memaw from her mother. They give hints about the family's years in Autreyville. They also paint a picture of a much different Nell than I ever knew, a doting daughter, a vulnerable child to be protected and fretted over. This Nell is the little girl whose mother chased her across the field with a razor strop, the one who hid behind her mama's nightdress.

In a letter dated May 8th, 1966, Miss Linnie writes from a nursing home in Moultrie:

Nell Darling,

As this Mother's Day is nearing its close, I thought I'd better start thanking you for my lovely card and gift. Thanks a million, dear, but don't you try to help us till you are well again. We should be helping you! Must say nitenite now, will try to conclude in the A.M. if I live. Dad is already asleep. Tell Bobsy I still have the Valentine he made me in '43. Tell him I might let him have it back for ten dollars. Who knows?

I still love and pray for him and Gene, too. I remember a little girl as well who sat on the doorsteps in Autreyville long ago with an old wash pan, washed one foot and said, "Now, by grabs, I am not going to wash the other one!" Remember her, dear? Her name was Nell.

She continues the next morning:

Monday A.M. Trying again. Hello Nell, my darling. How is my little girl on this rainy morn? I had a happy Mother's Day, I think. I wore a beautiful orchid from the flower shop (real, too!) brought by guess who? Columbus Gregory and his wife visited with us a while. He is pastor of Greenfield Church now and a wonderful preacher, too. He's also manager of the Coca-Cola plant and one of your old boyfriends. Or at least wanted to be.

This story of an old suitor piques my interest; it's so alien and discordant, this idea of Memaw as a flirty young teenager. Over the course of writing this book, I've formed a Facebook group with my Hamner cousins, all the living children and grandchildren of the little group on the porch that June night, at least the ones I've been able to find, and so I ask the lot of them if anyone knows anything about Mr. Columbus Gregory. Lana, Memaw's niece through her younger brother, Russel, has the answer.

"Russel used to talk about playing with Columbus when both of their parents were farmers in the community of Hog Creek in Autreyville," she says, then adds: "He also told me that Columbus and Nell were sweethearts for a bit."

Hog Creek is the tiny waterway that crossed Pryor Road where we first stopped the car that day with Polly. At that point, it's little more than a trickle but continues through farmland and woods until it meets Tallokas Road, from which point it joins Okapilco Creek. The Hamner farm was somewhere between these two streams. On Thursday, June 16th, 1921, the *Bainbridge Post* claims that officers in Moultrie told reporters they suspected John Henry Williams had an accomplice. With packs of dogs, they conducted a manhunt along "Pilco Creek" where they believed the man was hiding. It's the only reference I find to an accomplice. The mention of the creek makes me wonder if the baying hounds passed right behind my family's property. Uncle Russel would have been four at the time but perhaps old enough to be playing by the water with his sister's future "sweetheart."

None of my Hamner cousins are surprised that Miss Linnie helped the black families hide from the mob.

"It's so like her to do something like that," Lana says. "I remember when they had their store in Bridgeboro, she used to give every child that came in, black or white, a penny bag with a Nabisco cookie from the jar she kept near the register. Mama always said it was a wonder they made any money with all the stuff Linnie gave away. She just doted on children."

"When was this?" I ask.

"Well, I first met them in 1947, so it was after that."

So, the store I had originally imagined as the setting for confrontation on the porch was only their home two decades later. And yet it remains a central symbol here, for as I have said before, it represents the essential character of Memaw's parents—their compassion, their gentleness—and also the profound regard their neighbors held for them. It's a character I can reconcile neither with the people who raised the woman that helped drive my father toward suicide nor with the man who went out that night to join a posse that devastated a community.

There's always this terrible schizophrenia about the South and the people we love. The issue of race is where affection always breaks down. Aunt Nancy was my only adult ally in Keystone other than my father and thus, a refuge, but she could suddenly rant about "n——s" and fill me with an intense and complicit shame. My father, with whom I could discuss nuclear physics and the inherent corruption of politics, would stubbornly insist on such Antebellum notions as the irreconcilable differences between the races. And my great-grandmother could both save her neighbors from the mob and whip her daughter for playing with their children.

I know almost nothing about Miss Linnie's husband, my great-grandfather, Claude Hamner who, according to Memaw, rode off to join the posse that night with her older brother Fred at his side. The grandchildren called him Pap and remembered him for his big round belly and suspenders. I know just two stories about Pap. One comes from Aunt Nancy, and it's about a daughter's rage and a hidden demon coming out.

"Oh, Claude was just the sweetest man," Nancy says. "How he raised that demon I will never know. I remember once Nell told me that her daddy played the 'meanest trick on her.' That's just how she put it, too. She wanted herself a fancy pair of stockings she'd seen in a store window in Moultrie. They were real expensive, made of silk, I think she said, and she knew her parents would never be able to afford them, but oh, she wanted them anyway and raised a big fuss about it, so all anyone could talk about was Nell hankering after them stockings. One day, her daddy appeared at her bedroom door with a little present wrapped up all pretty-like, in a bow and the whole works. She was just sure he'd bought her those damn stockings, so she snatched it out of his hand and tore it open to find nothing but an empty box. Her daddy laughed and laughed. He thought it was the funniest thing! Well, she came at him like a bobcat, just a'punching and a'clawing at his face. Yeah! Her brothers and sisters had to pull her off, and she just a'kicking to get free of them so she could have another go. 'Daddy was just covered in scratches,' she said. She was so proud of this story and her little temper!"

I don't know how accurate this tale is, or if Memaw was maybe simply poking fun at herself when she told it.

I have a handful of pictures of Pap, his face always hidden in shadow by a wide-brimmed farmer's hat, except for one where he sits on the porch swing with his left foot tucked under his right leg. He looks to be in the middle of telling a story, a quiet half-smile warming his expression. A crutch sits behind him propped against the wall, and he's looking down at something in his hands. A young Memaw sits across from him, scratching at her ankle. I recognize her profile. The square angles and set of the mouth are my own. It's the same profile as my father's. You cannot escape your genes.

In all the letters I have from Memaw's mother, there is only one line from Pap, scribbled diagonally over the top of one of his wife's paragraphs:

Dear Nell,
I will try to write a few lines. I am not any good. I can't see too well, but maybe you can read this. I hope you are much better. Just remember, you are a Hamner *and can take it!*

***

Polly, Delal, and I find the "schoolteacher" the man in the truck told us about. She lives a few blocks south in a small brick house on a large expanse of land. We're hesitant to approach the front door at first, or at least, I am. In Lakeland, after all, whenever my mother and I are out driving around, she'll panic if I turn the car around in a stranger's driveway. "Hurry up!" she'll say. "We're liable to get shot!" She has a point. This is the age of cell phones and emails, and strangers do not just show up on your front porch unannounced. Moreover, there's a Rottweiler sleeping on the front steps. Still, our curiosity gets the best of us, and if this woman really interviewed the people in the town, we stand to learn a lot from her. I push down all my nerves and invoke Dad, his way with strangers. That's in my genes, too. Without hesitation, he would have loped up the steps, given the dog's head a scratch, rang the doorbell, and started jawing. So, that's what I do.

"Come on in!" the teacher says after we explain who we are. "It sounds like y'all ran into Mr. Pryor."

"Couldn't tell you," I say. "He didn't mention his name."

"Well, the Pryors had a few things stolen a while back, so it fits your story. I'm Mandy."

Mandy's house is dark, all the blinds pulled tight against the Wiregrass July sunlight. She ushers us into the living room where a teenage girl sits curled up in a recliner channel-surfing. A tiny Chihuahua puppy peers warily at us from her lap. When we come in, the girl lays the remote on the chair arm and stands, the dog held in the crook of her arm, sniffing in our direction.

"This is my daughter, Augusta."

Augusta puts the puppy down and shakes each of our hands.

"Nice to meet y'all."

"And that's Ronald at your feet. Augusta named him after her favorite president."

"Really?" I ask. "But you weren't even born when Reagan was in office. Why pick him?"

The girl shrugs. "I just like him, I guess. What he stood for."

"These folks are here investigating that lynching," Mandy explains. "Remember that class project I did last year?"

Polly, Delal, and I are invited to sit on the couch, and Mandy takes her daughter's place in the recliner. Augusta stands behind her mother.

"What can I tell you?" Mandy asks.

"Anything," Polly says. "We heard you did a lot of research and interviews even."

"Well, my students and I talked to a lot of people at the church. Many had parents or grandparents who lived here at the time. See, I was doing a unit on bias and how different people could see the same incident in radically different ways. Some of those we talked to felt basically that John Henry had committed the crime and deserved what he got, and just as many thought what happened to him was a horrible thing to do to a person and wrong no matter what."

"It was about half and half, wasn't it?" her daughter says.

"Did anyone say whether John Henry had actually committed the crime?" Polly asks.

"Let's see," Mandy says. "I did encounter a few people who questioned it. Some even went as far as to suggest that he could have been framed and used as a scapegoat. The folks who said that were in their early fifties and remembered hearing their elders talk about it."

"Did they say who they thought was the actual killer?" I ask.

Mandy hesitates. "No, no one had any ideas about that. One of my students heard a story that Mr. Williams had a job on a turpentine farm and that the owner regarded Williams as a hard worker. He really respected him and supposedly even spirited him off to safety when the mob started gathering."

"But he was caught almost immediately," I say. "At least, that's what all the papers say."

"Maybe it's the guy who loaned the sheriff his car," Polly suggests.

"This whole thing started," Mandy says, "because I was looking for an incident to engage my students on the subject of bias. It was a gifted class, and they could be demanding. They liked wrestling with big real-world issues. So, I decided to focus on lynchings, what with the Black Lives Matter stuff in the news and everyone so divided. Then I found out a lynching happened right here, not a mile from where I live! I couldn't believe it at first and started digging around. The store the little girl was coming back from is just a block up the road."

"We saw it," Polly says. "We were trying to figure out where the lynching happened exactly 'cause the papers said the murder took place a mile from the store and that John Henry was killed in the same spot. That's when the man in the truck came and told us the pond had been on his land."

"That pond's all dried up now," Mandy says. "And they pulled out the stump where Mr. Williams died just last year. Mr. Pryor let me see it before they did. Some people have pictures of the body, but they only admitted it after I promised not to reveal their names."

"Pictures!" I say. "I remember an interview I read that said whites were distributing pictures to all the black people in the county as a warning. I couldn't quite believe that was true."

"I don't know if anyone distributed them, but they exist. So, what have y'all found out?"

We put forward all we know to see if something strikes a chord, any of the dead-ends and clues Polly and I have unearthed from newspaper archives, family stories, and census records, all the dangling artifacts that have invited lots of guessing but revealed no answers.

"I heard the Wilkes family kind of fell apart," I say. "My grandmother told me the mother, Laura Wilkes, died in a mental hospital. Of course, I found her 1952 obituary which said she lived in a house in Moultrie right up to the end, so that was probably just an old rumor. I did some research on the girl's sisters, too, because some of the articles on the lynching say Loreena's body was discovered by the mother and 'another young daughter.' According to the 1930 census, Loreena's sister, Vera, is living alone with her mother. If it's just the two of them, I'm guessing they had an especially close relationship, maybe because they went through that trauma together? By 1940, though, Vera has a different last name and is living in Autreyville as a boarder, which maybe means she's been married in those ten years and already gotten a divorce. I know that out of all the kids, only Vera is buried with her parents and Loreena up at the Hopewell Cemetery. I can't say for certain, of course, but all this makes me think she was the sister who found the body and that it left its mark on her."

I hear my mom's admonition that morning over breakfast when I told her why I hadn't been surprised at Dad's suicide: *You can't assume you know what goes on inside people's heads.*

"Interesting," Mandy says. "I didn't know anything about that."

"In my family," Polly says, "there's always been this story that my grandfather helped Williams' wife escape the county. I remember Mama saying he got her to Atlanta, but my brother says it was Florida. Did you run across anyone who knew what had happened to his family?"

Mandy shakes her head.

"I'm curious about the school project you did," Delal says. "You said the kids helped research?"

"Why don't I just grab the computer and show you?"

Mandy opens a presentation with a black-and-white picture of a few girls smiling at the camera.

"I started with this photo and asked the kids what they thought was happening. They all guessed a festival or a picnic. Then I zoomed out."

The next picture reveals the charred corpse of a human being hanging from a branch just above the grinning children.

"The students were shocked," Mandy says. "They couldn't understand what they were seeing. Then, I told them that something similar had happened right here, and we all, as a class, decided to investigate. We read accounts from Northern papers and black papers, then we compared them to what we read in Georgia papers and analyzed the whole lot for bias. In the interviews, they had to think about the issue of bias as well and evaluate each person's response for evidence of it."

"Did you have any black students?"

"No, but it was a really diverse class. There was an Indian girl and Asians and white children and a Mexican girl."

"I'm just stunned you did what you did," Delal says. "We have a similar history in Turkey, too, and a lesson like yours would be incredible but completely impossible."

"Not everyone here was happy with it," Mandy says. "But most people were very cooperative. You know, I will say that after scouring all the sources, both me and my students were very skeptical that John Henry Williams was the real murderer."

***

There's a picture in Memaw's box of memorabilia of a man named Shelly Pryor. He leans against a white lattice fence with his legs crossed at the knee. He looks dressed for church, with slacks, a white button-down shirt, and a spotted tie. His hair is light and greased back, his eyes deep set. He wears an expression hard to decipher. On the back, someone has written in faded black ink, "Here you go. Guess what kind of smile this is." Below that, in much darker blue are the words, "Shelly Pryor, drowned June 19, 1948." Pryor was the name of the man in the truck who told us the lynching had happened on his land.

I go back and scan the census. In 1920, twelve-year-old Shelly is living just four farms away from Loreena Wilkes, her widowed mother, and four sisters. All the accounts in the papers stated that both the murder and lynching happened close to the Wilkes' home. One article in the *Moultrie Observer* says that the pond was almost visible from the Wilkes' farmhouse. Was it on Shelly Pryor's property, the very same bit of woods and fence we stopped at that morning?

Poking a little more into the boy's history turns up something curious. In 1930, Shelly Pryor has moved away from home and is living as a boarder in Liberty, Texas where he works for a logging company. He's a Southern boy on his own, seven hundred miles away from home and family. What makes me pause is his death certificate. I have been talking about megaterraces throughout this book, echoes of disaster in the landscape and strange parallels written in time. On June 19th, exactly twenty-seven years and a day after the lynching of John Henry Williams, Shelly Pryor is found drowned in Gum Slough, a pond in a swamp just south of Liberty. He is forty years old, the same age as John Henry when he was burned to death on Pryor land. His death mimics the deaths of both victims of June 1921.

I call it an echo in history, but Delal has another explanation, one far less philosophical.

"Someone took revenge."

It makes me stare harder at that picture and puzzle over the question on the back.

What does that smile mean?

***

After talking with the teacher, Delal, Polly, and I leave her house and look for a place to sit down, talk, and process what we've learned. With no restaurant or cafe for miles around, we settle on the BP gas station back up on the highway where at least there is a table at the deli. Delal gets a hot dog, I a sweet tea, and together we spend an hour discussing politics, race in the South and Turkey, and the lynching of John Henry Williams.

Polly reviews what her mother told her.

"I told you my grandfather was in the KKK, but my mother always insisted it was the 'good' kind. It never occurred to me there could be a good KKK. I always assumed she was trying to justify her dad's involvement and that was just her way of reconciling what she believed about her father with what she believed about the Klan."

The KKK did busy itself with more than just harassing black people. Polly says her mother told her about a young Autreyville husband notorious for abusing his wife. Klansmen rode up into his yard one night and gave him a beating he would never forget. They saw themselves as a higher-order moral police, free from the restraints of man's law and beholden only to God. No doubt when they burned John Henry Williams, they believed they were serving justice as dutifully as when they attacked the wife-beater. The thing with John Henry, though, was he had already been formally condemned to death when they seized him from the steps of the courthouse. There was no need for any vigilante effort. The Colquitt County judge had convened an extraordinary session to try Williams that morning. With the pressure of a mob of hundreds outside, the court convicted him of murder after only a few hours and sentenced him to hang. What Williams' killers wanted was more than an eye for an eye. They wanted a spectacle, a message to the community they had spent the last week tormenting. Do not overstep your place, or this is how it will end.

Polly's grandfather was also at different times Justice of the Peace, a school board member, and possibly a county commissioner, which perhaps shows how embedded the Klan was in the local government at the time.

As I have mentioned, Williams was arrested and taken to the house of Polly's grandfather, Van Crosby, for safekeeping. Sheriff Beard and several deputies guarded him. According to the June 14th edition of the *Moultrie Observer*, the crowd that gathered wanted to "help" with the investigation. The wet clothes used as evidence were discovered by a group of these helpers roaming the nearby woods who "rushed them immediately to the home of Crosby."

According to Polly's story, her grandmother had been asked to testify that Williams came to the house that morning dressed in those muddy clothes and asking for work. That story had made little sense from the start. Why would a man, fresh from killing a girl and desperate to hide the evidence, stop to ask for work wearing the very clothes he had committed murder in? And wouldn't there have been blood? Who was the "party" that discovered the clothes anyway? Clearly, it was not the sheriff or his deputies. Could the real killer or his relatives have been part of that group? Was the idea for having Mrs. Crosby testify cooked up then or later because they worried the jury in Moultrie might not convict their chosen scapegoat?

In any case, once the clothes were brought to the Crosbys, the mob was whipped into a frenzy. The *Observer* reports there were many shouts of "Let's kill the n——!," but somehow the sheriff was able to spirit John Henry away in the high-powered automobile of a Mr. Mayo Kendall, a businessman and newly-elected state senator. A high-speed chase ensued, the one I have already described, where hundreds of automobiles from all over south Georgia pursued them to Thomasville.

I imagine it was Mr. Kendall whom Mandy was referring to when she spoke of a turpentine mill owner aiding in John Henry's escape. Williams must have worked for him. However, so frightened was Kendall at the idea that people thought he helped the black man, he published a statement in the *Observer* the morning after the chase, right on the front page: "I wish to explain the part I took in assisting the sheriff in moving the negro that was under arrest in Autreyville, Monday. The sheriff pressed me and my car in to help him get the negro away. I went with them to Thomasville and put them out, and the sheriff of Thomasville took the negro in custody. I only acted as I was instructed to by the sheriff who told me I had to do it or be handled by the law. I merely write this to explain to the people, as I have heard on my return home that some thought I did this of my own will."

There seem to have been two kinds of white men in Autreyville that week, two opposing forces in Crosby's yard. Sheriff Beard, many of his deputies, and Van Crosby belonged to one. They did not necessarily have any sympathy for Williams or even entertain much doubt about his guilt, but they did believe in their duty to make sure he had a fair trial. The other—and judging from Kendall's appeal to "the people," the majority—wanted the kind of butchery the South was notorious for.

Where did Claude and Fred Hamner lie? If they were joining a posse that night, as Memaw claimed, after Williams had been caught, then they probably weren't on the side of Sheriff Beard and Mr. Crosby. I don't know, of course. I can't know, but circumstantial evidence does not look good. Maybe they had to go out or risk being targeted themselves, as Kendall's plea on paper intimates.

Maybe they were reluctant observers of the violence, or maybe they tried to restrain the worst of their fellow citizens' rampage. But if it's true that they rode proudly with the KKK that night, then it makes what Linnie Bridges did all that more extraordinary, even heroic, defying her husband, her community, and possibly even her own feelings about race to save her neighbors.

Another item to consider concerns Loreena Wilkes' death certificate. There are two, both issued by the State of Georgia's Bureau of Vital Statistics. The first is dated June 25th, 1921. The cause of death is listed as "throat nearly cut in to" (sic) with B.L. Lanier as witness. Lanier is one of the Wilkes' neighbors. This death certificate is signed by the local registrar, Van T. Crosby. The second certificate is filed a year later on the anniversary of Loreena's death. Instead of Lanier, it lists her mother as the witness, though Laura Wilkes' name is typed, not signed. The document itself is full of mistakes. It misspells Loreena, claims not to know her age, but says she "looks fifteen" and states her father was William "Pilkes." The cause of death is now "raped and murdered by a negro."

I don't know what to make over the two death certificates. It could mean nothing. But in the beginning of 1922 when the second one was filed, the chief of Colquitt County's police force, J.O. Stewart, was being investigated for corruption. In fact, a few taxpayers had submitted a petition to have him thrown off the force. One of the crimes he was suspected of was being "involved" in the lynching of John Henry Williams. He was one of the guards charged with escorting John Henry out of the courthouse on June 18th. His duty was to protect Williams from the mob, but it was suspected he was actually one of their number. The other crimes he was accused of were perjury and forging official documents.

One last fact nags. On June 17th, the *Moultrie Observer* announces the trial of John Henry Williams will commence the following day and "is not expected to be drawn out." It then says, "The evidence alleged to connect Williams with crime is largely circumstantial." One piece of this circumstantial evidence is a set of footprints leading to the murder site. They were made by a size eight shoe, which supposedly matched Williams' foot. According to average height and foot ratios, a man with a size eight shoe should be about five-foot-five inches or shorter, which strikes me as rather small for a grown man. I found a draft card from 1918 for a black day-laborer named John Henry Williams living in Moultrie. Though it's hard to be sure it's the same man, the general details match. The card lists his height and build as medium. It's true that in 1918, five-foot-five was closer to average height for a grown man, but my great-grandfather was about six feet tall and also listed as "medium" on his 1918 draft card. What if the part about Williams' shoe size was made up? What if it were too small? Whose size eight shoe was that?

Both Polly and I want to accumulate doubts. That's our bias. We have a need to prove Williams innocent. Given the flow of American history until this point, it is not an illogical assumption. Yet, what if he were guilty? Would that make any difference? Was it true, as I've heard from many relatives, that his crime was so heinous, the crowd's reaction was understandable? If such a reaction were natural and not racially motivated, then logically it would happen any time such a crime was committed.

I take a look at other court records in south Georgia around the same period. In Tifton, in 1915, a man named W.N. Cribb was charged with raping his ten-year-old daughter, found not guilty and released. In Sylvester, Georgia, a case of rape against a man named Lawborn was dismissed because of a lack of hard evidence. In Moultrie, a man named Ed Baker is accused of raping a young woman for the second time, found innocent and let go. In none of these cases does a mob throng the courthouse having already assumed guilt. The suspects are not pursued and burned to death after being declared innocent by courts. No one takes the law into their own hands. They are not mutilated and torn apart for souvenirs.

I propose another scenario for Loreena Wilkes' murder. What if she had been walking home that day and met at the edge of the Pryor property not John Henry Williams, but one of the Pryors, perhaps Shelly, who at thirteen, was just a year older than her, a teenage boy who wore a size eight shoe? Neighbors of the same age, they must have been friends. Perhaps they both went to the Hog Creek School just down the road with all the other white children, including the Hamners. What if Shelly raped and killed her, then hid her body in the pond? What if, when his family found out, they decided to save their son's hide by blaming the black man who recently moved in next door? Fresh out of a convict camp, he would be an easy target. What if it was one of the Pryors or a loyal friend who made the damning report claiming they saw Williams in the area of the murder chipping wood? What if the same man later joined the search parties hunting for evidence, went to Williams' cabin, stole a set of overalls, then dunked them in the pond before coming to Van Crosby's house with their find? Maybe that's why Williams' house was one of the first burned that night the mobs attacked the black community, to keep any conflicting evidence from turning up. Maybe Shelly Pryor was sent away after this, as far away as possible, because enough people knew or might find out he was the real killer, and then he died in the manner he did, with so many parallels to Wilkes and Williams, because in some strange way, time remembers even when everyone else forgets? Or maybe someone from the Wilkes family simply found out where he was and took revenge.

This is all wild speculation, of course; a story concocted from circumstantial evidence based on my own prejudicial assumptions mixed with a bit of pseudo-religion, but if that's true, then it's no different than the methods used by the mob that week to convict and execute John Henry Williams.

***

One last story, one that undoubtedly would fall under Dad's category of not important, but nice to know. Sheriff Thomas Beard, who made such an effort to keep John Henry Williams from the clutches of the mob when, according to lynching tradition, most sheriffs either surrendered their quarry happily or else joined the butchery, was part of a sheriffing family from Crosland. Crosland was the small town right next to Dad's birthplace, Omega. Thomas' older brother Wade Willis was sheriff of Clay County, and in February of 1900, he took three black men into the woods with a large crowd of white men and whipped two of them to death, leaving the third severely wounded in the hospital. Their crime? The sheriff suspected them of stealing overcoats from a hotel in the town of Doerun. "The crowd inflicted other indignities and bodily mutilations upon the men," says the *Tifton Gazette*. Given the unholy litany of "mutilations" in the history of American lynching, I can only shudder.

Thomas Beard's nephew, Malcolm, moves to Tampa, Florida, right next to my hometown of Lakeland, and becomes sheriff of Hillsborough County. There, according to minutes from the Hearing Before the United States Commission on Civil Rights, he does an admirable job providing for a secure integration of schools in September of 1971, the month I was born.

Last in this list is Thomas' son, Thomas Valentine Junior, who became deputy sheriff of Colquitt County, following in his father's footsteps. He is mentioned briefly in a book called *Unsolved Civil Rights Murder Cases, 1934-1970* by Michael Newton. On July 27th in Moultrie, Deputy Marshal Beard arrives at a possible murder scene to take testimony from train engineer R.V. Holt. "I saw an object lying on the railroad tracks," Holt says. "At first, I thought it was a white piece of paper, but as the car drew nearer, I could see that it was a man. It was too late to stop. I applied the emergency brake and blew the whistle." Deputy Beard found the body lying face down in the grass and noticed a wound at the back of the left ear but could not tell if the injury was from the train or something else. The man was black, "tentatively identified as Sutton Matthews." I think of Dad.

***

When I started this book, I had hoped, by the end, to have the answers to all the questions surrounding the murder of John Henry Williams. I went to the Colquitt County courthouse and poked through the archives but could find no court records before the 1940s. I went to Hopewell Cemetery just east of Autreyville and visited the Wilkes' family plot. Seven mildewing gravestones stood at the head of stone slabs, all enclosed in a ring of red bricks. Loreena lies just behind her parents and grandparents. Next to her is her sister, Vera Wilkes Culpepper, and at her feet, the headstone of a child named Francis with the dates eroded away. I went to the last known address of John Henry Williams, the convict camp in the 1920 census. It's now a patch of half-wooded lots and stockyards behind the Colquitt County Sheriff's office.

I turned up nothing. The past kept its silence.

The person who could have provided me with the answers I wanted, my personal eyewitness, was dead. Memaw passed away in 2007. When she first told me about the lynching, I had been too shocked to even think of the questions that would later come to mind, much less ask them, and after that, I never spoke to her again. For eight years, I neither called nor visited nor wrote. I had made my peace and moved on.

Nell Hamner, the little girl who fled from her mother through the field in Autreyville, died of heart failure at the age of ninety-three. The death certificate lists dementia as an overriding complication. In fact, at the end, Memaw's mind was almost a total blank. She didn't even know her name. And yet, the past was there, like it is for all of us, untiring in its pursuit, whether we are aware of it or not, speak of it or not, admit its significance or not. Memaw had inflicted her own catastrophe on a small piece of history, and in the end, she was overtaken by the echoing shockwaves. You cannot kill someone and go untouched.

The day her heart stopped beating was March 18th, Dad's birthday.

SIXTEEN

As I start the final chapter, it's April 2020, the Covid-19 virus pandemic is in full swing, and the whole world is in panic. In Istanbul, we are under quarantine, as are my friends and family in Georgia and Florida, Tokyo and Tucson. In the face of the latest global disaster, so much of what I've written for the last two years seems insignificant, a pointless dive into dead history, and yet when I dig around in the Moultrie newspaper archives online, looking for information about the convict camp where John Henry Williams lived as an inmate, I run across an article dated October 22, 1918. The subject is an inspection of the chain gangs and how many prisoners are infected with the Spanish flu: "Of thirty-six men," the reporter writes, "all but two are stricken with influenza. So far, only four deaths have occurred."

The story is surrounded by others preoccupied with the same subject. They could be talking about today. One article announces the banning of public assemblies, another complains that Moultrie doctors are not reporting new cases so they can't be accurately counted. In an editorial, a woman demands the schools be closed as they have in other counties across the state and insists the school board stop referring to such calls for closure as "hysteria." A paragraph in the top left mourns the unexpected death of local bigwig, B.B. Beard, from the disease; he was Sheriff Thomas' brother. I imagine that when and if this book is ever published, our current pandemic will have been forgotten, too, even as we continue living on the scars we pretend not to see. That's the peril of remembering only the nice things.

I go out on our balcony to take a break. It's raining lightly and gulls circle over apartment buildings up the hill and around the slender minaret of the mosque that broadcasts prayers every night, imploring God to protect the nation from the scourge. On the street below are the pink blossoms of a cherry tree and a wet gray cat slinking across the road. Her head is lowered, ears flattened. She's on her way downhill, toward our apartment. She sniffs packets tossed on the pavement for anything edible, then looks up toward me and pauses. I get the feeling she's in search of my father, the patron god of strays.

***

When Memaw died, I was living in Boston and teaching in a language school downtown. Karin emailed me the news. I saw it first thing in the morning when I got to the office. "It isn't necessary for you to come," she wrote. She only thought I might like to know.

"Okay," I typed in reply. "Thanks."

Not necessary for me to come. I closed my mailbox and waited to feel something. It had been eleven years since Dad had killed himself, and the memories were rusty. They felt like part of someone else's life. My desk had a view of the crosswalk beneath the commuter rail tracks near North Station. Outside it was a typical New England March day, gray and cold. A late-season blizzard was settling in. People went in and out of the subway clutching their coats as snow spun around them like ash. Cars piled up behind a city bus trying to cut across the lanes at a red light. Horns honked furiously.

The great villain had died, and the world didn't blink.

At first, I had no intention of traveling to Florida for the funeral. I had made my peace with my grandmother. I'd been free of her for years, free of the South she represented. I had assimilated to life in Tokyo, Tucson, and now New England. I wouldn't go backward.

My sister, Michele, tried to persuade me otherwise when I told her that night over the phone. "Your memaw always talked about having money set aside for you," she said. "If you don't go, you won't be able to claim it."

"I think that was all bullshit," I answered. "Anyway, if it was ever there, it's gone now. Uncle Gene got power of attorney over her estate years ago. He controls everything."

"You can't let that man keep you from your inheritance."

For as long as I could remember, everyone in the family had been obsessed with Memaw's money and property. They all thought she was rich from her marriage to Grandpa Zillman and secretly held a fortune in stocks, savings, and CDs. Aunt Nancy, for her part, was convinced every item in Memaw's house was a priceless antique. To me, all this preoccupation with money and land and things was part of the disease that plagued the family, and I wanted no part of it.

"Even if she had left me anything," I told Michele, "I would give it away."

"You can do what you want with your inheritance," she said, "but it's not about you. You represent your father now. You have to go down there to remind them he existed."

I left work that night and deliberately planned a night impossible in the South. The snow had gathered over the cars, the streets were white and empty, and the flakes were still falling. I dined at a Portuguese restaurant in East Cambridge, washing down a plate of cod with green wine, then walked to my favorite Irish pub, drank a beer, and bantered about the upcoming Red Sox season with the foul-mouthed bartender. He turned the flame on his Boston accent to high, and I found myself unconsciously mimicking him.

"Think this is Schilling's last season? Man's ovah fahty fah Crissake!"

I needed to demonstrate how thoroughly I could blow off the past.

But that night, I had an intense dream about Florida. I don't remember much, just sunlight reflecting off the surface of a lake, the dense wall of green cypress along the shore, breaths of humid air, and a feeling of absolute belonging when I wade into the warm brown water and go under, the eternal summer, the egrets and threat of moccasins and gators in the weeds. It was home. It had always been home.

I bought my tickets the next day.

***

We gather at a fishing ramp on the west end of big Lake Santa Fe, all the Gibbses that are left, Uncle Gene and Aunt Nancy, my four cousins and their families. Karin's youngest brother, Ray, unloads his pontoon boat from the trailer on the back of his truck. Uncle Gene clutches a white box in his hand. It looks like Chinese take-out, exactly the same as the one that held my father's ashes. He gives it a friendly jostle.

"I hear her in there," he says, "bitching we didn't dress nicer for the occasion."

"Better watch it," my second oldest cousin, Mark, says. "If her ghost is lurking about, she's liable to sink our boat out of spite."

We all laugh, not quite disbelieving.

"She was pretty nice at the end," Karin says. "Once she'd forgotten everything."

Well, Memaw, I think, *this is your eulogy.* We still don't know what to make of you.

"I brought some carnations," Wayne says. "This lady at work got them as a present for her birthday or something, but she was allergic, so I took them off her hands."

"Oh, Jesus fucking Christ," Uncle Gene mumbles.

We climb in the boat. As I cross the floorboards, they creak and bend. I hear a snap.

"Watch it," Ray's wife, Donna, says. "That one's rotten."

"This thing's been sitting out in the yard a while," Ray explains. "But I think she's all right. Just watch where you step."

"Another thing to piss off your memaw," Aunt Nancy says. "She'd have wanted us to rent a yacht. Well, we best be on our guard. Get your silver bullets ready."

The motor starts after a few tries, and with Ray in the driver's seat, we head out. The passage to the lake is gorgeous. We putter through a corridor of tall cypresses forming a colonnade of green and shadow. The water is shallow here, honey gold over a rippling sand bottom with cypress knees poking out like stalagmites. A line of turtles sits on a half-submerged log. We emerge through a curtain of Spanish moss, and when we get past the weeds that crowd the mouth of the inlet, Ray hits the gas and we lurch forward, speeding toward the opposite shore. The waves bang hard against the floorboards, the water spray hits my face and bare arms. The weather couldn't be more perfect—blue skies, bright spring sun, and a warm wind blasting across the body of the boat.

"So far, so good," Donna says, and almost immediately there's a thump and the motor cuts off. We drift in the middle of the lake, spinning circles.

"Guess I spoke too soon."

Ray stands and heads toward the stern. The whole thing tips backward with his weight and sends Memaw's box of ashes sliding toward the water. I scoop it up just before it tumbles off. A sheet of lake water rushes over the bottom of the boat, covering our shoes.

"Everybody to the front!" Wayne shouts, and we all scramble forward, at which point the boat tips the other way, sending more water flooding over the prow.

"Goddamn it!" Uncle Gene says, and we manage to redistribute our weight so Ray can work on the motor at the stern without sinking us all.

"I think it just needs gas," he says.

What follows is a delicate balancing act where Ray and Wayne orchestrate their moves so that when Ray comes forward again to get the gas can from next to the driver's seat, Wayne moves back to provide ballast.

"Better sing to her or something, Jeffrey," Uncle Gene says and nods to the white box in my lap. "She always liked you."

Ray starts the boat. "Yep," he says. "It was the gas."

We finish crossing the big lake and slip through the pass toward the little.

"I haven't been on little Lake Santa Fe since Memaw moved," I say. I scan the shoreline looking for familiar sights and see the heads of the pine trees on the east side where I used to imagine the shape of the tyrannosaur. I can still see images from the nightmares I had where I'd watch it stalk the trees, turning its head as if sniffing, as if sensing me across the lake. We pass docks jutting out into the water. A man with a cane pole waves to us, a little yellow-haired boy at his side. The boy is on his knees looking into the water where an orange bobber bounces on the waves. Spanish moss in the cypresses on either side of their dock dances in the wind. It's the landscape from my dream in Boston. It's the place I know most deeply, bodily. It's home.

We circle the boat in front of Memaw's old house.

"I don't even recognize it," Aunt Nancy says. "You sure that's it?"

"That's it," Uncle Gene says.

Ray does a couple turns in front of the dock where Dad and I spent so many nights trying to catch the giant gar. Our wake rocks the lake weed on the left side, then Ray veers east, and we head full speed toward the opposite shore. He slows the boat to a crawl when we approach the middle of the lake. We face the patch of trees where my dinosaur used to keep watch. Beyond that wall of pines is another world.

"This is as good a spot as any," he says, switching off the motor.

"Nobody make any sudden moves," Donna says, "or we'll capsize. We're here to throw her in, not ourselves."

"Hand her over, Jeffrey," Uncle Gene says. "Let's get this over with."

"Shouldn't we say something first?" I ask.

"Well," Aunt Nancy laughs. "As they say, if you ain't got something nice to say...."

"Hold on," Wayne says. "I have a spare funeral program in my pocket."

"A spare *what*?"

"I brought it from Uncle Jimmy's funeral last month. Maybe we can read from it?"

Jimmy was Aunt Nancy's brother.

"Great," I say. "She'll love that, a secondhand prayer."

"And for one of my family members," Aunt Nancy adds. "Us 'Shanty Irish.' She's going to sink us for sure."

Wayne holds out the program to me. "Jeffrey, I think you should be the one to do it."

"Me?"

"You're the only one left of your dad. Just skip all the stuff about Jimmy. It's got a pretty passage in there somewhere. Yep, there. It's from the Bible, I think."

I look down to where his finger taps the page. "It's the twenty-third psalm," I say.

"That's a good one, isn't it?"

"Well, then," Uncle Gene says. "Get to it. We ain't got all day."

I look at them all. It's quiet, no birds, no boat motors, just the wind and the sound of the water lapping the gunwale. Nothing had changed in Boston when Karin told me the news, but here, at the heart of it all, we hold our breath, and I feel like the world is about to shed its skin.

I begin. "The Lord is my Shepherd. I shall not want. He maketh me to lie down in green pastures."

Uncle Gene opens the box and tears the plastic seal.

"He restoreth my soul. He leadeth me in the paths of righteousness for his name's sake."

He dumps the ashes into the water, giving the bag a rough shake.

"Come out of there, goddamn it," he grumbles.

A cloud of ash wafts over the water. Clumps of yellow-gray float on the dark surface.

"Yea, though I walk through the valley of the shadow of death, I will fear no evil."

As soon as I hit the word 'evil,' the fish start jumping, snapping up Memaw's ashes as if they were breadcrumbs. I start to snicker. I hear Karin giggle, too.

"For thou art with me. Thou preparest a table before me in the presence of my enemies."

The water is practically boiling at this point. It's like every fish in the lake has converged on our boat. No sooner does a spot of ash fall from the bag that something gobbles it up.

"That's the last thing I eat out of this lake," Aunt Nancy says, and we all get to laughing so hard, I can't go on.

"Oh well," Wayne says and tosses the secondhand carnations right into the middle of the feeding frenzy. They float together for a second, a bright spot of red, then slowly drift apart.

"That was a nice touch, after all," Uncle Gene says, thrusting his chin toward the flowers.

On the way back, he sits beside me, sucking thoughtfully on his pipe. His trucker's cap is pulled down over his eyes, and his hair sticks out the back. It's all gray now. The last time I saw him it was still jet black. I wonder what he's feeling after dumping his mother in the lake. Maybe he's thinking about his younger brother. Maybe that's why he chose the spot next to me. He's the last of that tormented nuclear family.

"You know, Jeffrey," he begins, "she had a CD set aside for you and Karin in the bank. But all that money went to the nursing home. There's nothing left."

***

That night, back at Memaw's house, I wander through the rooms one by one, touching the walls, the furniture, the pictures. Aunt Nancy follows close behind. She's moved in already because her place on Lake Geneva is literally falling down. My uncle is still there, though the roof of the living room caved in last month. She talks nonstop as we walk together, but her eyes never leave my hands. I get the feeling she's afraid I'm going to pocket something valuable. There's another feeling, too, a powerful one that comes from outside of me, like I'm walking with the weight of my father's right to walk here. We both feel it.

In Dad's old room, I find a watercolor he made as a young man, a European street at sunset. What in the world ever possessed the alcoholic outcast from Wiregrass country to paint such a thing? To my astonishment, I find more evidence of my father's artistic leanings in the bottom drawer of Memaw's dresser. There's a typed short story, the paper yellowed. Beneath that is a detailed drawing of a gas station in Omega and another paper titled "An Excerpt from the Disturbed Mind of Robert L. Gibbs, Jr. Re: This hard life we try to live." "In all the hustle and bustle of these modern times," it begins, "all of the old-school normalcy has ceased."

"Dad wrote?" I ask aloud.

"Yeah," Aunt Nancy says. "Your memaw said he scribbled a few things when he was younger."

"He never told me. All those years I talked about being a writer."

"Take them if you want," she says. "I don't know who she left the dresser to."

In my old room, I find a box of old quilts and afghans.

"Some of those might be worth a fortune," my aunt says.

"I wouldn't sell them."

"You can have one if you want. There's plenty of the damn things. I don't know who gets the bedroom set, though. That's a nice bed frame, mahogany. I think it's an antique."

"Wasn't there a will?" I ask. "She was forever asking me what I wanted when she died."

"She just left the house to Gene; that's all I know. He controls it all. Mommy's dearest."

Under the quilts is a box of loose pictures. One after the other of Uncle Russel in his Air Force uniform, and then an old family photo album from back when Memaw was a Gibbs. The front page has a family register with a list of names. Next to my father's is the date, "Died, April 23rd, 1996." No one else's has been updated with a death date, not Pepaw's or Uncle Russel's or her parents' even. The same is true of an old Bible, so ragged the pages are falling out. In the front is a family tree. Memaw has crossed my father's name out and written beneath, "Killed by a train." Again, no one else's death date has been noted, not Linnie and Pap's, not Robert Lenward Senior's. Had she dug out these old records just to record his passing?

"There's nothing in that but pictures," Aunt Nancy says.

"I know," I say. "That's what I'm after."

"Well, you can have all those of your daddy." She's peering over my shoulder and then looking back as if someone were watching both of us.

Underneath the Bible is photo after photo of my father, from the beginning of his life to the end. There's one of him as a baby, sitting in a chair too big for him with a Pinocchio doll clutched in his right hand. There's another of him as a little boy, posing in a gray shirt and tweed jacket. "Jacksonville" is scribbled on the back. There's one of him in a white tuxedo with his prom date. I flip it over and see Memaw's handwriting, "Mary, His love." Several are misshapen cut-outs of him alone; someone has clipped off everyone else with a pair of scissors. Another photo shows him and my mother rigging a sailboat, another as a teenager sitting on the trunk of an old Chevy with his arms folded across his skinny chest, another dressed in a suit and tie with Linnie and Pap at either side. There's one of him as a toddler, wearing a hat with ear flaps, a bewildered white puppy at his feet, another standing at a picket fence as a baby with a bottle in his mouth, Uncle Gene in suspenders behind. In still another, he's posing as a twenty-something in front of a barn with his arm around his mother. He's spinning me around in the shallow water next to the dock at Santa Fe, he's in the living room holding a sailing trophy, he's driving a motorboat down a river as a beanpole of a teenager with no shirt and a tackle box at his feet. Under the pictures are graduation and wedding announcements, old report cards. Half a ratty valentine has slipped to the bottom of the box. It looks like a gingerbread man with hearts for eyes. "To Mama, from Bob," is written across the neck.

"Well," Aunt Nancy says, "all she lived for was Gene, Gene, Gene, but I guess your daddy crossed her mind once in a blue moon."

This is my inheritance. Her memory and his, this box of thwarted love and regret.

***

On my and Delal's last morning in Georgia, we have breakfast with Lisa again at the Cracker Barrel in Tifton. "Honest to goodness Southern cooking served on old-fashioned plates," a sign out front brags. It's such a strange place to end this, a chain restaurant that turns memory into merchandise. These rustic farm tools and black-and-white photos hanging on the wall are like objects at a theme park, marketing a concept to a town that lived the real thing, but they aren't true artifacts. They have no ghosts. The old lady on the porch of the log cabin in the picture above our table most likely came with the kit the corporation ships out to its franchises, but I've got dozens just like it of relatives who were born in the farmland that starts just beyond the parking lot. I see the road from the window, Highway 319, Alabama Avenue, which runs from here west, toward Omega and Moultrie, past the graveyard with Dad and Pepaw, and then to the Colquitt County Courthouse, with a turn-off for Autreyville before it finally crosses into Florida. I think, *This restaurant is a perfect metaphor for my father's family, a facsimile of the real thing created by people who've never seen it, a changeling without love or a soul.*

"That was Gus Patrick that just left," Lisa says out of the blue.

"Who?" I ask.

"Your cousin, Gus Patrick, a bigwig in the Patrick clan. He would have been your daddy's second cousin, I guess, on his father's side."

"I know the name. I mean, where is he?"

I look toward the door and then out the window.

"He's already gone. I would have introduced you, but I wasn't sure how it would go."

"What do you mean?"

"If he knew who you were. After the way you buried your daddy. You know, without asking, in their plot."

I nod. "I guess I kind of put a burr in his britches."

"Now, I don't know about that," she demurs.

I'm thinking about this as we head south out of Tifton toward the Florida border. On the right are a series of billboards. One shows Jesus hovering over a

269

cemetery filled with B-movie zombies. "Which Kind of Undead Do You Want To Be?," it asks.

"I feel kind of embarrassed," I tell Delal.

"About what?"

"That I can't be introduced to a long-lost relative because I pirated his cemetery plot."

"Why'd you do it, then?"

"I don't know," I say. "No, that's not true. I did it because he'd been forgotten by everyone, and I wanted them all to sit up and take notice."

"There's no official record of him being there?"

"No."

"Nothing filed away with the city or county?"

"No."

"So, if someone wanted to find him and went poking around in all those archives like you've been doing, they wouldn't turn up a thing?"

"No."

"Then, it's like he never existed. Forgotten all over again."

The word comes out without me even being aware of it, "Daddy."

And then I'm crying like I haven't cried for him since that night in Karin's truck two decades before.

***

Mom asked me why I wanted to remember "the bad things." I think it's like those pictures on the wall of the Cracker Barrel. They mimic life but are soulless because they've been robbed of their context. They have no impact. Who was that old woman in the photo above the table? What had her intentions been, the cut of the sins she wore and the craters she left in the timescape? How could anyone love her without knowing such things? How could she have any gravity? She's been robbed of her story, unremembered and slapped on the wall as you would stick a plastic flamingo in your lawn when you first move to Florida because you have no substantial understanding of the place you occupy.

My family contributed to the forgetting of a human being when Autreyville burned John Henry. He got neither a grave, a stone, nor a word to mark his impact on the world. Maybe there was a kind of justice in Dad's pirated headstone and inglorious death or in Memaw's complete erasure from history. She had no headstone either, legal or otherwise.

When I explain this writing project to friends, to Delal, or to Florida family, or to anyone foolish enough to ask what I do all day shut up in my room, they inevitably want to know what in the world my father's suicide could possibly have in common with the lynching of John Henry Williams. I don't say I don't know. I smile, tell them I have faith in my guides, and then change the subject so that no one can ask what those guides might be. I have barreled ahead, hoping in the end that it all ties together.

But here at the conclusion, I'm still confounded by that same question. I stare and stare at the blank screen, scribble something about scars and tragedies, then erase it. I write, "The lynchings still have an impact on the families and towns in which they happened just as my father's suicide has its impact on us, however much we try to forget." It's true, but it's bullshit to pretend that's why I wrote hundreds of pages. I erase it and write, "All these deaths have the same source" and erase that, too. Then in a rush of irritation and frustration, I type, "Just what are you trying to say about race and society then, smartass?"

And then I know. Nothing. Because I'm not qualified to say anything about those things. What I am really trying to talk about is who I am, as Jeff, as a Gibbs and Hamner, as a Floridian and Southerner, as a white man and an American and the son of a suicide and an alcoholic and as the descendant of a place and people that mutilated and burned their fellow human beings. I am not just an individual, but a coming together of all these histories. I am filling out my shape as fully as I can and claiming its gravity, the full story of our collective past, with its sins and trespasses, its impacts and ghosts, its catastrophes and echoes of catastrophes across time, and all the responsibility that it carries. I am staking claim to all my identities.

***

It's now April 23rd, 2020, the twenty-fourth anniversary of Dad's death. In Turkey, it's Children's Day, an official holiday celebrating another anniversary, that of the first parliament of the Turkish Republic. There are fireworks, balloons, dance shows, and flags, or rather there would be if not for the pandemic.

I have been writing this book for more than two years. Memaw has been gone thirteen years, Uncle Gene eleven. Here, in the final pages, I want to yield the stage to the last of them, the woman without whom this project would have been impossible, my Aunt Nancy. She has been one of the most colorful characters in my life. Most people in the family would say the same. I've always felt she deserved to be immortalized in writing. However much her views on race disturb me, she was the only adult in the clan who didn't feel like a threat, who I knew was on our side. She made living among the Hamners and Gibbses feel as close to a home as it could.

Aunt Nancy is now in a nursing home in Gainesville, well into her eighties and suffering from a variety of health problems, ranging from broken knees and hips to hypertension. Whenever we meet in person or even talk on the phone, she bursts into tears and says, "I worry I'll never see you again!"

I know she doesn't have long, and when she goes, that awful wish I made in Karin's truck after Dad died will come true. They will all be dead at last, and in passing, she'll take with her a gift for storytelling and all the memories she has kept so faithfully for decades. Thus, she'll also take a good chunk of who I am. When everyone else was too proud or ashamed or indifferent to explain the history that led to what we'd become, she was generous with her knowledge.

The last time I saw her was at Karin's house. She was talking about her favorite show, *Naked and Afraid*, and we kids, ever in pursuit of explanations, were prodding her away from the topic of reality TV and toward stories about Memaw. Karin told her I was writing a book about the family.

"You are?" she said. "You'll need to write a couple volumes, then."

We'd discovered some old photographs, including several of Linnie and Claude. Among them was a sepia-toned portrait of a woman who looked remarkably like Miss Linnie, but something was off. The nose was wrong, and the eyes seemed too big.

"I think that's Linnie's mama," Aunt Nancy said at last. "My great-grandmother Dean." She gave it a shake and squinted. "Or maybe it is Aunt Linnie when she was younger. Lord, I don't know. My old eyes can't see a damn thing anymore." She handed me the photo. "Miss Linnie was the sweetest thing you ever did meet. Oh, just the kindest woman in the world. I think someone must have switched your memaw in the hospital when she was born. I hear the leprechauns do that sort of thing." She shook her head. "Of course, Nell couldn't stand her mama. She couldn't stand anyone kind. She thought being kind was weak, see. I remember…"

She stopped.

"Now, how did that go? There was something about stockings."

"What?" I asked.

"A story I used to tell all the time. Nell and the stockings. Her daddy bought her these stockings for her birthday, only he got them from a discount store, and she was so mad he bought the cheap ones, she ripped them up with her bare hands and tossed them in his face."

"That's not how you used to tell it," I said.

"It isn't?"

"You used to say he gave her an empty box, and she thought it was the stockings she wanted from a fancy store, and she got so mad she kicked him."

"Are you sure?"

"Well, no. Maybe I've got it wrong."

She grinned and shrugged. "Oh, it doesn't matter anymore, anyway. She was a crazy old bat. Memory goes like everything else. Flush it down the commode with all the other bullshit. It's...now, what do they call it? Hearsay. That's it. When you write that book of yours, you tell them that from me. This is all hearsay, see? You tell them that's all it ever was. Hearsay."

And she burst out laughing.

ACKNOWLEDGMENTS

I would like to first and foremost thank the folks at April Gloaming for taking a chance on *The Peril of Remembering Nice Things*. I would also like to thank all of those who helped critique and edit its many drafts, including Michael Goertzen, Ned Entrikin, Stephen Freer, and David Joiner. David, especially, helped me navigate the twists and turns of publishing with an indie press. Numerous other writer friends from Frederike Geerdink and Jiyar Gol, to Louise Callaghan and Karen Branan provided invaluable advice. The actual fleshing out of this story owes the most to my mother and sister who tolerated all my questions as I tried to sort out family memories. I owe a lot to my cousin Karin for being so honest and brave in walking back with me through some of our darker times, and of course to her mother, the inimitable Aunt Nancy, whose treasure trove of stories was the early inspiration for this book. I must also mention my therapist, Banu Hummel, who, after an agonizing session about my father one autumn day said, "Why don't you write it down?" Polly Yates was a thoughtful guide in southern Georgia and was generous with all of her time and her own resources on the lynching of John Henry Williams. She is braving a great many Southern taboos in her own explorations. My second-cousin Lisa has also been very generous with her time and input. Another cousin, Ginger, was invaluable in painting a portrait of my father's childhood. The folks at the Colquitt County Library and the Tift County Genealogy Room were also quite helpful. Alexsey Vays was invaluable with his help on the website. Most of all, I would like to thank my wife, Delal, for enduring years of me squirreling myself away on weekends and evenings, for believing in me, and for providing a glimpse into a way of seeing things that I, as a white man, could never ever have had otherwise. She was a critical and challenging voice. If this book has any insights of more universal significance, it is thanks to her. Finally, I have to thank my son Robin, just for being there and representing a hope for the future.

ABOUT THE AUTHOR

Jeffrey Wade Gibbs was born and raised in rural Florida, shuttling back and forth between his mother's people in Lakeland and his father's in the woods of the north central lake region. He grew up fishing, boating, and wandering the woods while learning the dark twists and turns of his Southern heritage at his father's side. He attended the University of Central Florida where he majored in creative writing and then left the South to teach English in Tokyo. Since then, he has made his way around the world, working as a teacher and writer in Japan, India, and now Turkey, where he lives with his wife and son. He earned his MFA in Creative Writing at the University of Arizona and was fortunate enough to take workshops from visiting writers, Barbara Kingsolver and F. Scott Momaday, and studied under the late Oprah Book Club author, Aurelie Sheehan. His short stories, essays, and poems have appeared in *Chaotic Merge*, *Diagram*, *Fiction Southeast*, *3am*, *The Opiate*, *The Sand Journal*, *A Minor*, *Hyperallergic*, *The Boston Review*, and *Big Truths Little Fictions*, among others.

Printed in the USA
CPSIA information can be obtained
at www.ICGtesting.com
JSHW031109021224
74618JS00007B/20

9 781953 932297